Henry Charles Beeching

Pages From A Private Diary

Henry Charles Beeching

Pages From A Private Diary

ISBN/EAN: 9783744665971

Printed in Europe, USA, Canada, Australia, Japan

Cover: Foto ©Thomas Meinert / pixelio.de

More available books at **www.hansebooks.com**

PAGES FROM
A PRIVATE DIARY

"*L'homme qui a le temps d'écrire un journal intime nous parait ne pas avoir suffisamment compris combien le monde est vaste.*"—RENAN, *Feuilles Détachées.*

FOURTH IMPRESSION

LONDON
SMITH, ELDER, & CO., 15 WATERLOO PLACE
1899
[*All rights reserved*]

Printed by BALLANTYNE, HANSON & Co.
At the Ballantyne Press

TO

MY VERY GOOD FRIEND

J. St. LOE STRACHEY, esqr.

THE ONLY BEGETTER OF THESE ENSUING PAGES

These "Pages from a Private Diary" are reprinted from the Cornhill Magazine *with a few alterations and omissions.*

PAGES FROM A PRIVATE DIARY

May 7th, 1896.—My birthday, and so as good a day as any and a better day than most for beginning these extracts from my journal. I had thought of compiling a history of the parish by way of "Typical Developments," but it turns out that the new vicar is setting out on the same enterprise; and it is perhaps more in his way than mine. Besides, there is very little history to tell.

> " Our village is unhonoured yet in story,
> The present residents its only glory,"

as Sophocles says in the Coloneus (ll. 62, 63).

The house-martins have begun to think about building on the north side of the house. I had the old nests taken down for the pleasure of seeing these "amusive" little creatures, as Gilbert White would call them, once more at their loved masonry; and this year I nailed boards across the corners of the windows for cleanliness' sake. At first they were rather puzzled, and sat on the cross-pieces looking out on the world like tiny Dominicans; then a pair began building in one of the obtuse angles below; then they took themselves off to a window on the east side which had not been tampered with; finally, as there was not enough accommodation here for several families, the rest have swallowed their feelings and begun to build as usual. The nightingales are staying longer in the garden than in any year I can remember. There is a tradition that they used to build in the hedge overhanging what was once a more or less public road, but have not done so since the road was added as a shrubbery to the garden. I suppose now that we have a parish council they feel at liberty to withdraw their protest. Swinburne and Matthew Arnold are the last poets who have dared speak of the nightingale as Philomela. We all know now that it is only the cock-bird who sings, and poets have had to note the fact. Indeed the only virgin source of inspiration left for modern poetry is Natural Science. She is the tenth muse. There must have been some people who backed the Faun in his contest with Apollo, and I confess that in the daytime the blackbird affects me more than the nightingale, and in all moods. Sometimes it has all the jauntiness of the Pan's pipe heralding a Punch and Judy show, at other times the plangent note, "the sense of tears" which is Pan's contribution to serious art. I think it is partly John Davidson's interest in blackbirds that attracts me to him above the other sixty or seventy young gentlemen who make modern poetry. In the "Thames Ditton" passage of the first "Fleet Street Eclogues," he speaks of their "oboe-voices," and again of their song as "broken music"—one of his cleverest adaptations of a Shakespearean phrase.

8th.—My old gardener has at last condescended to retire. He has been on the place, I believe, for sixty years, man and boy; but for a long time he has been doing less and less; his dinner-hour has grown by insensible degrees into two, his intercalary luncheons and nuncheons more and more numerous, and the state of the garden past winking at. This morning he was rather depressed, and broke it to me that I must try to find some one to take his place. As some help, he suggested the names of a couple of his cronies, both well past their grand climacteric. When I made a scruple of their age, he pointed out that no young man of this generation could be depended upon; and further, that he wished to end his days in his own cottage (*i.e.* my cottage) where he had lived all his life, so that there would be a difficulty in introducing any one from outside. I suppose I must get a young fellow who won't mind living for the present in lodgings. I make a point as far as possible of taking soldiers for servants, feeling in duty bound to do so; besides, I like to have well set-up men about the place. When they are teetotalers they do very well. William, my coachman, is a teetotaler by profession, but, as the phrase goes, not a bigot. He was a gunner, and the other night—I suppose he had been drinking delight of battle with his peers—he brought me home from ———, where I had been dining, in his best artillery style, as though the carriage were a field-piece.

9th.—C., who is just home from Cairo, came to dine, and we had much talk about things military which need not be recorded. It seems the Sphinx's cap has been discovered, but one cannot imagine this increasing his majesty; hats are such local and temporal things. C. remarked that some of the papers had been speaking of the Sphinx as "she"; confusing it with the Greek sphinx that asked riddles and made short work of the unfortunates who failed to answer them. But is not his beard in the British Museum? The Egyptian sphinx has far too much serenity to play either the poser or the cannibal. But there is a riddling sphinx of the Nile, a very modern and undignified personage; and the Egyptian question, one may hope, has at last found an Œdipus in England, one might almost say in Lord Cromer. For Lord Cromer typifies, even to exaggeration, in the eyes of native and European, our characteristic qualities, strength of hand, and strength of purpose, devotion to athletics and distrust of ideas. His memorial is written in Milner's book, and no praise can be too high for his exhibition of the "Justum et tenacem propositi virum"; the man who knows his mind and won't be bribed. It is curious to notice the new type that is being created by young England in Egypt. The usual British alertness, not to say menace, of manner is soothed down into an Oriental dreaminess, as though time had never been called money, and there was no such superstition as free-will; but of course the Orientalising is only superficial.

11th.—To-day falls our customary beating of the bounds. But the new vicar is for still older customs, and wants to revive the Rogation-tide procession with a litany, especially in view of the present drought. Tom, who is patron of the living and parson's warden, refused to take part and "make a guy of himself," as he expressed it; and Farmer Smith, his colleague, said very bluntly that he would have no papist nonsense in *his* fields, and "besides, there couldn't be any rain till the wind shifted." So, as the substantial men stood aloof, the vicar had to content himself with the choir-boys, who celebrated the new forms with too much of the old spirit. I suppose my wandering life has purged me from a good deal of insular and Protestant prejudice, for I confess there seems more sense and present advantage in the religious rite than in the civil, when boundaries are all registered in maps. But we have lost whatever instinct we ever had for picturesque ceremonial. The other day I saw the town council of ———— turn out to meet a Royal Princess; the majority wore gowns which were much too short for them, and their hats were the various hats of every day. In short, they were ridiculous, and seemed to know it.

This Jingoism in America is too silly. A little while ago it was England, now it is Spain. A schoolboy translated Horace's "Dulce et decorum est pro patria mori" by "sweetness and decency have died out of the land." Jingoism is the schoolboy's version of patriotism.

13th.—It was to-day, how many years ago, that I put a certain serious question to Sophia. The crisis came as we stood by the lily-convally bed in the old Manor House garden at ————. There was only one lily with any of its bells fully out, and I gave it her, and now I reckon any year normal which brings its lilies into flower by the 13th, to let me pay my annual tribute. This year they came a few days too soon.

The copses and commons—our Berkshire commons are little forests—seem this year more beautiful than ever. The bloom of all the flowering trees, thorns, chestnuts, &c., even the elms and oaks, has been abnormal. The primroses are yielding place now to the wild hyacinths, which show through the trees in broad belts, and smell almost as strong as a bean-field. Soon the bracken will supersede both. My poet Davidson speaks somewhere of these hyacinths as—

> . . . "like a purple smoke
> Far up the bank."

The description is very just. I have a notion that this is what Fletcher meant by "harebells dim," if we accept that emendation,[1] for what we now call the harebell comes too long after the primrose to be connected with it. The beeches are in their full spring beauty, but the oaks are devoured by caterpillar, and too many of them are lying all abroad and naked, like giants stripped of their armour. The depression of agriculture, which town Radicals affect to disbelieve in, is having this result amongst others, that every stick worth cutting is being cut, except in the parks of the big landowners or on the glebes of the clergy, who are debarred from "waste" by law. Old philologers used to explain Berkshire to mean Bare-oak-shire; and the nakedness of the land will soon justify the name.

[1] "Primrose, first-born child of Ver,
Merry Springtime's harbinger
With *her bells* dim."

14th.—To-day is the centenary of the vaccination of James Phipps by Jenner, which Gloucester, his birthplace, has been celebrating in so becoming a fashion. "No prophet is accepted in his own country." A stranger giving himself out as from Gloucester, probably some wag who knew our nervousness, called a few days ago at the village shop, and the excitement in consequence among the well-to-do has been extraordinary. Tom's wife at once issued a placard appealing to all mothers to set a good example by being re-vaccinated. It appeared in the shop window next the new muzzling order, and seems to have got mixed up with it, for the postman carried about the news that in —— village "all the women were to be muzzled and all the dogs vaccinated." Yesterday was fixed for the doctor's attendance, and old Widow ——, who is eighty-eight, was the first voluntary victim. This morning I offered my wife and children and slaves. The cook, I am told, ripped up her sleeve with a pair of scissors, and then went off into hysterics; the ruddy David turned the complementary colour, but remembered the story of the Spartan boy in the "Sixth Standard Reader," and did not scream or struggle. Rumour brings in momentarily fresh stories of heroism.

Why did Mr. Austin receive the laurel? Tom, who thinks that to love Lord Salisbury is a Conservative education, is annoyed when I put the question; but I am convinced it arose from a confusion between Swinford and Swinburne, very natural to one more familiar with scientific than literary distinctions. Our arguments, however, never become really serious, as Tom is not concerned to defend the honour of any poets but those who belong to the county, and these, so far as we know, are only two, Chaucer and the laureate Pye. Chaucer's connection with Donnington is doubtful; but the Pyes are a Farringdon family, and the poet Pye planted that conspicuous clump of trees above the town on the west known as Farringdon Folly.

15th.—The wave of Conservatism seems to have brought with it a revival of interest in heraldry. Or is this merely due to the savage mania for collecting book-plates? I bought to-day Miss Austen's "Persuasion" in a rather pretty edition, and found *her* coat-of-arms printed inside the cover by way of *ex-libris*. The publishers seem to carry this piece of folly through all their reprints, Shakespeare, by way of eminence, having his achievement treated in two styles. Perhaps the new taste may spread in time to the upper classes, and prevent ladies printing their family crest on envelopes within a shield. One observes too, that printers and publishers are reviving their old signs; Longmans publish "at the Sign of the

Ship"; the new poetry is sold "at the Bodley Head," or "the bodiless head" as a humorist called it, and I have heard the suggestion made that the new type of "evil and adulterous" novel should not be procurable except "at the sign of the prophet Jonah." This would be a useful guide to us country bumpkins. But to return to Miss Austen. I notice that the first page of this last edition of "Persuasion" piously preserves the awkward misprint of a full-stop in the middle of the description of Sir Walter Elliot and the Baronetage:—"There any unwelcome sensations arising from domestic affairs changed naturally into pity and contempt. As he turned over the almost endless creations of last century, &c."

16*th*.—Read debate on Navy Estimates. Virgil has put our foreign policy into a single line, "Pacem orare manu, præfigere puppibus arma," which one might translate, after Dryden, "Provoke a peace and yet pretend a war."

The *Spectator*, surfeited for the moment of cat and dog stories, has been opening its voracious columns to a collection of Irish bulls, very curious wildfowl. Many of them present no recognisable bullish features; others are bulls in appearance only, and for the most part confusions of metaphor that happen to be amusing, of the type of the familiar "he never opened his mouth without putting his foot in it" (which is not a bull, because *it* does not refer to the mouth, though it seems to). The story about "never being able to keep an emetic on the stomach" is in the same way a bull only in appearance; for the remark has no sense at all if the man knew what an emetic was, unless he meant it humorously; and in neither case would it be a bull. It is of the essence of a bull that it should be nonsense in form only, not in matter. One of the best of those in the *Spectator* is the following :—" When one counts the accidents, dangers, and diseases which beset the journey of life, the wonder is a man lives till he dies." The Irish have no exclusive property in mixtures of metaphor, though their greater imaginativeness makes them more figurative in speech than the common run of Englishmen, and their impetuosity tends to confusion. The following passage is from the carefully written memoirs of one of the greatest English scholars of the century, Mark Pattison :—" Even at this day a country squire or rector, on *landing* with his *cub* under his *wing* in Oxford, finds himself much *at sea* as to the respective advantages or demerits of the various colleges" (p. 16); and of course Shakespeare mixes his metaphors freely.

18th.—I notice that household tempers get tinder-like in a prolonged drought, from the commander-in-chief downwards. Add to this that all the servants' arms have "taken." Time and a few drops of rain will allay these fevers. But meanwhile the rain does not come. "Why don't you let David"—the ruddy buttons—"help you with that, Laura?" "Please, sir, me and David hates each other." "My love, why is Proserpine all blubbered?" (Proserpine is so styled because she works upstairs in the morning and downstairs in the afternoon.) "Oh, John, she has broken Uncle George's Venetian glass, and I have been speaking to her. I never saw such a careless girl; but there, they're all alike."

19*th*.—At luncheon, Miss A., the Scotch governess, asked me if I liked buns. I replied that I liked them if they were made with sultana raisins and not currants. She blushed, and explained that she meant the poet "Buns." This, it seems, is the patriotic manner of pronouncing Burns. Or let me say *a* patriotic manner. For I recollect being taken to hear a lecture in Edinburgh by a Scotch friend, who when it was over inveighed against the speaker's accent. "Why," said I, "I thought it was Scotch!" "Scotch," said he, "it was Fifeshire, man." Miss A. may hail from Fife. Well, I pleaded to an enthusiasm for certain verses of the poet, and asked for her favourite passage. It was this:—

>"To catch dame Fortune's golden smile,
>   Assiduous wait upon her;
>And gather gear by every wile
>   That's justify'd by honour.

> Not for to hide it in a hedge
> Nor for a train attendant,
> But for the glorious privilege
> Of being independent."

Poor Miss A.! She showed me the Burns number of a Scots journal in which persons of importance gave their pet quotations. No one seemed to care for the best things. I suppose in the case of songs that are actually sung, it soon becomes impossible to criticise the words. I find even Dr. Service mentioning as the best of Burns's songs, " Mary Morison," " My Nannie O," and " Of a' the airts the wind can blaw." Now, unhappily, I am no songster, and do not know the tunes of any of these; but I should unhesitatingly assert that to mention the first two in the same breath as the third is "to unstop the string of all degree." In " Mary Morison " the only lines that deserve saying as well as singing are the final couplets of the second and third stanzas—

> "I sigh'd and said amang them a',
> Ye are na Mary Morison."

and

> " A thought ungentle canna be
> The thought o' Mary Morison."

But these are not sufficient to compensate the insipidity of the rest. " My Nannie O " opens well; after that there are irreproachable sentiments; but for " the golden cadence of poesy, *caret.*" " Of a' the airts" is a creature of another element. The first verse, perhaps, comes as near the border-line where simplicity joins tameness as is safe for a great poet, and the last two lines are not good; but what amends in the second stanza! Even here I should not like to pin my faith to the fourth line, but the rest is as perfect as a song can be, both in pathos and imagination. It is an interesting study to compare the two versions of "Ye banks and braes of bonnie Doon." The extra two syllables in the even lines of the later version seem to me to give the sorrow weight; the shorter line is jerky in comparison.

> "Ye flowery banks o' bonnie Doon
>   How can ye bloom sae fair!
> How can ye chant, ye little birds,
>   And I sae fu' o' care!
> Thou'lt break my heart, thou bonnie bird,
>   . That sings upon the bough:
> Thou minds me o' the happy days
>   When my fause luve was true.
>
> Ye banks and braes o' bonnie Doon,
>   How can ye bloom sae fresh and fair!
> How can ye chant, ye little birds,
>   And I sae weary fu' o' care!
> Thou'lt break my heart, thou warbling bird,
>   That wantons thro' the flowering thorn;
> Thou minds me o' departed joys,
>   Departed— never to return."

Burns never wrote anything so "simple, sensuous, and passionate" as the first four lines of the amended version, the epithet " little " seems to me exquisite ; but the second quatrain is spoilt, the last line being as bad as anything in his English songs. This inequality is a curious point about Burns ; where he is equal throughout, as in " Auld Lang Syne " and " John Anderson, my Jo," neither of which has a word one could wish other than it is, it is because the pitch is not very high ; in the poems where he touches sublimity, the pitch is never maintained throughout. Few people would wish a line away from " My luve is like the red, red rose," but few would deny that the first two stanzas are better than the last ; and in the " Farewell to Nancy," which contains his finest as well as his best known verses—and surely the love lyric in England has never so perfectly crystallised a tear—

> " But to see her was to love her ;
> Love but her, and love for ever.
> Had we never loved sae kindly,
> Had we never loved sae blindly,
> Never met—or never parted,
> We had ne'er been broken-hearted ! "

there occurs what is perhaps the worst couplet he ever wrote—

> " Deep in heart-wrung tears I'll pledge thee.
> Warring sighs and groans I'll wage thee."

And he actually repeats these lines to end with. Of course, Burns was a superb satirist, and to enjoy his satire one is content to make acquaintance with the Scotch Kirk, and the Scotch de'il, and even with Scotch haggis.

21st.—Rain at last, but too late and too little to save the hay. My wife and daughter have for a long time been involving me in a bicycle controversy. In vain have I repeated that my prejudices are against the exercise for women; they fixed upon the word "prejudice," and called for reasons. I appealed to custom; Sophia thought it enough to point to the fashion; Eugenia, knowing how penetrable I am to a quotation from Shakespeare, overbore me with "What custom wills, in all things should we do't," &c., from "Coriolanus." So I yielded, and it was arranged they should take lessons, and this morning I was permitted to accompany them to see their progress. E. was decidedly graceful, and carried herself well; but what shall I say of my dear wife?

22nd.—To Oxford; wandered through the Bodleian gallery and looked at the old curiosities, and many new ones, such as the Shelley papers. How like Lord Salisbury is to the portrait of his great ancestor riding on a mule! Has Mr. Gould allegorised this? Walked about and told the towers. Probably St. Mary's spire will satisfy nobody. Why has B. N. C. put so monstrous a lion and unicorn over its new porch? Magdalen looked beautiful, but not so beautiful as before the bridge was widened for the tramway. Somehow the narrow bridge helped the height of the tower. But the modern spirit hates privilege, even the privilege of beauty; and only Radicals may job. There was much talk at luncheon about the admission of women to degrees. It seemed to be the married dons who had led the attack. Possibly they have lived so long on terms of insipid equality with the other sex that they do not realise the effect of mixed lectures upon impressionable undergraduates. Courtship is like "hunt the whistle"; you can't play at it with any interest after you know the game. But there are always fresh generations coming up to whom the whole thing is new; and, let dons say what they please, the universities, no less than the public schools, exist for the training of youth. Happily, the undergraduates so far take the Conservative side. The Radical party forget, too, that if it became as much the fashion for girls as for men to reside at a university, they would no longer be all "reading girls," as at present, but a smart set, and what the effect would be Ouida alone could prognosticate. In the afternoon strolled round the Parks, but was driven by weather into the Museum. The anthropological collections seem well arranged, and very interesting, especially the musical instruments. Who would have guessed that the guitar is a development from the bow-string? The new Professor of Art was lecturing in the theatre to a few, but doubtless fit, ladies. Of the matter I could not judge, but the style was excellent—simple, dignified, and finished, without the over-elaboration usually affected by art-lecturers. One passage especially struck me— upon the splendid audacity of pigments in attempting to render human character, and succeeding. Went to the service at Magdalen Chapel, and afterwards dined with ———, and had dessert in common room; vintage and anecdotes were both old and sound, so that no one desired new; "across the" chestnuts "and the wine" renewed my friendship with ———.

23rd.—This morning's *Standard* celebrates the close of the session by a leading article, in the conventional three paragraphs, on the Beauties of Nature. But the new wine retains a strong constitutional smack from the old bottles. The "golden tassels of the laburnum" overhang "hundreds of villa residences," each "a typical English home," and when we escape from the suburbs it is to contemplate the "county seats and splendidly timbered parks, through which run rights of way preserved for the public from generation to generation." It always was the landlords who preserved rights of way, and commons too. But it is not only the striking features of the landscape, it is the inscrutable spirit of the Universe itself that is to be whipped into the Government lobby. "Nature is a *Conservative* force, admonishing us all to keep together, to act together," by joining her flocks of sheep or leagues of primroses; her method is "a wise, slow continuity, evolving and revolving," like the Great Wheel, no doubt, and "patient under passing disappointments," as, for example, when it gets stuck. It is a great faith, and ennobles politics with a religious sanction. But it is a game that two can play at; and it strikes me that the Radicals could make out a better abstract case for themselves as followers of Nature. Take, for instance, the following passage from a scientific writer; what a capital text it would make for a dithyrambic leader in the *Daily Chronicle!*—" Physical life may be said to be the continual struggle every moment against surrounding and imminent death; the resistance of an undiscoverable principle against unceasing forces; and it holds its own and lasts *by replacing waste, by repairing injuries, by counteracting poisons.*"

25th.—Whit-Monday is a high day with many of the Benefit Clubs in our neighbourhood. It has, in fact, taken the place of the old Berkshire feast or "revel," which was already fast decomposing when Hughes described it in "Tom Brown's Schooldays." There is only one old man in the village, so far as I can learn, who ever took part in a "back-swording" contest, and he only once. His story is that an "old gamester" asked him to make play for him, promising to let him off easily; but the incessant flicker of the single-stick before his eyes so roused his bile that, being a brawny fellow, he beat down the old gamester's guard by sheer force and "broke his head." He has no sentimental regret at the disappearance of backswording, which, as he describes it, must have been brutal enough; and he insists that the wrestling was as bad, the shoes of the wrestlers being often full of blood from cuts made by the sharp leather. A degenerate age is content with cricket and football, which are vastly better civilisers both of thews and temper. All the morning on Whit-Monday, the purveyors of amusement, mostly gipsy, are getting their stalls, and cocoa-nut pavilions, and merry-go-rounds into place; then the town band arrives a little before noon and plays the members into church. Dinner follows in the big barn, the gentlemen interested in the club carving the joints. When everybody is well wound up, the annual meeting is held, the honorary secretary makes an inaudible report, new officers are elected, the Queen's health is drunk, and everybody proposes a vote of thanks to everybody else. Then the whole company migrates into Tom's park and gardens to watch the cricket-match, or sing or loaf as their fancy leads them, except a few thirsty enthusiasts who prefer playing skittles at the Blue Boar for a cheese to make them thirstier. In time comes dancing, and in time the band marches out of the park drawing the youths and maidens after it.

29th.—The scythes have begun in the bottom meadow; there is no more cheerful sight and no more delicious sound, when the grass is worth cutting, but this year it is all " bennets." " It shall be called Bottom's Dream, because there is no bottom." Turned over Bacon's Essays. He is not Shakespeare, but he is often as surprisingly modern, sentence after sentence seems written with an eye to current events. Take this, for instance: "To be master of the sea is an abridgment of a monarchy [*i.e.* a monarchy in miniature]. Surely at this day, with us of Europe, the vantage of strength at sea (which is one of the principal dowries of the kingdom of Great Britain) is great; both because most of the kingdoms of Europe are not merely inland, but girt with the sea most part of their compass; and because the wealth of both Indies seems in great part but an accessory to the command of the seas."

And here is our Armenian policy. Among unjustifiable wars Bacon ranks those "made by foreigners under the pretence of justice or protection to deliver the subject of others from tyranny and oppression."

And here is a judgment on the Transvaal Government: " All States that are liberal of naturalisation towards strangers are fit for empire."

Here, too, is one side of the Colonial Secretary: " Wonderful is the case of boldness in civil business: What first? Boldness. What second and third? *Boldness*. It doth fascinate and bind hand and foot; therefore we see it hath done wonders in popular states, and more ever upon the first entrance of bold persons into action." This is, of course, the passage from which Danton stole his " Il nous faut de l'audace, encore de l'audace, toujours de l'audace."

Here is a good criticism on the Drink Commission: " In choice of committees for ripening business for the Council, it is better to choose indifferent persons than to make an indifferency by putting in those that are strong on both sides."

Finally, the following judgment of a great soldier on duelling might well be commended to the notice of the German Emperor: " It were good that men did hearken to the saying of Consalvo, the great and famous commander, that was wont to say 'a gentleman's honour should be *de tela crassiore*—of a good strong warp or web, that every little thing should not catch in it.'"

30*th*.—The post this morning has more waste paper than ever. There are six prospectuses of joint-stock companies, most of them offering gold mines. Will Africa never cease blowing bubbles? It is not insignificant that money-lenders' letters are increasing in proportion. There are a couple to-day. One gentleman suggests "remunerative but not exorbitant interest," and writes in a boyish hand that is very frank and engaging. Indeed, I opened the letter first, thinking it was from Harry. The other fellow puts a crest on his envelope, a hound's head with the motto, "Fides in adversis," which is even more touching. It strikes me that "a crocodile's head, the eyes distilling tears, all proper," with for motto "Beati pauperes," or "Dare quam accipere," would be much more appropriate. Then there is an enormous circular from a gentleman who is urgent that I should go with him on an educational tour to Jericho, or a co-operative cruise to shoot polar bears. And then there are the wine-lists. There is no such good reading to be had, if you lunch alone, as an advertiser's wine-list; to a person of imagination and gouty tendency it is more stimulating and far more innocuous than the wine itself. Indeed, I suspect that what these vintners sell is not half so precious as their description of it.

June 1st.— The pitiful accident reported this morning, that befell the Russian crowd in the Khodinsky Plain waiting for their coronation mugs —between three and four thousand being crushed to death—impresses one with the vast size of modern nations. The description in Matthew Paris, which I have just been reading, of the crowd at the coronation of our Henry III. presents an almost ludicrous contrast. We are told that the citizens of London went out to meet the king in holiday attire, and vied with one another in trying the speed of their horses; and that the Constable of Chester attended the king and kept the people back *with a wand* when they pressed forward unduly.

2nd.—Came to visit Aunt Julia at Barchester. The ecclesiastical atmosphere of the Close is somewhat rarefied and hard to breathe; but for a few days I rather enjoy it. And the cathedral music is capital. The factions seem in a flourishing condition. The Dean has put down a Turkey carpet in the sanctuary, which the Archdeacon's party resent as an unspeakable outrage, considering what has been going on among the Christians in Anatolia and Crete. On the other hand, the Archdeacon's daughter has become engaged to a minor canon. Aunt Julia, who is a staunch supporter of the Dean, told me of the engagement with a light in her eye and a deprecatory movement of the hands that meant, "What could you expect?" I asked if she knew the gentleman. Her reply was, "My dear, I have seen the young man going backwards and forwards to his duties." She went on to say that of course she should call after the wedding, but it would make a great deal of awkwardness, as it was her custom to do no more than leave cards on the wives of the minor canons. This phrase of "leaving cards" always reminds me of a story, which may be in Joe Miller, but we tell it of a distinguished ecclesiastical neighbour. He had a new groom, fresh from one of the racing-stables, who was to accompany him one day in a long round of leave-taking calls, and was sent into the house before starting to get some cards. When they reached the last house, the order came, " Leave two cards here, James," and the reply followed, " I can't, my lord; there's only the ace of spades left."

4th.—The papers are enthusiastic about the victory of Persimmon, or rather the Prince of Wales, at the Derby. Nothing succeeds like success, and the Prince is popular, so that even we who for local reasons wished "Tueful" (as we call him) to win, take our beating philosophically. But why should the Stock Exchange burst out into singing "God bless the Prince of Wales?" Could it be that these gentlemen were interested in Turf reform, and foresaw in the Prince's good fortune, with a horse of his own breeding, a good time coming in which everything should be straight and aboveboard? It is not racing, however, so much as betting and the misery it leads to, that offends thoughtful people. Everybody has read " Esther Waters," with its scenes of sordid tragedy. If the Prince of Wales were to discountenance heavy betting, a great deal of good might be done. For betting, like drinking, though a natural taste, is much under the influence of fashion. The

"Paget Papers" contain a letter from the last Prince of Wales who won the Derby, in which he speaks of drunkenness in these engaging terms: "The rest were bad enough, God knows, except myself, though my every glass was a Bumper to your health. I can safely swear I never flinched one, dear Arthur, and you well know I am not even upon indifferent occasions a *shirker*. Since that day the old girl has never ceased being tipsy twice a day," &c.

We have moved away from those days, and not long ago one of the Royal princes spoke of drunkenness as "the only enemy that England had to fear." If the Prince of Wales would only say that now of gambling!

> "Lordës may finden other manner play
> Honest enough to drive the day away,"

said Chaucer, and he was brought up at court.

6th.—Old Juniper is dead. He called in the village carpenter last night to receive directions about his funeral and to make his will. The poor here are very cautious not to employ the gentry in these testamentary matters, as they fear the knowledge of their little savings might impede the flow of charity. Tom, who is precentor and wears a surplice in church like Sir Thomas More, whom he much respects, used to make a point of the choir being present at all funerals. But one spring an epidemic so increased the mortality that he got tired, and the sixth corpse was condemned to be buried plain. So now the vicar summons a few boys from the school; and certainly singing the Psalm very much lightens and seems to christianise the service. One has to see a country funeral to appreciate the real luxury of woe. The deceased may have been all that was disagreeable and degraded, and his death may be acknowledged on all hands to be a good riddance, but the conventions must be respected. The mourners walk behind the bier in a longer or shorter procession of pairs, a man to the right with a woman on his left arm, and a handkerchief in his free hand. The exact position of the handkerchief varies with the locality; here it is pressed to the right cheek. In church they remain seated, leaning forward in an ecstasy of uncontrollable grief during the whole service; then the procession is re-formed. This is Bacon's "custom copulate and conjoined," and a mighty power it is, and perhaps in a dim way it makes for righteousness. On the Sunday following the burial all the mourners that have not scattered to distant homes come to church, where they expect some pulpit reference and an appropriate hymn.

9*th*.—Sophia's birthday. It is desperate work finding presents in the country. However, at —— I picked up a rather pretty piece of mosaic binding, which I have filled with writing-paper to make an album.

I have long meditated keeping an album myself of another sort, a commonplace book, what Milton calls a "topick-folio." This is one of those resolutions that come with every first of January, and too often go with it; though a very fat volume lying here on the table has its first few pages filled with the harvest of several new beginnings. Laziness has something to do with the irresolution; the habit of reading in the Balfour position perhaps more; more still the conviction at the moment that if a passage is very good there is small risk of forgetting it (a terrible mistake!); but most of all that paralysing sentence in Marcus Aurelius, "No longer delude thyself; thou wilt never read thine own notes, nor the extracts from books which thou wast reserving for thy old age" (iii. 14).

10*th*.—The cuckoo to-day has a decided hiccough. Saw some young partridges as I drove in to ———. The barber was more interesting than usual. He has received a commission from some distinguished person to count how many light and how many dark-haired people he operates upon in a month. The theory, as he propounded it, was that the dark-haired people were clever, but weak, and the light-haired strong and foolish, and that having been for centuries oppressed by superior force, the aboriginal black-haired folks are now coming to the front again. He called them Hibernian (query Iberian). "Shy-traffickers, the *dark* Iberians come." Lunched at club. Talk turned on eccentric wills. Dr. —— had a friend who picked up an old gentleman's hat in Piccadilly, and, before returning it, wiped off the dirt, which so delighted the old gentleman that he asked for the young man's card, and left him his fortune. The legatee was killed in the Soudan three months after. The moral seems to be, have polite relations, and inherit the consequences of their virtue.

11*th*.—Went to P.'s wedding. Everything went happily, and everybody seemed contented. There was an extempore sermon, which began by dividing itself into three heads; and this a little frightened me, but the heads proved to be without tails. The service itself is one of the best in the Prayer-Book, being short and to the purpose; but it would be better still for a few slight changes. For example, the officiating clergyman emphasised a distinction between the man's "plighting" his troth and the woman's "giving" hers, which is surely a distinction without a difference. Then what does "With my body I thee worship" mean? And might not the wife's promise be brought a little more up to date? New women, new promises. In older days the woman had to promise to be "bonnair and buxom in bed and at board." We like them to be so still; but we "hold it not honesty to have it thus set down." Might not the "obey" follow the "buxom" into limbo? My wish for P. and his wife is that they may hit the mean, as in other things so in their conjugalities, between the extravagant complacency that Lamb ridicules and some people's *brusquerie*. Of the latter I heard an amusing instance the other day. B. said to his wife, "Why are your dresses half an inch longer than any other woman's? To which she replied, "Because I am your wife. Otherwise the other women's dresses would be half an inch shorter than mine." And a new sting has been introduced into connubial controversy by chatter about heredity. Two young friends of mine were overheard wrangling the other day as to which was to blame for their very much spoilt daughter's wilfulness. On second thoughts I am not sure that we have done altogether well to get rid of that old promise. The unsoured Milton found in it his youthful ideal:

> "Come, thou goddess fair and free,
> In heaven yclep'd Euphrosyne,
> And by men heart-easing Mirth,
> . . . .
> So *buxom*, blithe, and *debonair*."

All moral novelists agree that conduct at board is nine-tenths of wedded life. Is it not Anthony Hope who says, "Her eyes looked as if they would expect too much of me at breakfast"? and there is the same feeling, heightened to mania, in Q.'s "You are too fat, Lydia." Yes, "to be buxom at board" is to be perfect, and of all boards none is so difficult as the breakfast-table. The old conventual practice of having a person to read some dull book or an office during the meal might be introduced with advantage into country houses where the post comes in late. But for the "obedience"? No doubt all males must hold Milton's theory that obedience is their due, but the un-success of Milton's practice is strongly in favour of disguising the claim:

> "Therefore God's universal law
> Gave to the man despotic power
> Over his female in due awe;
> Nor from that right to part an hour,
> Smile she or lour:
> So shall he least confusion draw
> On his whole life, not sway'd
> By female usurpation, or dismay'd.
> *But had we best retire? I see a storm.*"

The same chorus in "Samson" enumerates, not without surprise and chagrin, all the fine male qualities to which the other sex can be impenetrable, and gives up the puzzle of affinity as hopeless:

> "It is not virtue, wisdom, valour, wit,
> Strength, comeliness of shape, or amplest merit,
> That woman's love can win or long inherit;
> But what it is, hard is to say,
> Harder to hit."

Ladies, I am told, find it no less puzzling to account for the fascination exercised by many of their own sex who are neither beautiful nor witty. Mrs. ———'s drawing-room is the rendezvous of all the bachelors and married men in the countryside, of whom I am the least. Why do we go there? Let me examine myself. I go because she makes me feel comfortable and contented; because she seems to say always the right thing, the thing I want said to me. She moves like a goddess in a magical atmosphere of sympathy. I go in bruised and battered and resentful, and feeling all my tale of years, and come out like Æson from Medea's tub, young and sleek and self-satisfied. I was there when Major Ursa himself, the biggest bear in the country, was lugged in by his wife against his will, all bristles, to pay some social debt, and saw him take leave in less than twenty minutes, purring like a pussy. And now he comes without Mrs. Ursa.

15th.—There has been thunder about all day, and this afternoon some twenty good flashes of lightning, but no rain. After dinner I was reading, over my cigar in the garden, Dr. Garnett's selection from Coventry Patmore, which seems to contain that poet's salvage. After enjoying my favourite poems, I turned once more to the very spirited but to me incomprehensible piece called " To the

Unknown Eros," and found it no more luminous than usual.

> "It is a Spirit though it seems red gold;
> And such may no man, but by shunning, hold.
> Refuse it, though refusal be despair;
> And thou shalt feel the phantom in thy hair."

As I reached that line, though I was unconscious of any wilful act of refusal, red gold not being much proffered in these parts, I felt the phantom in my hair—just at the nape of the neck—and a very unpleasant sensation it was. When I recovered my presence of mind, the phantom proved to be a very big moth, which had settled there and was flapping its wings. I do not suppose this is altogether what Patmore meant, but it was an apt illustration. It is an *annus mirabilis* for *Lepidoptera*.

19*th*.—Went to town for several days. We have been reading aloud in the evenings lately Doughty's "Arabia Deserta," which is a powerful piece of writing, though mannered; and a passage in praise of precious stones has taken such hold of the feminine mind that I have been afraid to act as escort in shopping thoroughfares. This is what D. says: "The Oriental opinion of the wholesome operation of precious stones, in that they store the mind with admirable beauties, remains perhaps at this day a part of the marvellous estimation of inert gems amongst us. Those indestructible elect bodies, as stars, shining to us out of the dim mass of matter, are comfortable to our fluxuous feeble souls and bodies; in this sense all gems are cordial, and of an influence religious. These elemental flowering lights almost persuade us of a serene eternity, and are of things (for the inestimable purity) which separate us from the superfluous study of the world" (i. 315). Certainly pearls are very beautiful objects, and their wearers as certainly find them "comfortable" and "cordial"; and the two or three thousand pounds one has to pay for a necklace may be an exceedingly good investment into the bargain if it persuades us of a serene eternity. Conscience would be for once on the side of the expense. The lady at the Royal Academy whom Sargent has painted in her pearls does look to have a very tranquil soul, as though separated from the superfluous study of the world. What pearls they are, and what paint! But if I had the money to spend I should buy my immortality directly of Mr. Sargent rather than of Mr. Spink. How good the Chamberlain is too! People may grumble that there is not much revelation of character in the face beyond keenness and will; but is there in the living face? And to make the eyes big and yearning, as Watts too often does, by way of "divinely through all hindrance finding the man" behind them, is not to paint a portrait.

20th.—Sunday. Went to —— Church. Service Gregorian, preacher Gorian. At least he thought he was, but what he really resembled was an earwig endeavouring to extricate himself from a filbert, and frantically waving his flippers. The matter was what that shrewd judge, Mr. Pepys, would have called "unnecessary." What a bore it must be to have foolish imitators! In the afternoon to St. Paul's, where the service is said to be the best in Europe; but ah, the reredos! How awful for three or four venerable clergymen to have the responsibility of decorating a cathedral! The days of bishop builders are gone by, and probably the professional architect has it all his own way, except for the occasional pressure of public opinion. I could not get near enough to the choir to judge of the new ceiling, but the general colour effect seemed good.

21st.—Stood for some time on the doorstep drawing in the electrical force of London, and feeling like a mouse in oxygen. It is only we country cousins who really enjoy London, just as it is only Londoners who really enjoy the country, and the enjoyment on both sides may be a good deal due to misunderstanding. A little chap from Seven Dials is said to have called a lark "a bloomin' cock-sparrow in a fit," and I may be doing even greater injustice to the passers-by when I fancy them pulsing with the high fever of existence. I am glad London has found singers of late. Some very genuine poets have not been kind to it; "that tiresome, dull place," says Gray; and Cowper is more impolite still; but then he was mad. In Kensington Gardens I met K. for the first time since our disagreement. He treated me very civilly, like a stranger, though we had been close friends for ten years. That is the worst of your idealist; all his friends are angels and all his opponents ——; so that to cross him is to experience, in his estimation, the fall of Lucifer. He sadly lacks humour, or, what comes to the same thing, a sense of proportion. To console myself I walked round the Albert Memorial, and found Hiram and Bezaleel an excellent tonic. Tom met us in the afternoon at the Academy, and took us, as usual, to criticise the construction of the hayricks. He was much impressed by a picture called "Whoa, steady!" wherein were represented two plough-horses, the one capering while the other stood impassive: he vowed he had never seen so steady a horse in his life, and was determined to purchase it, if he could find out from the painter where it lived. I could not get him to admire Clausen's "Crow-boy," who was evidently, he thought, one of the present soft generation, spoilt by too long keeping at school, even if he had not got, as he suspected, St. Vitus's dance; La Thangue's ducks, too, very much puzzled him. We dined at ——'s, and talked about ghosts. L. gave us the only true and genuine account of the

Glamis ghost, in whose room he had slept since its happy decease. I told the story of my grandfather and the headless horseman, and of the ghost who rolls my lawn every 29th February. F. had seen too many ghosts to believe in them. She told us how, when the clock struck twelve, a party consisting of an old gentleman and three girls used to appear nightly in her bedroom. Once she determined not to open her eyes, but a strange rustling all round the room roused her curiosity, and when she looked there were ears of corn mixed with poppies thrusting themselves from behind each picture frame. The old gentleman seemed much amused.

22nd.—To my dentist, who gave me the laughing-gas, and "charmed ache with air"; dreamt that I was being dragged down through a sea of blood. Went to the club to write letters and lunch, and recover tone; then walked through the Park to make calls. How rare it is to find ladies in society who know what they think about anything! They hand on opinions like counters, all of which are of equal conversational value. If your ears are long enough, you may hear the judgments you have just expressed, original as you may think them, being passed on to Mr. X. as the merest commonplace. One pleasure of an excursion to town is the sight of pretty dresses. In the country the dress of the upper class becomes plainer and plainer year by year as that of the classes below waxes in flamboyancy. Perhaps some ladies push the principle to an extreme. One of my neighbours while waiting for the train at —— station, where she is not known, was accosted by a farmer and asked, "How many did her master keep?" (*i.e.* how many servants); and the —— photographer pronounces it impossible nowadays to obtain an artistic picture of any county lady, because their dresses fit so ill. Ladies whose husbands have made a fortune recently, and buy a country "cottage with a double coach-house," should be clever enough to take the hint.

23rd.—Came down in the train with Archdeacon ——. One of Smith's newspaper boys amused me very much by pressing on him the sporting journals. He told me of a very sharp lad who once offered him the *World,* and when he shook his head, explained "*Christmas* Number, sir." I have no doubt our Berkshire breed is very virtuous, and it is far from stupid, but one does sometimes wish for a little of the cockney smartness. It strikes me that "paiper," for "paper," which must have come to London from Essex, is less fashionable along the line than it used to be, and may quite go out, like the *v* for *w,* of which Dickens made so much.

26th.—Q. has reprinted some of his *Speaker* "causeries," and delightful table-talk they are.

Q.'s criticism has the flavour of first principles that one associates with Oxford scholarship and philosophy. For the honour of Oxford I am glad to see a protest against Mr. Hardy's system of the universe, and also an additional paragraph on Davidson's "Ballad of a Nun," a poem that, with all my admiration for D., I have never been able to read a second time. Q. explains that the style on a first reading blinded him to the sense. In that misfortune he was not alone. On a certain Monday morning late in '94 a *queue* of respectable middle-aged ladies thrust its way along Vigo Street into the "Bodley Head," asking for copies of the "Ballad of a Nun" by a Mr. Davidson. When the pressure was a little eased, the publisher ventured to inquire the cause of the sudden demand, as the Saturday papers had not contained any remarkable review. The answer was that the Archdeacon of W—— had charged them on their souls' health to procure it. Dear Archdeacon! He knew the story from the *Gesta Romanorum* or from Miss Procter's version, and too carelessly assumed that D. meant the same thing. The one of Q.'s papers I incline to regret is that upon Samuel Daniel, and for an entirely selfish reason. Loving Daniel, I should be sorry if he were "boomed." My feeling about him is very much that excusable jealousy which made Q. himself refuse Gigadibs the explanation of a certain "Troy" custom. (See the preface to "The Delectable Duchy.")

27th.—The roads are execrable. This year they should have been better than usual, as the District Council has taken them over, and the contractors have no inducement, as the farmers had, to delay mending them till too late for the flints to work in; so the metal was put on in good time, but the drought has made them thoroughly rotten again. Down in the vale they use granite instead of flints, and if the parsons and farmers who compose the council would only take to cycling, we should soon see flints discarded here also. We should see also the hedge-clippings swept up. I have been learning to bicycle; what I especially dislike about it is the second or hind-wheel jolt after one has kept one's temper over the first. What I especially enjoy is the exhilaration of running downhill. I find, too, that my ideas flow more easily when in rapid motion,—this may be a sign of decrepitude,—but if I descend to register them they are gone. Some scientific genius should invent a bicycle-phonograph into which one could talk.

To bicycle amongst country villages is a very good way in which to test their *ethos*. In some places the traveller is laughed at, or tripped up, or stoned, or the children spread tacks across the road; in others, perhaps only a mile or two distant, he is as safe from molestation as in a London suburb. I have noticed—and the experience is not palatable to my Radical friends, but it is this—that where the natives are barbarous it is a sign that there is no resident squire or no competent parson.

July 1st.—The young wrynecks, alas! are dead, no doubt killed by their parents through my folly in taking one out of the nest. They are very uncommon birds in the neighbourhood, hence my wish to examine them. They dug their hole in an old apple tree just below where it had lost a branch, so that the wood was rotten; and not more than five feet from the ground, so that I could watch them easily. Of course, I had to widen the orifice before I could remove the youngster. The snake-like twist they can give to their neck, and their snake-like hiss, make them rather uncanny birds, and may account for their use in divination by Greek wizards. They were spread-eagled on a wheel, and turned, or perhaps whirled, round. Simætha, in Theocritus, uses such a wheel to charm back her faithless lover, Delphis. The poor birds must have rejoiced at the advent of Christianity, modern Christian witches preferring to conjure with robins and other birds of bright plumage.

2nd.—The Agricultural Rating Bill passed its third reading by two county Radical votes over the Government majority. The Committee debates have slowly exhibited, or perhaps evolved, the Government position, at last clearly stated by Mr. Balfour in his concluding speech, that the Bill is meant not only to relieve a greatly distressed industry in redemption of election pledges, but also as a contribution towards remedying the present monstrous injustice in the assessment to local rates. It is to be hoped that the Government will sooner or later overhaul the whole bad business, but not without more deliberation than they thought necessary before overhauling our educational system. The Janus-faced contention of the Opposition that the proposed relief is, as regards the landowners, an enormous subsidy, but as regards the agriculture interest generally a drop in the bucket, reminds me of an ancient story about a little girl and a piece of cake:

Little Girl: Is that *large* piece of cake for grandfather?
Mamma: No, dear, for you.
Little Girl: What a *small* piece of cake.

The new vicar, who is not so good a Conservative as we could wish, is indignant with the Government for not allowing the relief to the clergy on Tythe Rent Charge. At present, he tells me, he pays half as much rates as Tom; and when the Act comes into operation he will pay exactly the same amount, for Tom, who farms his own land, will get the reduction. This certainly seems preposterous in regard, for example, to the road rate, for Tom wears the road much more with his carriage horses and plough teams than the vicar with his one pony and "humble vehicle." I noticed in the Rate Book to-day that Tythe Rent Charge is now entered as "buildings." It was "land" for the sake of being rated, and ceases to be "land" when rates on land are reduced. But how can it be "buildings"?

4*th*.—A curious example presented itself this morning of our growing sensitiveness to criticism, and also of our ready invention in the manufacture of scandal. A person who makes mineral water at some distance from here sent in his card and asked to see me, and on being shown into the library began this catechism:—"Sir, did you pay a visit to —— last Friday week? Did you stop to lunch? Did you say at lunch that my soda water was enough to give everybody typhus fever?" I endeavoured to persuade the little man that he was misinformed, that I did not so much as know that he existed; still less, if possible, that he made mineral waters; that I could not, therefore, have censured them; and that so far as my memory served the topic did not arise; so that his friend the footman must have confused two people and two occasions. I then warned him that perhaps the circulation of such a report was not the most advantageous form of self-advertisement, because a man's mineral water should be not only pure, but above suspicion. He left in some excitement, generously accepting my disclaimer, but determined to find the truth somehow. I was tempted to suggest that he might find the truth at the bottom of his well, but he would not have understood. Poor lady! No wonder Lucian thought her ἀμυδρὰ καὶ ἀσαφὴς τὸ χρῶμα—wan and washed out in complexion; but it would be a pity she should have typhus.

6th.—The garden sun-dial came unriveted from its pedestal some months ago, and has been laid aside ever since, as it seemed to the ladies a pity to lose the opportunity of decorating it with a motto. We are all gone crazy about mottoes in this part of the world. Every new house that is built must have its motto, and the selection gives a good deal of entertainment both to the house-builders and their neighbours. Well, fashion must be followed, so this morning I have been reading through Mrs. Gatty's collection of sun-dial mottoes, being stimulated to industry by my stop-gap gardener's inquiry whether he might not put a pot of hydrangeas on the pedestal. So I explained its purpose. The best mottoes seem to be the best known, such as—"Non nisi cœlesti radio," "Horas non numero nisi serenas," "Pereunt et imputantur," but one cannot use these. A favourite device was to print "we shall," and leave "di(e)—al(l)" to be supplied by the local wits;

but that is too *macabre*. I remember an uncle of mine choosing "Sensim sine sensu" from the *De Senectute*, and being very indignant with a friend of his, a fine scholar, who tried to convince him that he had pitched upon an interpolation. On the whole, I doubt if I shall find anything better than my first idea of " Cogitavi dies antiquos" (" I have considered the days of old"), from the 77th Psalm. It is dignified, and to a reflective mind monitory without being impudently didactic, and I am fond of the Vulgate. The seventeenth-century preachers and essayists were fortunate in being able to quote it, " to saffron with their predicacioun," but it should be kept for sober occasions. Matthew Arnold was something too liberal in his use: it became a mere trick of style with him.

7th.—I notice that one of the papers in a report of the Queen's Review of her Jubilee Nurses, says, "The nurses curtsied *thrice simultaneously*, which had a novel and pleasing effect."

8th.—Made our annual excursion to White Horse Hill. We lunched, as usual, at the "Blowing Stone." Five minutes' practice once a year for half a century has not taught me the trick of blowing it, and Sophia remains the one member of the family who can rouse the fog-horn blast by which Alfred is *said* to have gathered his forces. It was almost too warm for the climb, but we persisted, and were rewarded at the top by the breeze over the downs. I drove Sophia in the light pony-cart along the Ridgeway to Uffington Castle, and (to quote the words of a recent *Spectator*) " enjoyed the sensations of a British chief driving his spring-less car to the fortress of his tribe." But, more fortunate than this writer, we did not smash our chariot in effecting an entrance into the camp. The vale lies stretched out below in vast and level panorama, "like the garden of the Lord," and there is no such lovely sight, to my thinking, anywhere. It is a little sad, too, for all the towns one sees are slowly decaying, largely through their own folly in refusing the Great Western Railway. Reading had more foresight, and in the half-century has more than trebled its population. Perhaps it is not so sad after all, for Wantage remains what it was to Bishop Butler if not quite what it was to King Alfred, and Farringdon has still its memories of Saxon kings (not to mention Pye), while Reading is like a strong ass couching down between the two burdens of Sutton's seeds and Palmer's biscuits. After tea we drove on to Uffington village for the sake of Hughes's memory. But the church is a splendid specimen of Early English architecture, and well worth a visit for its own sake, as our American cousins are sure to find out soon, and make it a shrine of pilgrimage. The vicar should open a subscription list for some memorial, as they are doing at Rugby.

The school-house still stands as it did when Tom Brown and Jacob Doodlecalf were caught at the porch by the choleric wheelwright, only the date over the door is not 1671, as you see it in the illustration, but 1617. The inscription just indicated in the picture is as follows:—

> "Nil fœdum dictu vitiiq; hæc limina tangat
> Intra quæ pueri. A.D. 1637."

The "pueri" is emphatic, and is explained by one of the rules of the founder on the walls within:—

"Whereas it is the most common and usual course for many to send their daughters to common schools to be taught together with and amongst all sorts of youths, which course is by many conceived very uncomely and not decent, therefore the said schoolmaster may not admit any of that sex to be taught in the said school."

The room is now used as a village reading-hall. Tom Hughes's "Scouring of the White Horse" describes with a wonderful vividness, which was one of his gifts as a writer, the "pastimes" that used to be held on occasion of the scouring, and it remains their memorial. For now the old idol is kept clean by the tenant without ceremony. It is a quaint notion—an ancient idol scoured by a muscular Christian. People who write in the papers are not old enough to remember the hideous Clapham School religion, from which "muscular Christianity" helped to deliver us. There is a good sketch of it in Laurence Oliphant's "Piccadilly." Its outward symbol was black kid gloves, and its passwords were many, perhaps the most odious being the word "engage." When a clergyman called, it was quite customary for him to say, "Shall we engage?" and then and there you were expected to let him hale you into the presence of your Maker. Its organ in the press was a paper called the *Record*, which ruled the religious world with a rod of iron. Any parson caught thinking for himself was noted, and

> "Without reprieve condemned to death
> For want of well-pronouncing shibboleth;"

the "death" in question being not only professional, the disfavour of Lord Shaftesbury and loss of preferment, but "the second death" as well, with quarters assigned in the disciplinary department of paradise. The persecution of that good man Frederick Maurice, the prophet of the musculars, the memory of which has been preserved, like a fly in amber, by Tennyson's delightful ode to him, helped to disgust moderate people; and meanwhile the Oxford school was growing in influence. Of course "muscular Christianity" could never have become really popular with the clergy, as it reduced them to the position of second-rate laymen.

10th.—There was a nut-hatch very busy in one of the limes this morning. The bees are also busy there; but listening to them as they "improved the shining hour" made me less and less inclined for business myself. In fact, I fell asleep. A modern poet notes "a hum of bees in the queenly robes of the lime" as one of the most delightful noises in nature, and so it is; though his line, when I quote it, makes Sophia shake her petticoats. On my way to ——, to consult my lawyer about a boundary dispute with G. P., I met a party of three magpies, which should bode good fortune. Prosit! The hedges are in their full summer glory—

"lovely to see
With mullein, and mallow, and agrimony,
With campion and chicory handsome and tall,
And the darling red poppy that's gayest of all,"

to quote a very old-fashioned poetaster. Indeed, such is summer's pomp and prodigality, that many things slip by without being enough enjoyed. That ancient allegory of the pursuit of pleasure, which still eludes the pursuer, is wonderfully true even of such a mild delight as the enjoyment of summer; one cannot really set to work to enjoy it; the enjoyment comes when it wills in chance waves; but I have ever an absurd feeling that, while I am occupied with business indoors, flowers are wasting their sweetness, and birds their melody, and summer is growing old. But to go out is not necessarily to find enjoyment.

The visit of the Artillery Company of Massachusetts to their elder brethren in England should help to patch up the sentimental alliance between the two countries. But sentiment will not last unless it is supported by courtesy and tact. Now it is a curious and unfortunate thing that while individual Americans often excel Englishmen in these qualities (one need go no further for an instance than Colonel Walker of the H.A.C., and that fine phrase of his about her Majesty, "her queenliness as a woman and her womanliness as a queen ")—the bulk of those prominent in politics seem singularly destitute of both, and there is no diplomatic tradition. There is an interesting *Tatler* (No. 41) about the Artillery Company, describing a sham fight in the streets of London on June 29, 1709; which shows that the H.A.C. was to the wits of two centuries ago what the Rifle Volunteers were to *Punch* in the sixties.

11*th.*—There seems a chance of the Parish Council meetings becoming more lively. Both Tom and his wife are on the council, Tom being chairman, and they regard it as a highly useful means of registering their benevolent *ukases*. But the vicar, who has been elected this year, is full of notions and wants to democratise it. As a first step, to ensure publicity for the discussions, he has persuaded a few old women to attend the meetings, all the men being too busy in their gardens and not very keenly interested. Last night there was a debate about housing. The vicar maintained that certain cottages (not Tom's) were a disgrace to the village, and that the people who live in them were very respectable people who had a right (ominous word!) to decent houses if they could pay for them. Tom replied that if he or any one else built new cottages for these people, other people anything but respectable would be only too glad to come into the empty ones. That is true enough. The solution, of course, is for Tom to buy the cottages in question, and either reconstruct or pull them down; and this, if no one suggests it to him, he will probably do. But such debates as last night's will soon bring up the council to the level of interest of Lord Salisbury's circus.

15*th*.—St. Swithin's: just enough rain for the "apple christening."

H.M. Inspector paid a "visit without notice" to the school. At least it was without notice so far as the schoolmaster was concerned; I had known the awful secret for three days past, as he had proposed himself for luncheon. So I happened to call at the school and found him there. He is a good inspector, if a trifle "tarrifying," as we say here. Most inspectors are terrifying; so much depends upon their verdict, and it is difficult for them to keep the sense of their importance out of their manner. One inspector I know exercises a quite extraordinary and basilisco-like fascination by virtue of a rather stony blue eye, and a lapis-lazuli in his finger-ring of the same tint. These in a remarkable way react upon and reduplicate each other. He, too, is a good fellow, but full of fads, and the worst of these is grammar. I heard him once take a class in grammar. He asked, amongst other useless things, the meaning of "intransitive." Happily no child knew, so he proceeded to explain. "Intransitive means *not going over;* an intransitive verb expresses an action that does not *go over* to an object. For example, the verb *jump* is intransitive; if I say, 'the cat jumps,' I describe an action that doesn't '*go over.*'" O mad inspector! I fear your teaching proved more intransitive than your cat's jump. At luncheon H.M. Inspector amused us with professional anecdotes. At a remote village school he had surprised the infant mistress watering the children with a garden rose before the examination began to keep them fresh. Another story was of a child whom he asked to explain the word "pilgrim." "Please, sir, a man who travels about." "But I travel about. Am I a pilgrim?" "Please, sir, a *good* man." As an example of what is meant by "visualising" in children (and the want of it in inspectors), he told us of a small boy who could not add nine to seven. The inspector, to make the sum easy, put it thus: "Suppose you had nine apples in one hand and seven in the other, how many would you have altogether?" "I should have two jolly good handfuls."

16*th*.—The papers report this morning the unveiling of three monuments: a bust in the Abbey of Thomas Arnold, a statue to Newman at the Brompton Oratory, and a granite column crowned by a bust of Shakespeare in the churchyard of St. Mary, Aldermanbury, to the editors of the first folio, Heminge and Condell. It was interesting to notice as characteristic of our tolerant age that several distinguished persons passed from the first of these celebrations to the second. The names of Heminge and Condell are less *répandus;* but their service to literature cannot easily be exaggerated, and it is pleasant to think that the great public should recognise who it is they have to thank (under Shakespeare) for eighteen of his thirty-six dramas. "We have but collected them," they say, "and done an office to the dead to procure his orphans guardians, without ambition either of self-profit or fame; only to keep the memory of so worthy a friend and fellow alive as was our Shakespeare." *Fellow* implies that they were players —Heminge a poor one, "Stuttering Hemmings," he is called; but besides being players, they were the leading proprietors and managers of the Globe and Blackfriars theatres, and so the owners of the plays they allowed to be published. In Shakespeare's will there is an item interlined: "To my fellowes, John Hemynges, Richard Burbage, and Henry Cundell, xxvj^s viij^d a peece to buy them ringes." The commentator Steevens has some amusing remarks on the greasy condition of most copies of the first folio that have come down:—

"Of all volumes those of popular entertainment are soonest injured. It would be difficult to name four folios that are oftener found in dirty and mutilated condition, than this first assemblage of Shakespeare's plays, 'God's Revenge against Murder,' 'The Gentleman's Recreation,' and 'Johnson's Lives of the Highwaymen.' Though Shakespeare was not, like Fox the Martyrologist, deposited in churches to be thumbed by the congregation, he generally took post on our hall tables; and that a multitude of his pages have 'their effect of gravy' may be imputed to the various eatables set out every morning on the same boards. It should seem that most of his readers were so chary of their time, that (like Pistol, who gnaws his leek and swears all the while) they fed and studied at the same instant. I have repeatedly met with thin flakes of pie-crust between the leaves of our author. These unctuous fragments, remaining long in close confinement, communicated their grease to several pages deep on each side of them.

It is easy enough to conceive how such accidents might happen—how Aunt Bridget's mastication might be disordered at the sudden entry of the Ghost into the Queen's closet, and how the half-chewed morsel dropped out of the gaping Squire's mouth when the visionary Banquo seated himself in the chair of Macbeth. Still, it is no small eulogium on Shakespeare that his claims were more forcible than those of hunger. Most of the first folios now extant are known to have belonged to ancient families resident in the country." Would that our ancient family possessed its copy, how succulent soever!

18*th*.—Met some people who have long lived at Woodbridge, and tried to glean a few fresh stories about Edward Fitz-Gerald, but with no success. All they could tell me was that he never entertained and rarely accepted invitations; that he walked about a great deal always wearing a plaid, always apparently lost in thought and recognising nobody, being indeed also short-sighted. He seems to have been regarded by the neighbours with a certain awe as a student and man of letters, though no one quite knew what he wrote or studied. The story lingers in the place that he once instructed his boatman to sew him up in a hammock when he died and pitch him overboard. But I am told that his tomb is now a place of pilgrimage, I suppose to young gentlemen who think the quatrains of Omar Khayyám the last word in the criticism of life. The pity of it, that Fitz-Gerald should have sacrificed so exquisite a literary gift to refurbishing such antique pessimism, and the irony of it, for a man who was always censuring Tennyson for his effeminating sentiment and calling on him for trumpet-blasts. I suppose if a man will live alone in the country and dine daily on vegetables and his own heart, there is no resisting pessimism. But Fitz-Gerald would himself have recognised that the quatrains were the poem of a mood. C. gave me lately E. F. G.'s Sophocles, with his autograph, and the funny churchwarden-Gothic bookplate designed for him by Thackeray. I remember being once told by the late W. B. Scott that Fitz-Gerald and Charles Keene were friends for a long time on the ground of a common attachment to the bagpipes before either knew the side of the other that the world now cares for.

19th.—Sunday. Megrims, so did not go to church. Who was it said that the one pleasure that never palled was the pleasure of not going to church? I have a notion that it was the Bishop of ———. Anyhow it could only be by reference to a constant type that the aberration would interest. Having Fitz-Gerald in my mind, I took down the first volume of "Wesley's Journal," a book of which E. F. G. thought highly, to read by way of sermon. It covers the years of Wesley's missionary expedition to the new colony of Georgia. One does not know which to wonder at most, his toughness of body or his toughness of mind. Both were extraordinary. What would one of even our hardest-worked London clergy think of the following Sunday programme :—

- 5–6.30 A.M. First English prayers.
- 9. Italian service for the Vaudois.
- 10.30–12.30. English service and sermon.
- 1 P.M. French sermon.
- 2. Catechising of children.
- 3. English evensong, followed by prayer meeting, &c.
- 6.30. German service, at which, however, Wesley attended only.

For another proof of his very remarkable physique, one might take this account of a travelling adventure, which was by no means unparalleled in his Colonial experience :—

"Mr. Delamotte and I, with a guide, set out to walk to the Cow-pen; when we had walked two or three hours, our guide told us plainly, 'He did not know where we were.' However, believing it could not be far off, we thought it best to go on. In an hour or two we came to a cypress swamp, which lay directly across our way; there was not time to walk back to Savannah before night, so we walked through it, the water being about breast high. By that time we had gone a mile beyond it, we were out of all path, and it being now past sunset, we sat down, intending to make a fire and to stay there till morning; but finding our tinder wet we were at a stand. I advised to walk on still, but my companions being faint and weary, were for lying down, which we accordingly did about six o'clock; the ground was as wet as our cloaks, which (it being a sharp frost) were soon froze together; however, I slept till six in the morning. There fell a heavy dew in the night, which covered us over as white as snow. Within an hour after sunrise we came to a plantation, and in the evening, without any hurt, to Savannah." (Wednesday, December 23, 1736.)

Every page of the journal testifies to the scholar no less than the gentleman. He quotes obscure Greek epigrams; he reads to his Savannah flock exhortations of St. Ephrem Syrus. Fancy Mr. H. P. Hughes reciting the rhythms of this saint to a congregation at St. James's Hall! On his voyage back to England he reads Machiavelli to see what can be made of that political dissenter, and comes to a decided conclusion:—

"In my passage home, having procured a celebrated book, the works of Nicholas Machiavel, I set myself carefully to read and consider it. I began with a prejudice in his favour, having been informed he had often been misunderstood, and greatly misrepresented. I weighed the sentiments that were less common; transcribed the passages wherein they were contained; compared one passage with another, and endeavoured to form a cool impartial judgment. And my cool judgment is, that if all the other doctrines of devils which have been committed to writing since letters were in the world were collected together in one volume, it would fall short of this: and that should a prince form himself by this book, so calmly recommending hypocrisy, treachery, lying, robbery, oppression, adultery, whoredom, and murder of all kinds, Domitian or Nero would be an angel of light compared to that man." (January 26, 1737.)

22nd.—Read at the Club Mr. Gladstone's attack on the minor poet in Henley's *New Review.* "He may write if he likes, but he must not print." The advice has an air of wisdom, and it may be offered with even more urgency to translators of Horace. For translation, though undoubtedly a useful exercise, cannot deserve printer's ink and paper unless the translator be a poet of equal genius with his author. And poets do not, as a rule, think it worth while to translate each other. Why is it that Horace appeals so irresistibly to the prosaic mind—even of good men? Why, for instance, should the venerable hand that gave us an annotated Psalter give us also a version of Horace? For my part, I sympathise strongly with the poet, still happily living, who, on being asked to English an ode of Horace, replied, "I should as soon think of doing Moore into Greek anapæsts or Tupper into Greek elegiacs." Mr. Gladstone suggests that when a man discovers he is not a great poet he should cease to print. But how is this simple-sounding discovery to be made? The poet does not, like the orator, appeal to the crowd, and estimate his greatness by the poll. He knows that if his gift is original it must at first be vocal only to the understanding few, for the crowd read only what their demagogues bid them. It was Bright who made Sir Lewis Morris's vogue, and for how many reputations is not Mr. Gladstone responsible! The recent competition for the laureateship, which to thoughtless people seemed so ridiculous, meant no more than that poets, like other authors, prefer a large to a small sale, and so wished to secure the great public that buys only what has the *cachet*. But Mr. Gladstone would reply, let the young poet consult the critics.

Alas! who are the critics? His critic may be the man he snubbed yesterday at the Club; or some young puppy fresh from the university bent on using his milk-teeth at all costs; or some editor, with a bee in his bonnet, determined that Bilson shall be the greatest living poet, and every other father's son, Tomson, Dickson, and Harrison nowhere. Austin Dobson has an interesting apologue, called "The Poet and the Critics," in "At the Sign of the Lyre." If, on the other hand, the young poet gets praise, it will probably be because he is himself a member of the press-gang. The public, then, being uninterested, and the critics interested, the young poet must fall back on himself. But if he understands how bad his first book is, it will only be because he has the power to make the next better, and so he will try again. Similarly he will try again, if he thinks his book good. So that the situation is really hopeless, and must be left.

24th.—Stayed in town to attend the presentation of the statuette of Sir Thomas More to the Chelsea Library. It is curious that London should be content with such a meagre memorial of one of her greatest sons.

Went afterwards to a meeting of a little society to encourage the employment of men who have served their time with the colours. Could not a similar society be started to find occupation for retired officers? Surely we are as a class the most pitiable people in the world. A day arrives when we lose our chief interest in life. The routine work of duty, the slave that bore the burden and heat with a light heart and easy conscience falls dead; and we must look about for a successor. Sometimes the by-work is set to the mill, and loses much of its zest in consequence. L. turns his lathe now all the morning, instead of at odd moments, and his house is fast filling with useless little pots; H. scours the country collecting grandfather's clocks for the sake of the brass corners on their faces; M. has taken up with the Church Association, and pesters the bishops with resolutions against Rome. They are fairly happy; but how many I know at Eastbourne and Southsea and other watering-places, who are sorely conscious, except for a month or two in autumn, of the passage of time—"time's discrete flow," as the psychologists call it—the odious *now, now, now.* "A man's life's no more than to say *one*," said Hamlet; but that was his hopelessly unpractical turn of mind, or possibly his fulness of matter. To many it is to say *one, one, one,* as the clock ticks.

27th.—Went to the sale at —— Manor. Fuller long ago remarked that Berkshire land was skittish and apt to throw its rider; but since the great fall in prices it has been changing hands very rapidly. The old yeomen of whom the county has long made its boast—Mavor attributing to Mr. Pitt the saying "that no minister could command ten votes in Berkshire"—are finding it impossible to go on farming at a loss, and are selling their land to rich strangers from town. The old manor-houses are pulled down and mansions take their place. It is a sad change for the yeomen and their friends, and perhaps for the country, but profitable for the peasantry, who will get better paid and housed.

28th.—What a topsy-turvy sort of vanity is that

which takes pleasure in being like distinguished people. I met a curate this afternoon at our Member's garden-party who is the very twin of the Archbishop of Canterbury,[1] only that he is of course "less consequential about the legs." He had the archiepiscopal carriage and look, even to the smile, which is a good smile, though not quite so good as the Pope's;—*that* seems to have more centuries behind it. I know, too, several middle-aged gentlemen who are not unlike the newspaper pictures of the Prince of Wales. But how can the resemblance in any reasonable way feed vanity, as it certainly does? There is more interest in being like the mighty dead, because one may cherish a mild Pythagoreanism. For example, my own nickname at school was Socrates, and I have recently discovered that I might have sat for the portrait of Ravaillac. Sophia often asks me why I keep a picture of the poet Gray on my mantelpiece; the reason is that it is so very like her, especially about the chin; but I do not like to say so, as she might not be flattered.

August 1st.—I am not happy. The cause of my unhappiness is nothing very great, but, on the contrary, something very small indeed; so small that it might be deemed below the dignity of a journal were I not able to record it in classical phrase. "There is an insect with us, especially in

[1] The late Archbishop Benson.

chalky districts, which is very troublesome and teasing all the latter end of the summer, getting into people's skins and raising tumours, which itch intolerably. This animal (which is called a harvest-bug) is very minute, scarce discernible to the naked eye, of a bright scarlet colour, and of the genus of *acarus*." (White's "Selborne," Letter 35.) Everybody has his pet specific; in past years I have employed the oil of cajeput; but the success is indifferent, and the aura one moves in undeniably pungent. My wife has endeavoured to convince me that I should resent it in my neighbours.

2nd.—It is no longer the fashion to relate one's dreams at breakfast, but last night's dream, as much as I can remember of it, is worth recording. It was an episode in a police case. I was in a well-lighted train half asleep when another train flared by and roused me. Looking in its direction I saw reflected in the windows of the passing carriages a scuffle, gagging, and robbery that was being transacted in the next compartment to mine; and at the end of the journey I identified the criminal. I do not remember that this possibility has been used by any writer of detective fiction. The idea is of no use to me whatever, and I should be glad to exchange it for something more serviceable. My more usual dreams are dialogues. It seems an extraordinary thing that one should be able to converse with oneself and enjoy all the excitement of expectation as to what is to come next. I ask a searching question or deliver what seems a crushing retort, and wait anxiously for the reply just as if the interlocutor were another person. But probably this is the ordinary experience of the novelist or dramatist—the sort with imagination, I mean; only they see visions while I but dream dreams. At least, I know whenever I meet ———, he is sure to say, "Isn't that a magnificent thing so-and-so says in my new piece? it is so like him;" whereas his natural modesty would prevent his calling attention to his own good things. I have always regretted that the ingenious author of "Happy Thoughts" got so little way with his "Handbook of Repartee;" it would have been invaluable to me in waking hours when my wit is always *l'esprit de l'escalier*. But failing this, it would be useful to have an historical handbook—not "what to say to an Abbé or Fakir," but what actually has been said in the way of repartee to or by distinguished Fakirs and Abbés. The book would naturally begin with the best things of the Abbé de Talleyrand. Not the least interesting pages would be those devoted to Bus-drivers and Policemen; for the wit in these cases is sometimes as subtle as in the more polished examples, and I heartily sympathise with Burton, author of the "Anatomy of Melancholy," whose one amusement was listening to the wit encounters of Oxford bargees. The other day I overheard the following:—

A.—Does your mother take in washing?
B.—Yes, and she ain't particular to having a gentleman-lodger, but he must know how to behave hisself *like* a gentleman, yer know.

I thought this excellent in several respects; it did not take umbrage at the suggestion of the laundry, but accepted it and went even further into biographical particulars, and then produced the sting, where the sting ought to be, in the tail. As some help to the future author of the Handbook, I note that one useful form of repartee depends upon Paronomasia, another upon looking closely at Metaphors, a third upon Quotation. A good example of the first is the reply of Sir Robert Walpole to Sarah, Duchess of Marlborough, who was indignant at being offered the revived Order of the Bath, and would take nothing but the Garter: "Madam, the Bath must come before the Garter."[1] Of the second, this is the best instance that occurs to me at the moment:—

Ritualist.—At least you will own that Art is the handmaid of Religion?
Protestant.—Yes, and I wish Religion would give her a month's notice.

---

[1] This story proves incidentally that washing did not, like Christmas Trees and Crystal Palaces, come in with the late Prince Consort.

The third I will illustrate from the same witty scholar, whose praise is in the University. An Ibsenite was running down Shakespeare and saying his characters were not "alive." To which my friend replied: "Oh yes, they're *alive*, but not *kicking*; certainly not *kicking*." In many cases a repartee is helped by a stammer. Of this use Charles Lamb is the classical example, but my Oxford friend runs him hard.

4th.—To-day the ladies set off by train to Southsea, and I on my bicycle. I ran first to Farnham, so as to spend a few hours at the Volunteer Manœuvres. The hops in the neighbourhood looked well. Some were shown me that had grown in the same field for three hundred years, but it will soon not pay to grow them. After tea I resumed my journey, and joined the Portsmouth road at Petersfield. I noticed on the way that Wolmer Pond was nearly dry. In such a drought a hundred and fifty years ago search was made in the bed, and there was a great find of Roman coins. It might be worth while to try again.

5th.—I strolled after breakfast to see who of my old acquaintance might be here. For a time the pageant of bright faces was singularly attractive; then I longed for some one to chat with or, at least, nod to—apothecary, plough-boy, thief. I mused with Bacon, "Little do men perceive what solitude is and how far it extendeth; for a crowd is not company, and faces are but a gallery of pictures." Which meant that my liver was beginning to show its distaste for the seaside; luckily I soon met Colonel ——, and in talk over old times forgot my melancholy. The roads were all crowded with bicycles, and their smoothness justifies the exercise. Ladies outnumber men and are more dangerous to pedestrians, being too careless in turning corners without ringing their bells. It seems the fashion to read as one wheels. Some enterprising publisher should start a Bicycle Library, on light paper with big type. So far I have escaped injury, but Bob, the fox terrier, was run over this morning. No doubt he was a good deal to blame. This is his first visit to a town, and he has been trying to maintain the country etiquette of speaking to every dog he meets— which is dangerous among so many vehicles. There is a grand parade of bicyclists before dinner, when the skilful exhibit their tricks. Some enthusiasts appear again in the evening. And certainly the gliding motion of so many lamps, the noiseless noise of the machines, and the half-seen passage of ambling nymphs and caracoling cavaliers has a very pleasing effect.

7th.—A correspondent is good enough to inform me that the story I entered in my journal on July 2 about the groom's confusion between playing and visiting cards was told him at Constantinople in 1847 by a Turk whom he met at table in the Hôtel de l'Europe, but he told it of a lady. The Turk proved to be a certain Seyd Ali, well known at that date as an interpreter, in which capacity he served in Colonel Chesney's Euphrates Expedition. The tale is probably told in every society which uses both sorts of cards, and speaks of them as "cards" without a qualifying epithet.

11*th*.—It is astonishing that the Admiralty do not take more pains to interest our inland villages in seafaring. Only one boy has in my recollection gone from us for a sailor, and he did not get further than Portsmouth, being obliged to return as he had no certificate of good conduct. He was one of Tom's under-gardeners and had a soul above cabbages. So the next time vegetables irked him he went to Reading, and took his shilling in the ordinary way. He was much above the average yokel in intelligence—I fancy he had a dash of gipsy-blood in him—and is now a clarionet player in the band. Cheap excursions will do much good in breaking down the old horror of the sea. I remember a sick boy of my old gardener's being sent to a Convalescent Home, and charged by his mother on no account to go near the water. After his first day he wrote home a post-card, which his mother showed me in fear and trembling; this was its audacious message: "There is nothing to be afraid of, it comes up like a snale."

14th.—Whenever there is likely to be work with the House of Lords, I read the *Daily Chronicle*, as in old days we used to read the *Star*—"for sweetness and charity," as Matthew Arnold said. It has hardly been up to its best vituperative form over the Irish Land Bill. "Splendid fatuity" and "unutterable farce" are not epoch-making phrases; they lack discrimination; and "three ridiculous old gentlemen," as the description of a quorum, is unworthy even of the *Star* of to-day. Possibly the editor of the *Chronicle* has discovered the elixir, and secured perpetual youth; but even so, "old" is ungracious; and why "ridiculous"? So many peers in the present House have been made and not born, that their intellect and manners are probably yet pretty much those of commoners. But it takes indignation to make satire, and though a landlord is an evil beast enough (while a "proprietor"—subtle distinction—is an angel), none but a spiritual peer can rouse the *Chronicle* to a really fine frenzy. I have never forgotten a sentence that closed the story of the rejection of the Home Rule Bill. "Thus the Bishops completed the work which their ancestors, the Scribes and Pharisees, began eighteen hundred years ago." I have often thought that this sentence had something to do with the Radical collapse at the polls. Of course the *Chronicle* is not without virtues, not the least being its enterprise; and I have been shown once or twice a piece of literary criticism that it would be hard to overpraise.

15th.—The news that to-day is Hospital Saturday in Southsea was broken to us at breakfast by the maid bringing in a collecting-box.

> " The veins unfill'd, our blood is cold, and then
> We pout upon the morning, are unapt
> To give."

However, we had plenty of opportunity, when our souls were suppler, to amend our beneficence. The streets were crowded with young women dressed like nurses and wearing a red cross, who smiled and smiled, and pushed a box into one's waistcoat. For a time I smiled and put them by; but at last was driven to my bicycle. Even then they lay waiting at the thievish corners of the streets, and bade one stand and deliver. The young men seemed to like it, but my seat is perhaps not so good as theirs, and I took to a country road. I see one of the papers has an apposite article on bazaars and other church leeches, on the whole condemning them. They seem to me as justifiable as the smiles of these engaging damsels. Both are an attempt to divert by cajolery certain sums from the milliner and cigar merchant to the sick and needy. Good churchmen, of course, tythe their incomes for charity, but there are churchmen and churchwomen who do not, and it is for these that bazaars exist. In old days such were dealt with firmly by the priest at the deathbed; if we substitute the love of pleasure for the fear of pain, we employ no higher, but certainly no lower, motive. It does not seem in any sense fair to class bazaars with gambling hells; there is no question of doing evil that good may come; it is a fact that Flavia,[1] now as much as a century ago, requires some stronger stimulus than pure benevolence before she will put her silver penny in the alms-dish, and the fact must be taken account of. Goldsmith tells a capital story of the method Beau Nash employed to extort a subscription from a reluctant duchess for the hospital at Bath:—

"The sums he gave, and collected for the hospital, were great, and his manner of doing it was no less admirable. I am told that he was once collecting money in *Wiltshire's* room for that purpose, when a lady entered who is more remarkable for her wit than her charity, and not being able to pass by him unobserved, she gave him a pat with her fan, and said, *You must put down a trifle for me*, Nash, *for I have no money in my pocket.* Yes, madam, says he, that I will, with pleasure, if

---

[1] "If any one asks Flavia to do something in charity, if she likes the person who makes the proposal, or happens to be in a right *temper*, she will toss him *half-a-crown* or a crown, and tell him if he knew what a *long Milliner's bill* she had just received, he would think it a great deal for her to give." (Law's "Serious Call," p. 96; but see the whole witty description of this modish lady.)

your grace will tell me when to stop : then taking a handful of guineas out of his pocket, he began to tell them into his white hat, one, two, three, four, five. *Hold, hold,* says the dutchess, *consider what you are about.* Consider your rank and fortune, madam, says *Nash,* and continued telling, six, seven, eight, nine, ten. Here the dutchess called again, and seemed angry. Pray compose yourself, *madam,* cried *Nash,* and don't interrupt the work of charity; eleven, twelve, thirteen, fourteen, fifteen. Here the dutchess stormed and caught hold of his hand. Peace, *madam,* says *Nash;* you shall have your name written in letters of gold, *madam,* and upon the front of the building, *madam.* Sixteen, seventeen, eighteen, nineteen, twenty. *I won't pay a farthing more,* says the dutchess. Charity hides a multitude of sins, replies *Nash.* Twenty-one, twenty-two, twenty-three, twenty-four, twenty-five. *Nash,* says she, *I protest you frighten me out of my wits, L—d, I shall die !* Madam, you will never die with doing good; and if you do, it will be the better for you, answered *Nash,* and was about to proceed ; but perceiving her grace had lost all patience, a parley ensued, when he, after much altercation, agreed to stop his hand, and compound with her grace for thirty guineas. The dutchess, however, seemed displeased the whole evening; and when he came to the table where she was playing, bid him *stand farther, an ugly devil, for she hated the sight of him.* But her grace afterwards, having a run of good luck, called *Nash* to her. *Come,* says she, *I will be friends with you, though you are a fool; and to let you see I am not angry, there is ten guineas more for your charity. But this I insist on, that neither my name nor the sum shall be mentioned."* ("Life of Richard Nash, Esq.," p. 121.)

18*th*.—It would be an astonishing thing, but for the known laziness of human nature, that parents should allow their children to attend revivalistic meetings on the beach at seaside places. The religion of children should be simple and home-made, enthusiastic, if you please, but breezy and full of ozone; the reverse of morbid. Now the spiritual methods of these beach-combers are about as healthy as their physical methods. They collect a vast array of children together, and seat them cheek by jowl, dirty by clean, on a hot August day, in circles of an inferno, with a double row of nurses behind to keep out any stray whiffs of fresh air; and then instead of telling them, as our Catechism does, that they are Christians and should behave themselves as such, they call them sinners, who will probably die young, and then—the preacher will not answer for the consequences. In some cases, too, that I know of, the preacher has told children to come against their parents' wishes; a pretty religion, surely, that begins with the breach of the first ethical commandment. Parents that I have remonstrated with for allowing their children to attend these services defend themselves by saying that it *may* do the children good; a plea that shows the importance of the Johnsonian precept to free one's *mind* from cant.

19*th*.—My term of patience at the sea having reached its period, we have come for a few days' visit to the B——'s, near Guildford, to fill the interval before we are expected at P——'s place in Norfolk. I took train to Petersfield, as it seemed unnecessary to labour up the south slope of the downs, and then followed the Portsmouth road through Liphook, &c. The heather was in brilliant beauty, and a Scotsman whom I boarded on the road confessed that it put him in mind of his own country. I vowed that should I ever become a potentate, I would be "Sowdun of Surrye." My friendly Scot, by his pleasant society, more than halved the toil of climbing Hindhead. He pointed out the objects of interest on the road, such as the "Seven Thorns" Inn, telling me how the landlord resented Mrs. Oliphant's use of it in the "Cuckoo in the Nest." When we reached the top he showed me all the counties of England and the glory of them. The run from Hindhead down to Godalming will remain long in memory. The road was perfect; it was about mid-day, and exceedingly hot; but the rapid motion made a breeze, which seemed to insulate me from the flames. There was no one else on the road for the seven miles of descent; and this was perhaps as well, for my spirits were so much raised that I could not help shouting. I thought of Elijah going to heaven in a chariot of fire, and extinguished a scruple about the downward direction by a vague reference to Antipodes. Every now and then the wind brought a hot whiff of the bramble. In the valley there was shade once more, and the aromatic smell of firs; but what ointment is not spoilt by flies? I was so much cheered by the journey that I conceived a tenderness for any bicyclists I met, and would have accosted them had they not looked strangely on me. There should be (perhaps there is) some formal salutation for the road, or better several, one for meeting on a level, one of encouragement to the bicyclist going up hill, one of congratulation to the fortunate brother going down.

21*st*.—Was Mr. Watts present at Millais' funeral? The *Daily* ——, in one column, tells me that "conspicuous among those, &c., was the venerable form, &c.," and in another that "in accordance with his habitual practice, Mr. Watts did not attend the ceremony." It must be very difficult for an editor to maintain consistency among so many picturesque writers. I remember at the end of the Ashanti War that the same paper honoured Prince Henry as a patriot who gave his life for his country, and applauded the withholding of rewards from the survivors who no less had to face the dangerous climate. "It would be a remarkable arrow that should pick out only the brave," said the Spartan prisoner in Thucydides; so these gentlemen attributed too much discrimination to the malaria.

25th.—The papers report that the Pope has included Zola's "Rome" in the *Index Expurgatorius*. Was it not Pio Nono who, being asked by an author to do something for a book of his, after long reflection, replied, "I will tell you what I can do; I can put it on the Index"?

September 5th.—A chronicle of sport—so many guns and such and such a bag—is not lively reading for any but the particular sportsman, and it takes a meteorologist to find interest in a chronicle of bad weather; so for the early days of September I leave the record of birds and rain to the exuberant imagination. We travelled into Norfolk leisurely at the end of last month, taking Cambridge and Ely on our way. Sometimes we journeyed by rail, sometimes on our own wheels, and in the latter mode of progress seemed to renew the golden age when folks were content to ride on horseback, and had time to look about them. But even behind the horseman rode "black

Care"; nor does that Fury desert the bicyclist, though forced by the exiguity of the saddle to shift her position to one or other tyre, where she stands, like Fortune, on the ever-rolling circle,

> "Allowing us a breath, a little scene,
> Inspiring us with self and vain conceit,
> and humour'd thus,
> Comes at the last, and with a little pin . . ."

Cambridge was just emptying itself of what are called "Extension students," many of them school-mistresses who take the opportunity of enlarging the range of their interests or hearing the latest theories on some pet hobby. Without being in the least what Peacock calls a "Pantopragmatic" one may allow that lectures in this way fulfil a useful function; and probably there has never been since the days of the sophists so well-considered an attempt on the part of those who know to share their knowledge and spread enthusiasm. The ladies had not seen Cambridge before, and were becomingly impressed with its characteristic glories—the rosy-brown brick of Trinity and St. John's and Queen's; the "backs"; King's Chapel; and not least the marvellous statue of Newton "with his prism and silent face." We plucked a few mulberries, too, from Milton's tree at Christ's.

Coming from the undulations of a down country, we were much struck by the peculiar beauty of the eastern counties, the beauty of a flat landscape

—the long stretch of meadows to a dim horizon, broken by clumps of trees, an occasional windmill, or the glimpse of a white sail on a hidden stream. Even the geometrical canals had prospective.

6th.—Last Sunday and to-day we drove into Norwich for the cathedral service. The English Matins and Evensong are *sui generis;* how different they are from the corresponding Roman services, out of which they have been evolved, any traveller knows who has heard the choir office gone through in a foreign church, "entunĕd in the nose full seemĕly." They are English to the core, and are excellently fitted to express or suppress, to half reveal and half conceal, what the average Englishman calls his religious feelings. The double chant is a kind of symbol of the whole, and those Italianate clergy who hold by Gregorians deny their birthright. I could wish it were the custom not to begin singing till the "O Lord, open Thou our lips"; the Exhortation on G, as usually rendered, is about as silly and unimpressive a piece of ceremonial as was ever devised, and the General Confession is only a little better. I sympathise in this point with the hot-heads who are for getting back to Edward's First Prayer Book, which opened admirably with the "Our Father." More attention might be given in cathedrals as well as parish churches, to the reading of the lessons. A style is required midway between the dull monotone sometimes affected by the High Church school and the over-dramatic manner of others. At Norwich last Sunday a very exalted dignitary thundered out St. Paul's advice about buying your meat at the butcher's without asking too many questions, as though it were a matter of eternal spiritual import to all present, instead of a mere piece of antiquarianism. We lunched in Norwich, as I wished to hear Tom Mann, who was advertised to address a meeting in the afternoon. He had not much voice and strained it painfully, but he was impressive from the nervous energy and the air of conviction with which he spoke; and I was agreeably surprised at his moderation.

7th.—I have a great respect for the *Standard* newspaper; it maintains, as a rule, a dignity and a self-restraint which in these last days are becoming rare. But, too often, when an article is required on the British aristocracy, it puts the pen into the hand of our old friend Jeames de la Pluche. There is no mistaking his style this morning. The Duke of Marlborough has been feasting Conservative associations—a circumstance that would have inspired Theognis, who said, "You should eat and drink with the nobility, for from the good you will learn what is good." Twenty-five centuries pass and the spirit of Theognis takes flesh again in Jeames. "It is well," he says, "that these great gatherings should sometimes be held in the grounds belonging to members of the aristocracy whose ancestors have helped to make the history of England. For there is nothing better calculated to make men Conservatives in the best sense of the word than a knowledge of our national history, and the steps by which its glory grew. It may be true enough that the celebrated man, the founder of the ducal House of Marlborough, had his weak points. Addison's famous simile of the angel has often been laughed at, but *there is quite as much truth in it as in most similes*,[1] and it is well that the *people* should be from time to time reminded of the fact that *aristocracy* tends to develop qualities not less valuable in the domestic arena ['domestic arena' is good], than on the field of battle. The 'calmness' imputed to Marlborough at the most trying moments of his career is one of these." The party press is generally secure in appealing to popular ignorance. Still, to tell them that aristocracy tends to develop calmness of the

---

[1] What does this mean? The *Tatler* of the day (No. 43) praised it, apart from its "sublimity," on the ground that it complimented "the general and his queen at the same time."

> "So when an Angel by Divine Command
> With rising Tempests shakes a guilty Land,
> Such as of late o'er pale Britannia past,
> Calm and serene he drives the furious Blast;
> And, pleas'd th' Almighty's Orders to perform,
> Rides in the Whirl-wind, and directs the Storm."

Marlborough type, however true it may be, is not wise; it is not calculated to make them Conservatives in any sense of the term. Nor is it wise generally to encourage much investigation into the title-deeds of "our old nobility." Lord Verulam (than whom none knew better) says very pregnantly, "Those that are first raised to nobility are commonly more virtuous [*i.e.* capable],[1] but less innocent, than their descendants; for there is rarely any rising but by a commixture of good and evil arts." Lord Wolseley spoilt his apology for Marlborough by printing the Duke's portrait in the book, a portrait with *sui amans* written in every line of the "calm" and handsome face.

8th.—I spent a day looking at the best of the forty churches that Norwich can boast, but made no discoveries not already made in the guide-books. In St. Andrew's Church I visited the tomb of Sir John Suckling for the sake of his poet son, who is figured kneeling by it. The porter who showed me over what was once the church of the Dominicans, and is now two public halls, had the true ecclesiological instinct, and should have been a verger. "It is quite vexing," said he, "when I

---

[1] Cf. *Winter's Tale,* iv. 3:

"AUTOLYCUS. I cannot tell for which of his virtues it was, but he was certainly whipped out of the court.

"CLOWN. His vices, you would say.

"AUTOLYCUS. Vices, I would say, sir."

read the old histories to see there used to be a high altar here, with stalls all round it, and you could look the whole length from choir to nave. *Now* there's nothing to see" (with a wave of his arm to the civic pictures) " but these old celebrities —very interesting, no doubt, for the costumes of the period." I felt sympathy as well as pity for the old-fashioned fellow, who did not know that our masses are now evangelised by picture exhibitions.[1] I made my way also to Borrow's house and the site of Sir Thomas Browne's. They have recently been marked by tablets. The inmates of the former—a very pretty house, standing back from the main street and approached by a narrow entry—seemed amused at my interest in Borrow, of whom they had naturally never heard till the tablet made their house a shrine of occasional pilgrimage.

10*th*.—Rain. I found on the library table the *Romanes* lecture by Dr. Creighton on the " English National Character." It is specially interesting at the present moment from its main thesis, which is that from the first England has shown "a tendency to withdraw cautiously from the general system of Europe and go its own way. . . . Its dominant

---

[1] I once saw an example of sudden conversion. Arrius and Arria were strolling along the galleries at Hampton Court, looking very much depressed. At last Arrius saw a word that pierced home to him. It was "—— landing at Margate." He turned round to his companion and said, "Good old Margate, good old 'all by the sea! let's go and have a drink!"

motive seems simply to have been a stubborn desire to manage its own affairs in its own way, without any interference from outside." The Bishop illustrates this from England's relation both to the Empire and the Papacy. Some of the national characteristics are very happily sketched. "Who does not know the travelling Englishman aggrieved because he may not argue the rights of his particular case as against some general rule, which the native finds no difficulty in dutifully obeying? His grievance lies in the sense that the rules never contemplated his particular case." Never shall I forget the picture of —— swearing in choice Italian at a station-master because he would not let us have our luggage after office hours. The trunks lay behind a glass-door, conspicuous to all, and it needed but a turn of the key to release them, and there were excellent reasons why they should not remain there all night, but—rules were rules. The Bishop tells a good and characteristically English story of Robert Tomson of Andover, who sailed from Bristol to Cadiz with the purpose of making his fortune, learned Spanish, sailed to Mexico, suffered shipwreck and plague, reached his destination, found a Scotsman[1] there who befriended him, talked

---

[1] Is this not also characteristic, both as to the friendliness and the enterprise? In the dark days before the gospel of Free Trade was preached, we English were a little jealous of our northern brethren, as

theology, was delated to the Inquisition, sent back to Seville and imprisoned for three years, married a fortune, and lived happily ever after.

13th.—We came for a few days to this hotel at Lowestoft for a final breath of the sea air. There must be people who like hotel life, as they stay here for months together; but it is impossible to say of it, as Johnson said of taverns in his day, that "there is a general freedom from anxiety." On the contrary, the ladies seem anxious to outshine each other in their dresses, the men in their vintages. In my youth champagne was reserved for festival occasions; here it is drunk like beer. This is good for the exchequer, but it strikes me as ungentlemanlike. After dinner last night some

---

Boswell abundantly testifies. Among the recently printed Dartmouth papers is a letter written when George III. was king, which contains the following amusing paragraph:—"I am certainly the most unfortunate man in the world. Two Scotsmen, the only two, I am persuaded, who are not in office and employment, have plundered the house in Hanover Square. I wish the Administration had provided for them before. If I had been pillaged with the rest of the nation, or persecuted with the rest of the Opposition, I could have been contented, but these private pilferings are very unfair. However, by the vigilance of Sir John Fielding, and notwithstanding all the endeavours of Lord Mansfield and the rest of the Cabinet Council, the thieves are taken, and now my mother is much more alarmed at the thought of their being hanged than she was with the robbery; but I tell her she may be perfectly easy, that they are very safe, and will be in place and in the House of Commons next Parliament." It is undoubtedly a great advantage to belong to a little clan, if its members are vigorous and patriotic, and if I were an author I should certainly turn Scotsman or else Roman Catholic. Then I should be sure that my merits would not fail of recognition in the press.

singers came on to the lawn, and I had an opportunity of hearing the current comic songs. The one most applauded celebrated the cheap chicanery of some rascal who left his cabman in the lurch, &c.; the chorus was, "He's waiting there for me." This would seem to lend colour to Sir Edward Fry's indictment of our commercial morality. I had some talk with a literary lady, or rather she had some talk with me, but to me it was disappointing, being for the most part personal gossip. I did not see how she differed from any ordinary matron who gives away her "friends" with a cup of tea, except that the friends were people who write books. This reminds me that I met this morning young ———, whose novels are coming into notice. He asked my felicitations on his approaching marriage, which I gave with sincerity, and offered a piece of advice into the bargain—not to formulate his wife's faults, should he ever discover any. It is my experience that faults are less easily pardoned when "set in a note-book," and this is the business of the novelist. I regard this sage counsel with some complacency as the "something attempted, something done" that has earned my night's repose. For at the seaside I behave very much like the exquisite who "made a point of never doing any work between meals."

14*th*.—It is a long time since I have stayed in a

house fronting a public road, and either my nerves have become case-softened with age or the children of this generation are noisier than their predecessors. Hawkers and street organists I do not complain of; they have a use in the commonwealth, though I am far from believing they do not take a savage joy in wreaking what amounts to a revenge upon society. The noises that anger me are such as have no use. At this instant a girl, aged about twelve, is riding her bicycle up and down the street, ringing her bell furiously all the time for sheer delight in the din; a small boy, not to be outdone, is drawing a stick along the railings; a second hoyden is being dragged by her companions in a little cart, shuffling her feet on the pavement as she goes; and a very small child is making daylight sick with a bladder whistle. "Eating strawberry jam to the sound of a trumpet" was a child's notion of heaven. One comprehends why the celibate schoolmen assigned as many babies as possible a limbo to themselves.

> "Continuo auditæ voces, vagitus et ingens,
> Infantumque animæ flentes."

Had they lived in these days of emancipated children, they would have extended its hospitality to noise-makers of riper years.

17th.—This morning I watched the fishing-boats being tugged out of the harbour—a very picturesque sight. They were roped together in a long chain, and by their bobbing motion suggested a caravan of camels. The sails were red and weathered for the most part to beautiful tints. There have been two fatal accidents lately in hydraulic lifts; the last victim bore the distinguished but ill-omened name of Richard Plantagenet. The earliest reference I remember to a lift for people comes in the Greville "Memoirs"; it was constructed for Victor Emmanuel at Genoa. "For the comfort of their bodies he has had a machine made like a car, which is drawn up by a chain from the bottom to the top of the house; it holds about six people, who can be at pleasure elevated to any storey; and at each landing-place there is a contrivance to let them in and out" (March 18, 1830). The description is a little wanting in precision.

21st.—The weather cannot be better described than by our Berkshire phrase "wunnerful cas'alty." For several days the glass had been slowly rising, and no rain fell here all Sunday. By mid-day the oats that remained out were dry enough to carry, and the ricks were opened to receive them, when lo! a waterspout for some four hours.

The Vicar and his wife came to dine for the first time, and we had a small party, chiefly clergy folk, to meet them. He seems a good fellow at bottom, despite his curious and inconsequential streak of Socialism. He has a little the air of a disappointed man; the *fallentis semita vitæ* is, I suspect, neither his courage nor his choice, but his necessity in being married. He took a good degree at Oxford, and was expected to do something considerable, but his great book is still to write, and being something of a poet and little of a partisan, no politician, and not even a nephew of the Lord Chancellor, he has not attracted public patronage; and, as his children are growing numerous, he was glad to accept Tom's offer. I was a little afraid at one point in the meal that conversation would be stranded, and I heard Sophia open a discussion on the difference between a "pie" and a "tart," which is with her a signal of distress; but by introducing a clerical topic we got into deep water again. Some one referred to the *Times*' letters on the poverty of so many country livings, expressing strong resentment at the irrelevant irruption of grumbling laymen headed by a gentleman whom I blushed to hear described as "Giant Grim." It is odd that Churchmen should lag so far behind Dissenters in the matter of providing for their ministers. I noticed in church a few Sundays ago, that a full quarter of the offertory sentences enforce this duty, but these are seldom read: I suppose the parson can hardly be expected to read them. In the country farmers and even squires feel they are being generous in simply paying their tythe, forgetting that they inherited, or bought, or leased the land subject to that charge, so that it does not come out of their own pockets. "Us wun't be prosperous," said one fine old Berkshire farmer, "till us have fewer of they black parsons, and more of they black pigs." Happily for the Vicar, Tom redeemed his tythe before the great fall in prices. My neighbour T., who makes his money out of starch and farms for pleasure, sets a good example by paying his tythe at par instead of seventy per cent. Some one mentioned the cartoons in the *Westminster Gazette* dealing with the Armenians; and from that the talk drifted to the unpopularity of the clergy, which that paper had lately discussed. It is difficult in the country to arrive at a judgment on the matter. "Murmuring in their tents" is and always was the peculiar vice of the wilderness, and the parson comes in for even a bigger share than the squire. He visits too seldom, or too frequently, or at awkward hours; he is inquisitorial in distributing alms, or lets himself be hoodwinked by impostors; his preaching is too short or too long, commonplace or over people's heads. The older parsons professed to remark little change in the attitude of their parishioners to them, but the younger men complained that their advice was apt to be resented as interference. This is what one would expect; the new sense of independence would feel a little *déplacé* and ashamed of itself before old gentlemen who did not recognise its existence, especially if they were humorous and dictatorial, of the Menenius Agrippa type, like so many country parsons of the old school. While the port was going round, I ventured a few remarks about my sermon experiences while away from home. I had found the sermons as a rule good, but badly delivered. I quoted Byrom for a similar judgment last century, and suggested that each rural deanery should acquire the services of an elocution master for a number of lessons. A clerical neighbour, who has an irritating trick in the pulpit of connecting his clauses by the interjection *urrer*, demurred, on the ground that their congregations would prefer them, as at present, to speak "as a man to men." I explained that my suggestion implied nothing more than a little coaching in voice-production.

22nd.—I had a curious shock this afternoon. In the bookseller's at —— I had been turning over Ruskin's "Ariadne Florentina," looking at the reproductions of the so-called Botticelli sibyls, and by way of contrast Michael Angelo's aged Cumæan sibyl, which, with characteristic humour and unfairness, Ruskin labels "The Nymph beloved of Apollo." The inevitable law of association brought back to mind the place in Petronius (48), "Sibyllam quidem Cumis ego ipse oculis meis vidi in ampulla pendere, et cum illi pueri dicerent Σίβυλλα, τί θέλεις; respondebat illa ἀποθανεῖν θέλω,[1] which must mean, "At Cumæ I saw with my own eyes the sibyl hanging *in a bottle.*" The idea this conveys to one is of those shrivelled organisms that are preserved in spirits on museum shelves. While I was walking through the streets and musing how the sibyl came to be in so awkward a plight, I saw staring me in the face in an Italian warehouseman's window the startling announcement, "Respectable girls, about 18, wanted for bottling." I rubbed my eyes incredulously, but there seemed to be no mistake. Presently, of course, I saw I had been misled by an ambiguous use of the verbal noun.

24th.—I am sometimes glad to be old, and never more so than when I come across advice to parents on the education of their children. Eugenia was brought up on no scientific principle; "I 'spect she growed;" and I do not believe she is any the worse for that. Nowadays there are reviews edited by old maids to teach parents their business; associations of parents to encourage each other and exchange experiences; worst of all, syndicates to spy upon children and tabulate their little ways. I hope the children do

---

[1] [And when the boys called to her, "What do you want, sibyl?" she replied, "I want to die."]

their best to puzzle these too curious observers; one would judge so from some of the stories the professors collect. I am satisfied that what parents want is common sense and not psychology. Neither the mother of the Gracchi nor the mother of the Wesleys had psychology, but the latter, at any rate, abounded in common sense. These important reflections arise from a story just told me by a very young mother who yearns to be scientific, and make the punishment, in the words of a great moralist, "fit the crime." A few Sundays ago she had arranged a water party, and as her little Tommy had told a lie he was not to be allowed to join it, but was to go to church instead. The retribution struck her as most artistic; Tommy would get good and yet he would be miserable. What more could be desired in any punishment? I was sorely tempted to inquire why, if one was certain to get good in church, she sacrificed herself by arranging a picnic; however I could not resist telling her of the effect such a retributory worship had upon a little girl of my acquaintance. She showed no sign of contrition or rebellion till the Creed, when she curtsied elaborately and ostentatiously at the name of Pontius Pilate.

29th.—I went this morning to the funeral of my dear friend H. S. I had seen her several times lately, and I saw her also after death. The change is always striking. Sometimes the individual merges in the family type; sometimes it is only the care that seems wiped out in a great calm. In this case the calm had given place to care. The smile that had made light of suffering was quite gone; and one understood what a triumph the spirit had for so long been celebrating over the flesh, by the naked anguish of the flesh when the spirit had departed. That beautiful phrase of Jeremy Taylor's, "weeds and outworn faces," came into my mind; and I saw its truth as I had not seen it before. I was never less moved at a funeral; the poor coffined body seemed exactly expressed by a word I had always disliked, "the remains"; and I could not lament that it should be buried. For once I came near an appreciation of the splendid scorn in the familiar words, "O grave, where is thy victory?" Since her death I have not been able altogether to suppress a regret that on the last occasions of our meeting the conversation was on no higher than its ordinary level; but it seemed at the time right that it should be as it was, and her sense of fitness was impeccable. Moreover the art of not saying things is more difficult than that of saying them, and its success proportionately great. "None but a tragedian can die by rule and wait till he says a fine thing on his *exit*. In real life this is a chimera; and by noble spirits it will be done decently, without the ostentation of it." *Quære*, Does not this of Steele show him a finer gentleman than his friend Addison, with his "Come and see how a Christian can die?"

30th.—George S. writes this morning: "My mother always thought of everybody but herself, and the least return we can make for her unselfishness is to be glad for her sake that the long waiting is over. As you would guess from your knowledge of her, she was remarkably cheerful to the last, and it was difficult on the Saturday morning, in the intervals of her paroxysms, to believe the doctor that she could not last out the day. The only hint she gave us of being herself aware how near the end was, was to look round with a queer little smile when the doctor had left the room, and say, 'Do you know I *fancy* he's at the end of his tether?' Of course we understood, and respected her reticence. She passed away under the morphia, and we were all glad she should have been spared leave-takings. I still find myself nursing things to tell her; and one of my sisters had run upstairs to show her a very beautiful wreath sent for her funeral before she remembered. So impossible is it to realise the loss."

October 1st.—All one's letters to-day are bills; these are the angelic messages of comfort that our modern Michaelmas brings us. They sing an ever new song, an elegant and simple melody, which shapes itself somewhat differently in the ears of each, but to which none can be deaf. This is how Macaulay heard it:

> "Taxes, rent, sisters; carriage, wages, clo'es,
>   Coals, wine, alms, pocket-cash, subscriptions, treats;
>   Bills weekly these, and miscellaneous those,
>   Travel the list completes."

4th.—William Morris is dead and the generation is poorer by a most virile and versatile type. Johnson's epitaph on Goldsmith, with the change of a word, would well become Morris. "Nullum fere *ornandi* genus non tetigit, nullum quod tetigit non ornavit." When a great man dies it is impossible not to forecast, idly enough, the judgment of posterity. His name, certainly, one would say, must live with those of Sheraton and Adam and Chippendale. It *may* live with Aldus and Stephanus and Pickering; but I question whether our grandchildren will think his types so good as his designs; and at best they are reactionary. What will be his place in poetry? "Virgil," says R., "will live as long as the race, but he was content to write but twenty lines a day. Morris could write seven hundred." Yes; but how many did Homer write? There is undoubtedly something in Morris that is not of an age, or, at any rate, not of our age, even if it be not for all time. My neighbour at ⸺, who is the only soul for miles round to be called a soul, considers Morris more primitive even than Homer or Herodotus, who have already the reflective man's melancholy, whereas the so-called melancholy of Morris is more instinctive, being a straightforward recognition of the facts of life and death untainted by philosophy. He compares him in this respect, and in the fact that an extreme simplicity of sentiment is accompanied by an infinite refinement of the senses, with Pierre Loti, whom Lemaître has spoken of as " la plus délicate machine à sensations que j'ai jamais rencontrée." To this conjunction of a most complicated sensitive apparatus with the reflective powers of a child my friend would attribute Morris's socialism, which is always sentimental, not theoretic. It would help to explain also his want of humour and of dramatic power, which were real wants in his nature, despite Nupkins, G. B. S., and Mr. Watts-Dunton. My own favourite volumes are "The Defence of Guenevere" and "Sigurd," the latter for Sundays because of its excellent moral; but one cannot take up any of his verse anywhere without feeling in it the inexplicable magic. Inferior artists have copied his designs, but they cannot copy his poetry. They may have the seed, but they cannot raise the flower. He saw the world with his own eyes, and this is what we mean by genius, not any capacity for taking pains. Some one has told us that Morris could not

G

"polish or refine"; that if a thing did not please him it was not corrected, but done over again. The only correction I know of is in the "Song of the Nymph to Hylas," which was reprinted in "Poems by the Way," with the two best lines spoiled. Any comparison, therefore, with a poet like Virgil is beside the mark. Morris gives us, as a rule, not quotable lines, but a light in which we see things—an atmosphere. The verse oftenest in my mind is one printed I don't know when or where:

> "Christ keep the Hollow Land
> All the summer tide!
> Still we cannot understand
> How the waters glide,
>
> Only dimly seeing them
> Coldly slipping through
> Many green-lipped cavern-mouths,
> Where the hills are blue."

That is Morris in quintessence, a drop distilled from his peculiar and inestimable *murex*.

11th.—Lord Rosebery has resigned, and the Press, which used to scoff, is like a running river of tears, meant, of course, to drown Sir William. Thus an emancipated party gets rid of two leaders at once; and yet it does not seem happy. Tacitus, who has phrases for everything, puts the case in a pretty epigram: "Magis sine domino quam in libertate." How true that is of the Liberal party!

It is masterless rather than free, because for freedom one must not only be able to do what one pleases, but know what it pleases one to do. Mr. Asquith at the Edinburgh meeting figured as the faithful lieutenant—" miles alacer," to quote Tacitus again, "qui tamen jussa ducum interpretari quam exsequi mallet"—a prompt soldier, but with a turn for putting a gloss of his own on the commands of his general. Mr. Gladstone meanwhile comes in for a big share of the blame. Why must he be making speeches? "Retire men cannot when they would; neither will they when it were reason, but are impatient of privateness even in age and sickness, which require the shadow; like old townsmen, that will be still sitting at their street door, though thereby they offer age to scorn."

Sir William Harcourt has been discussing agriculture in Wales this week in a speech which would make every landlord's heart of us rejoice if only we did not know better. The speaker proves all landlords to be exceedingly well off by leaving out of count the working expenses of the property, say some thirty per cent. Sir William is only a younger brother, and Malwood is not a big estate, but even a younger brother might have some inkling of so elementary a truth as this. His ignorance—wilful, I fear—is on a level with that of the town curate who on being preferred to a country living urged his parishioners to be content with milking their cows once on the Sunday; or that of the town poet who said to his country hostess at breakfast: "This is capital honey; may I ask, do you keep a bee?"

13th.—Bob is growing into rather a good shot, as becomes his father's son, and, I may add, his uncle's nephew. He told me when we were out together to-day a curious tale of something that happened as he was taking a stroll on Sunday afternoon. Two pheasants rose some distance off, and he pointed his stick at them, and to his amazement down they came. When he got to the spot he found the solution of the mystery: they had flown against some barbed wire. Tom was abroad last autumn and did not shoot his covers, so that many of the birds are old and so untender. In such a case the prudent housewife cooks them with an onion inside. Bob gave me also some odd experiences of his in pursuit of relations. He has a strong clannish instinct, and spent some part of his holidays bicycling in the neighbourhood where our family used to be settled. In one of the villages he was amused to see his name over the grocer's shop, and went in to buy a bun, hoping to get the name on a paper bag. But they were too primitive to have advertisements. He saw, however, on the shopman's face a nose so like his own that it seemed to stamp him of the same stock. Bob's nose had always been a rather sore subject with him; at times he has meditated recourse to the nose-curer's, for it is not in itself beautiful, and it does not resemble any family nose we know of. But now it looked as if his own despised organ were really the aboriginal nose, and all others not genuine. He asked the man how long he had lived in the village, and was answered: "Mr. ——, my master, has been here these twenty years; I am only his foreman." So the mystery of the nose was no nearer being solved. In another village seeing the name on a gravestone, he asked the sexton, who happened to be in the churchyard, whether there were any people of that name still about. "Nobbut one," said the sexton, "who comes here in the summer." "In the summer? why in the summer?" "Oh, because he isn't out in the winter." "Is he so delicate, then?" "No, he's in the workhouse." This a little cooled Bob's zeal. He is a good boy and pleasant company, and I miss him greatly when the holidays are over. I am always amused at the cleverness of boys who are clever at all. They seem to know as much about most matters as their elders, and to be even more keenly interested. What is it we gain in growing older besides the "orbis veteribus notus,"—the globe known to the ancients — as the Oxford orator in my day used to call what tailors hint at as "the lower chest"? Let us hope the improvement is ethical; we learn perhaps a little more self-restraint, or at least concealment, unless we are great geniuses. The geniuses keep the lamb's heart among the full-grown flocks, to the no little discomfort of the flocks.

14*th.*—Tom and I went up with Robert to-day to matriculate him at —— College, and I believe we enjoyed the outing more than he did, being without *arrière-pensée*. The Warden was exceedingly civil, as Tom remarked, adding that it was as well some few heads of houses should be old enough to remember the Crimean War. Tom does not share the new feeling about Russia. He had not been at Oxford for many years, and what most struck him was the encroachment of the town upon the University. At Carfax he could hardly restrain his indignation; turning now to the municipal buildings, which seem to flaunt over "the House," and then to the blank where Carfax Church used to stand. Fortunately, the one offence served as a counter-irritant to the other, or I fear he might have been taken with an apoplexy. When we came opposite the new building of B.N.C., and saw the gigantic lion and unicorn, "That, I suppose," said he, "is where my old tailor has moved to out of St. Aldate's; he used to be 'by appointment to the King!'" However, he was put in good temper presently by the sight of a few young horsemen coming over Magdalen Bridge. "I should have thought," he said, "that so modern-spirited and ingenious a University as Oxford would have invented a new method of hunting adapted to the bicycle!" (this with a look at me and a marked paroxytone accent); then, after giving Robert a caution against wasting his time and money over horses, he launched out into anecdotes of his own youth, which bore a very pink complexion.

19th.—St. Luke is allowing us a second summer this year; the roads are drying famously; the farmers have got to work at their wheat sowing, and the ladies to their pleasant chatter about the "autumnal tints." It is a remarkable season for hedge-fruit, hips and haws and holly, and this, say the local weather-prophets, betokens a hard winter. The yew berries—those coral lamps in a green night—have been especially numerous and beautiful; in fact, our solitary commons have become like the sacred grove at Colonus—τὰν ἄβατον θεοῦ φυλλάδα μυριόκαρπον. Walnuts, too, are plentiful. How much were walnuts a dozen in Queen Anne's reign? Here is the answer in a letter of Steele's:

"DEAR PRUE,—I send you seven pen'orth of wall-nutts at five a penny, which is the greatest proof I can give you at present of my being with my whole Heart yrs, RICHD. STEELE."

Outside the letter is written, "There are but 29 Walnutts;" but the "passionate lover and faithfull husband" made ample amends for the six he had diverted to his own use by a present the next day of "half a hundred more." To know what a walnut should be one must have travelled in Persia; in our northern latitudes it remains, as its name denotes, the "foreign nut," never properly ripening, and even when mollified by port presenting a grave problem to the digestion. The rooks seem very fond of them. Several times lately, as I have been driving, a sparrow-hawk has risen from behind the hedge, lying in wait, I suppose, for partridges. I saw yesterday three long-tailed tits, and to-day a kingfisher; and a few days since *six* magpies. What does that portend?

22nd.—By way of reaction from talking about Nelson and Trafalgar, and singing the glorious day's renown, I kept last night a very peaceful centenary in reading over again Jane Austen's "Pride and Prejudice," which, though not published until 1813, was begun in the October of 1796, as we learn from Mr. Austen Leigh's memoir. How real the characters remain! The proud Mr. Darcy and the prejudiced Miss Elizabeth Bennet are naturally the liveliest. The portrait of the former especially is painted with the finish of a miniature in a number of very delicate touches. We know his stare, his height.

"'I assure you,' cried Bingley, 'that if Darcy were not such a great tall fellow in comparison with myself, I should not pay him half so much deference.' Mr. Darcy smiled; but Elizabeth thought she could perceive that he was rather offended, and therefore checked her laugh."

This characteristic indisposition to be laughed at, in one who was so great a critic of others, is emphasised again in the final scene:

"Elizabeth longed to observe that Mr. Bingley had been a most delightful friend—so easily guided that his worth was invaluable; but she checked herself. She remembered that he had yet to learn to be laughed at, and it was rather too early to begin."

Everybody who can is allowed to make a contribution to our knowledge of the hero's character —Mrs. Gardiner, the old housekeeper, even the wicked Wickham:

"Mr. Darcy can please where he chuses. He can be a conversible companion if he thinks it worth his while. Among those who are at all his equals in consequence, he is a very different man from what he is to the less prosperous. His pride never deserts him; but with the rich he is liberal-minded, just, sincere, rational, honourable, and perhaps agreeable— allowing something for fortune and figure."

Change the words *rich* and *less prosperous*, and you have Miss Austen's judgment as well as Bingley's. Again:

"Lady Catherine has the reputation of being remarkably sensible and clever; but I rather believe she derives part of her abilities from her rank and fortune, part from her authoritative manner, and the rest from the pride of her nephew, *who chuses that every one connected with him should have an understanding of the first class.*"

The two most carefully elaborated scenes in the book are Darcy's first proposal to Elizabeth and his aunt's visit to Longbourn. Both seem to me quite perfect. In any one less accustomed than Darcy was to look at everything on the side on which it concerned himself, without imagination to see how it would strike others, or less unable, from long habit,[1] to dissimulate his feelings, the opening declaration would have been impossible, but in him it is in character. Equally well drawn are his surprise at Elizabeth's refusal of his suit, his shock at being called "ungentlemanlike," his dispassionate view of Bingley's courtship of Jane, and his frank, surprised defence of what was called incivility. " Could you expect me to rejoice in the inferiority of your connections, to congratulate myself on the hope of relations whose condition in life is so decidedly beneath my own?" It is interesting to remark that Miss Austen, whether

---

[1] Elizabeth Bennet's remarks over the pianoforte at Rosings about the duty of *practising* social virtues are quite a revelation to Darcy. "I certainly have not the talent which some people possess," said Darcy, "of conversing easily with those I have never seen before. I cannot catch their tone of conversation *or appear interested in their concerns*, as I often see done." "My fingers," said Elizabeth, "do not move over the instrument in the masterly manner which I see so many women's do. But then I have always supposed it to be my own fault —because I would not take the trouble of practising."

she studied Darcy from the life or built him up from suggestions, understood exactly how such a character would be produced. During the conversation on that famous walk to the Lucases, Darcy says:

"I have been a selfish being all my life, in practice, though not in principle. As a child, I was taught what was *right;* but I was not taught to correct my temper. I was given good principles, but left to follow them in pride and conceit. Unfortunately an only son, I was spoiled by my parents, who, though good themselves, allowed, encouraged, almost taught me to be selfish and overbearing—to care for none beyond my own family circle, to think meanly of all the rest of the world, to *wish,* at least, to think meanly of their sense and worth compared with my own."

The other dialogue—that between Elizabeth and Lady Catherine de Burgh—is still more finely imagined. Her ladyship's insufferable rudeness is always of the well-bred variety; it is that of a feminine Darcy, *sui amans sine rivali,* but without cultivation, and never crosses the line into vulgarity. It keeps its end steadily in view with great self-possession, and when finally defeated hurls none but social thunderbolts. "I take no leave of you, Miss Bennet; I send no compliments to your mother; I am most seriously displeased."

Of the minor characters I confess to admiring Mrs. Bennet most. To be witty the author had but to be Jane Austen, but to be foolish and inconsequent required no little imagination; and though Mrs. Bennet is not always equal to herself —as which of us is ?—she never quite sinks to caricature. Her high-water mark is, perhaps, her famous contribution to the old wrangle between town and country life :

"'The country,' said Darcy, 'can in general supply but few subjects for such a study [*i.e.* of character]. In a country neighbourhood you move in a very confined and unvarying society.'

"'But people themselves alter so much, that there is something new to be observed in them for ever.'

"'Yes, indeed,' cried Mrs. Lennet, offended by his manner of mentioning a country neighbourhood. 'I assure you there is quite as much of *that* going on in the country as in town.'"

Inimitable, too, is the new light on the question of entail. "Such things I know are all chance in this world. There is no knowing how estates will go when once they come to be entailed." Lydia Bennet also, for the same reason that I admire her mother, inspires me with unbounded respect. Mary alone I confess myself unable to believe in, and even to be told that she married "one of her Uncle Philip's clerks, and was content to be considered a star in the society of Meryton," does not convince me. I have no doubt the fault is in myself, because on the only other point in which I ever doubted Miss Austen, a prolonged residence in a country neighbourhood has persuaded me of my error.[1] It was a point in the character of the Rev. William Collins. In one of his apologetic speeches to Mrs. Bennet (which, like his complimentary epistles, ought to supply a word to the language; we should speak of "*making*" as well as "*sending* a Collins"), he says:

> "Resignation to inevitable evils is the duty of us all: the peculiar duty of a young man who has been so fortunate as I have been in early preferment, and I trust I am resigned. Perhaps not the less so from feeling a doubt of my positive happiness had my fair cousin honoured me with her hand; *for I have often observed that resignation is never so perfect as when the blessing denied begins to lose somewhat of its value in our estimation.*"

I used to think that the voice here was the voice of Jane Austen, for once breaking in and not inexcusably laughing at our reverend friend. But experience of life has convinced me I was wrong; and certainly the logic is the same as that of the famous dictum about dress: "I would advise you merely to put on whatever of your clothes is superior to the rest—there is no occasion for anything more." For the rest, Mr. Bennet is admirable, Charlotte Lucas is a very careful study of a very ordinary girl, and her little

---

[1] Sophia will have it that all through "Pride and Prejudice," which is the author's first book, the note is a little forced, and points out that Jane Austen showed herself half conscious of this by describing it as "wanting shade."

brother has expressed for all time a deep human sentiment when he declared he would not care how proud he was if he was as rich as Mr. Darcy. Of Jane Austen's heroines, Miss Thackeray said once in *Cornhill* that they were distinguished by a certain "gentle self-respect and humour and hardness of heart" from those of to-day, when "we have gained in emphasis what we have lost in calm, in happiness, in tranquillity." Miss Austen has suffered more than most authors at the hands of her illustrators. How delightful it would have been if her novels had first appeared in *Cornhill* with Walker's or Millais's pictures! For though it is undoubtedly a bore to read a novel for the first time in sections, nothing is pleasanter than to go back upon it in this way, tasting it like old wine. Mr. Cooke's persons are devoid of any character whatever, almost of expression; Mr. Brock's are not much better; and Mr. Thomson's, though they are more like real people, are not Miss Austen's people. Look at the conceited boy, for instance, who does duty for Darcy; Darcy was thirty. The name of the novel was borrowed from the following passage at the end of Miss Burney's "Cecilia":

"The whole of this unfortunate business," said Dr. Lyster, "has been the result of PRIDE and PREJUDICE . . . ; yet this remember, that if to PRIDE and PREJUDICE you owe your miseries, so wonderfully is good and evil balanced that to PRIDE and PREJUDICE you will also owe their termination." In the old editions the words glare at you in big capitals as they are here printed, and look to us like a reference to Miss Austen's novel—they are really a prophecy before the event. I note finally that a book-lover (whose name I know but will not say) burrowing the other day in the heaps of a London bookseller (whose name I know also but refrain also from saying), unearthed a nearly complete set of Miss Austen's novels in the original edition, which he bought for as many shillings as they usually cost guineas. The bookseller discovered his mistake before the buyer had left the shop, but, being a man of his word, *stuck to his first price*. Tell that in Gath!

23rd.—Lord Rosebery at Colchester made a political allegory of the oyster. He spoke of him as "an eminently self-contained character. His shell is his castle, his house is attached to a rock, and within that shell and attached to that rock he is absolutely aloof from the storms and catastrophes of the world." The moral is not difficult to draw. In politics let us be—not selfish, oh dear, no, but—self-contained. Being an old-fashioned person, I prefer the old-fashioned word selfishness! but, call it what you please, I prefer the old-fashioned moral of the oyster allegory as it is drawn in that delightful Buddhist sermon in Mitford's "Tales of Old Japan" (ii. 153):

"There is a certain powerful shellfish called the Sazayé, with a very strong operculum. Now this creature, if it hears that there is any danger astir, shuts up its shell from within with a loud noise, and thinks itself perfectly safe. One day a Tai and another fish in envy at this said—

"'What a strong castle this is of yours, Mr. Sazayé! When you shut up your lid from within, nobody can so much as point a finger at you. A capital figure you make, sir.'

"When he heard this, the Sazayé, stroking his beard, replied: 'Well, gentlemen, although you are so good as to say so, it's nothing to boast of in the way of safety, yet I must admit that when I shut myself up thus I do not feel much anxiety.'

"And as he was speaking thus, with the pride that apes humility, there came the noise of a great splash; and the shellfish, shutting up his lid as quickly as possible, kept quite still, and thought to himself, what in the world the noise could be. Could it be a net? Could it be a fish-hook? What a bore it was always having to keep such a sharp look-out! Were the Tai and the other fish caught, he wondered; and he felt quite anxious about them; however, at any rate he was safe. And so the time passed; and when he thought all was safe, he stealthily opened his shell, and looked all round him, and there seemed to be something wrong, something with which he was not familiar. As he looked a little more carefully, lo and behold, there he was in a fishmonger's shop, and with a card marked 'sixteen cash' on his back."

24*th*.—I saw at the club in one of the weekly papers an announcement of the death of the sister of Thomas Lovell Beddoes. I confess that, great as my interest in Beddoes has always been, I did not know that any sister was still surviving; I do not recollect any reference being made to her at the time it was deemed requisite to publish the sad story of his suicide. This was in 1890, when Mr. E. W. Gosse, a son of the distinguished naturalist, who has himself meditated the Muse, printed the poetical remains from papers given to Robert Browning by Beddoes' life-long friend and biographer, T. F. Kelsall. Beddoes' poetry will always be *caviare* to the general, but two or three things, such as "Dream-Pedlary," are creeping into anthologies. In my library I have a copy both of the "Improvisatore" and the "Bride's Tragedy," bound in that straight-grained morocco with stamped Gothic ornament which was then orthodox; they belonged to Beddoes' college friend, T. G. H. Bourne, and the former of them contains Beddoes' book-plate. I have also his Shakespeare, which is interesting from the passages marked; though they are not of any recondite beauty, nor especially concerned, as one might have expected, with "graves and worms and epitaphs." They are such as the following:

"Most choice, forsaken; and most lov'd, despised."

"Our indiscretion sometimes serves us well
When our deep plots do pall."

I am happy also in possessing a copy of the "Posthumous Poems" of Shelley, which Beddoes financed, and Leigh Hunt published, and Sir

Timothy suppressed. But probably this is not so scarce as Beddoes' own books.

November 2nd.—There was a curious demonstration in the farmyard this morning, suggesting to the philosophic mind that men are but chickens of a larger growth; at least proving that the commonwealth of fowls contains an element which we in our vanity are apt to consider especially human, for *human* and *humane* are the same word. Two cocks were taking steps to settle a dispute in the fearless old fashion with beak and spur; all the preliminaries of the duel had been gone through punctiliously, and the principals were about to engage, when a bevy of fair guinea-hens, some twenty in number, rushed again and again between the combatants, and at last succeeded in frustrating their purpose. The manners of guinea-fowl repay attention; at the first blush they appear foolish birds—indeed, as witless as a guinea-hen is one of our family proverbs—but this is a vulgar error; and perhaps some day I may collect into a letter to the press some *ana* upon the subject, to which the touching story of the dove's laying one *immortelle* on the bosom of his dead mate will be as moonlight unto sunlight. Here I note that they are the Quakeresses of their society. Observe their dress, how low in tone—the familiar slate-colour—but how rich in substance. Observe how they segregate themselves from the other barn-door fowls, and prefer to roost in a tree, from which in winter they sometimes fall down frozen, rather than sleep in a Gothic building with their fellow Christians. I have mentioned above a remarkable instance of their distaste for bloodshed; they carry this so far that it is a matter of great difficulty to catch and kill them. In one point only would they have displeased George Fox,—they are extremely loquacious; but then so is the new school of "Friends."

7th.—I journeyed to Reading to spend a few hours in the bookshops, for since Mr. Saintsbury went north to profess in Edinburgh, there is a little more chance of picking up there some unconsidered trifles. But in Broad Street I encountered the High Sheriff's coach taking the Lord Chief Justice to the Assize Court, and not having yet seen Lord Russell on the bench I joined the Hogarthian crowd and followed him in. Two or three things struck me; first, and most conspicuously, the utter boredom of the poor High Sheriff, who has to sit next the judge in a tight uniform, and look wiser than he feels; secondly, the good nature of the police, who handle the prisoners as if they loved them; then the half-stupid look of the prisoners, as if they had come by a dark stair into a great light, and the villainous look they have, due to the want of linen round the throat; but what struck me most was the very evident effort made by the judge to say something that might impress each offender who came before him. With counsel he was a good deal less patient, taking them in snuff in more senses than one. The cases were disgusting, and I did not sit long, but turned into the Biscuit Factory to see my favourite sight, the making of cracknels. It is the very type of hell. First the poor flakes of souls are thrown into the boiling waves of Pyriphlegethon and disappear; presently they rise to the surface, and are skimmed out and dashed into the biting lymph of Cocytus—

> "And feel the bitter change
> Of fierce extremes, extremes by change more fierce."

Since first I saw the sight—and I never go to Reading without seeing it, if it is to be seen—I cannot eat a cracknel, and they are my favourite biscuits, without calling to mind those mediæval pictures in which lost souls are being crushed between the jaws of a monster I will not name. It is not altogether an agreeable reminiscence. The Reading shopkeepers are an amiable set of men who display their wares with something of the enthusiasm more common among vendors of curiosities, taking an interest in the things it would seem for their own sake; though the curiosity-mongers sometimes carry their indifference to custom a little far. For instance, old A. showed me an enamelled snuff-box given by Napoleon to one of his generals, and all I could get out of him about it was, "Ah! I have refused a price for that;" what price I couldn't bring him to say. Perhaps he was on intimate terms with my banker, and knew it could not concern me in any practical sense. The jeweller, on the other hand, to whom I had to go about some repairs, brought out a magnificent peridot with the remark, "For this I am only asking 800 guineas." "Ah!" I said, "really, is that all?" I suspect this engaging habit of taking a customer's wealth for granted arises from their experience that "imputation" is a force in the market no less than in morals. People discover they can afford things because the dealer assumes that virtue in them. *Possunt quia posse videntur.* How many and how cunning are the excuses one considers it necessary to make to oneself for purchases! Now that a thing is cheap; now that it is so much more satisfactory to buy a really good thing for a five-pound note than to be always squandering crowns. It is the price we pay for keeping a conscience, that it will still be talking and must be cajoled! The oddest excuse ever devised for violent bibliomania is surely this of Coleridge's, which I came upon yesterday:—

"In case of my speedy death, it would answer to buy a £100 worth of carefully chosen books, in order to attract attention to my library and to give accession to the value of books by their co-existing with co-appurtenants" ("Anima Poetæ," p. 183).

Alas! to most of us that thought of speedy death is rather a deterrent. There are a few heroes who put *Nunc mihi, mox aliis* on their book-plates; just as there are a few philosophical poets like Lucretius who take a pride in the thought that all concourses of atoms (and books are, in a way, atoms) are but fortuitous and will soon dissolve; but who, except a philosopher, would buy books with his own auction catalogue before his mind's eye? And books are such a bad investment. "I was at a sale the other day," said a bookseller to me, "it was Lord C.'s, and if it had not been for an Italian, I could have bought at my own price." "Bless the Italian!" said I. I make it a religious duty to attend all the book sales within reach, just to help up the price for the sake of "the fatherless children and widows," but if ordinary book-collectors were wise they would stipulate in their wills, as I have done, that their books are not to be sold by auction, but valued by two trustworthy booksellers independently, and the larger offer accepted. The only book of any special interest I found in Reading to-day was a miscellaneous volume of first editions of Byron's poems with the autograph of Helen Shelley; and I bought little else, though I was haunted all day by that phrase of Coleridge's about "co-existing with co-appurtenants." Folios, quartos, dumpy duodecimos, seemed to be putting out forlorn hands to me, and entreating that I should end their exile and let them co-exist with some co-appurtenant on my happy shelves. And here at home I am conscious, as never before, of great gaps; *lacunæ valde deflendæ.* But that way madness lies! I suppose every one has a grain of malice in his composition somewhere, and if he is a book-collector it is apt to show itself there; perhaps as harmless a vent as it can take. Mr. Lang tells a moral tale of a certain Thomas Blinton who suffered a terrible purgatory for collecting the early amorous poetry of Bishops and Cabinet Ministers. My wicked passion is for presentation copies of books (not being minor poetry or otherwise uninteresting) by living authors; and it has usually been not the gratitude of men but the high price asked for the autograph that has left me mourning. A catalogue to-day advertises a copy of "Modern Painters," with the inscription "Coventry K. Patmore, Esq.,[1] with the author's sincere regards, 15 Jan. 1856," but the price demanded is exorbitant. I am particularly sorry to lose it because my secret cabinet already contains a presentation copy of a poem of Mr. Patmore's to another living and distinguished man of letters. Only once did

[1] See entry on Nov. 27.

I ever mention such a purchase to the donor of the book; it was in the early days of my zeal, and not being a maker of books I did not understand all the forces involved; but I received a severe lesson. I had gone up to town for a night, had found the book in a shop, and by a curious chance was dining with the writer, who was, and is, a great friend. Both my friend and his wife have a remarkable gift of silence, and the announcement of my discovery, made too light-heartedly, was received in a polar stillness that froze the blood. Both looked at their plates steadily while a man could count fifty; then my friend said, "For the time of year we are remarkably free from fog." Of course, being after all a man and no worm, I was obliged to recur to my topic, but I have never repeated the experiment.

16*th*:—One of the greatest charms of autumn is the opportunity it offers for improvements in the house and garden and estate. I think even Tom feels this new spirit in the blood, and in the intervals of hunting roams round his fields, planting hedges and making fences, and perhaps can be brought by the woodman now and then to cut any tree that is palpably noxious to a neighbour—a neighbouring tree, that is, not a human being; Tom has no sympathy with the modern notion that trees can prejudice health. The medical officer may tell us we shall never be without a spring epidemic till a whirlwind gets in and has a good game of ninepins; but Tom inherits my father's taste for planting and distaste for cutting, so that medical officers preach to deaf ears. And certainly the Hall stands well above the village, and out of harm's way. My "improvements" this year will be simple enough: a door knocked through a blank wall, a new flower border in the kitchen garden, a tree felled to open a view, and the Gothic porch taken down from the doorway, which is Georgian. This last alteration has cost me some searchings of heart; for the porch itself is of some antiquity. Sophia points out that on wet days our callers will have to stand in the rain till the door is opened; but a little rain hurts no one, and besides on wet days people do not call, or, if they do, they carry umbrellas. I suppose the passion for making improvements rests at bottom on the law of self-preservation, our surroundings being really a part of ourselves. It is a way of giving freshness to worn impressions, of bringing into notice again what is ever tending to slip below the level of consciousness. Even Eugenia, I have observed, though inclined to parsimony in matters of toilette, manages to vary her dress with considerable skill; and at least once a season Sophia rearranges the drawing-room furniture, and rehangs some of the dining-room pictures. We are all more or less obliged by nature to say with

Nebuchadnezzar, "Is not this great Babylon, that I have built?" If we did not, we should lapse, not only into vegetarianism, like that unfortunate monarch, but into vegetables.

19*th*.—Fogs are not pleasant even in the country, but they are clean, and sometimes they are beautiful. To-day, for instance, the plough teams were at work in the field called "Lynches" (I believe from its terraces), and the broadening purple-brown bands and the fallow between them were filmed over with a velvety opalescence very like the tender bloom on cold gravy.

I made a note the other day of my scepticism as to the civilising influence of picture galleries upon uneducated people. I had occasion to-day to show myself no less sceptical about another fashionable form that modern philanthropy takes, namely, to collect a savage horde of London roughs and take them to spend an afternoon in a friend's grounds. What good result is aimed at? Not fresh air, for that can be as well enjoyed in the public parks! If the parties were under the patronage of the Fabian Society I could understand them, and I should applaud their policy, for nothing could be so well contrived to make people envious. But what good object do they serve? It is difficult by your smiles, however gracious, to persuade a hundred people whom you have never seen before that you are pleased to see them; they are not deceived, and they are not in the least pleased to see you; they come frankly for what they can get. A lady who has been in the habit of conducting such parties, and to whom this afternoon I opened these views, was horrified at first by their "cynicism," as she phrased it; but presently she told me not a few stories which on reflection may perhaps lead her to spend her time and talents more profitably. On one occasion she had been remonstrating with some factory girls for picking their hostess's apples; they were quite small and green, for it was early summer; and the girls turned on her with indignant surprise. "Why, if we don't take them now, we shan't get another chance." If good ladies who practise such hospitality would extend it to unfortunate members of their own class, it would be appreciated. But it is far easier to wash the feet of ten beggars than entertain one poor relation. Speaking of the Fabian Society has put me in mind of an amusing circumstance relating to William Morris, that befell a year or two ago. We were paying our first call upon a newly-married pair, the husband (call him Mr. John Bull) being a typical country squire. Mrs. Bull has an inclination towards art, or perhaps I should say art-in-the-home. Some patterns of chintz had just arrived and were being inspected, and as we were old friends the examination was not stopped by our visit. Presently Mr. B. had an inspiration: "I suppose they're not from that Socialist fellow, who says I mustn't have a glass of sherry, because my fogger can only afford beer; what's his name?—Morris; because, if they are, I won't let him drink *his* sherry at my expense." Alas, they were Morris's! The discussion was not continued in our presence, but we were pretty sure remonstrance would be unavailing; and so Sophia consoled pretty Mrs. B. by saying she knew of a place where they made the most *delightful* copies of *really old* things for *ridiculously low* prices, &c. &c. I respect a man who carries his political principles into domestic life. I heard the other day that this same young gentleman had ransacked a whole toy-shop to find something for his heir-apparent not "made in Germany." But no one is absolutely consistent, and I know by pleasant experience that even Mr. Bull is not a stickler for British wine and tobacco.

27th.—The papers to-day announce the death of Mr. Patmore. The great poets at the beginning of the century died young, at the end they are living to full age; I say "great poets" because, if the quality of his best work be considered, there seems no reason why Patmore should not rank as such. Take away his five-o'clock-tea verses, his political verses, his Roman Catholic verses, with their mystical and somewhat nauseous Mariolatry, and there still remains a considerable volume that will live as long as any of the later verse of the century, because it has something to say and says it exquisitely. To mention "A Revelation" and "The Spirit's Epochs" from "The Angel in the House," "A Farewell," "The Departure," "Winter," and "The Toys," is to enumerate half-a-dozen poems that the world —unless it very much alters—will not willingly let die; but it is not to exhaust the list of successes. Many of the "Preludes" in "The Angel in the House," besides those already referred to, all written in the octosyllabic metre over which he attained such mastery, are excellent. An old favourite of mine is "The Wife's Tragedy," which mounts in pathos verse after verse till it reaches its height in that single-line simile; perhaps the best, certainly the most unforgettable, thing in Patmore.

> " Man must be pleased : but him to please
>   Is woman's pleasure ; down the gulf
> Of his condoled necessities
>   She casts her best, she flings herself.
>
> .   .   .   .   .   .
>
> And whilst his love has any life,
>   Or any eye to see her charms,
> At any time she's still his wife,
>   Dearly devoted to his arms ;
> She loves with love that cannot tire ;
>   And when, ah woe, she loves alone,
> Through passionate duty love springs higher,
>   *As grass grows taller round a stone.*"

It marks the accomplished artist that after achieving such success and popularity in one style, Patmore should in "The Unknown Eros" have achieved equal success, though not equal popularity, in verse of an entirely different stamp—a kind of choral ode, imitated probably from Drummond of Hawthornden. To take a specimen, from a passage where a poet for once speaks well of his critic:

> "How high of heart is one, and one how sweet of
>   mood;
> But not all height is holiness,
> Nor every sweetness good;
> And grace will sometimes lurk where who could
>   guess?
> The critic of his kind,
> Dealing to each his share,
> With easy humour, hard to bear,
> May not impossibly have in him shrined,
> As in a gossamer globe or thickly-padded pod,
> Some small seed dear to God."

Well, one hopes so, especially when one praises.

28*th*.—In turning over a chest of old books I found an album that had belonged to my mother in early youth, made about the years 1816–22. There were prints of many Berkshire towns and great houses, a vast collection of newspaper cuttings, and much manuscript verse. The cuttings were largely from poets' corners, the poets being Haynes Bayley, Mrs. Hemans, L. E. L., Barry Cornwall, and other extinct meteors; but some were anecdotes and some were conundrums—a form of merriment now happily restricted to children's parties. The main interest lay of course, and the only remaining interest lies, in the original contributions of the author's friends. Warren Hastings appears to have been much worshipped, and his retirement at Daylesford is sung very tropically—

> "Naught invades
> The still unbroken twilight of the shades
> Save the cool whisper of the tumbling rill,
> Which from the shelvy side of yon hoar hill,
> Now caught, now lost amid th' obtruding leaves,
> Foams down the craggy channel which it cleaves,
> Then through the vale with mitigated force
> Glides unperceived, forgetful of its source;
> As one by ceaseless persecution worn,
> Beset with ills, yet proof to fortune's scorn,
> Greatly retires, collected and resigned,
> Nor casts one look of self-reproach behind."

What a pity that Gray had anticipated that last line! I know a young poet who has written a very pretty ode which opens, "Let us go hence, she will not hear my songs!" which probably seems to him a considerable improvement on Mr. Swinburne's "Let us go hence, my songs, she will not hear!"

On another page of the album I came upon some doggerel which would seem to have been penned with a view to giving as exactly as possible the current pronunciation of certain words, the spelling of which was even more unhelpful than usual.

> "Once in merry Berkshire there l-
> -ived a charming little girl,
> With a charming dog called Smut,
> Tan as tan, and black as soot,
> Who could draw a cart, and fetch
> All he wanted, beg, and catch.
> Once, alas! poor Smut was lost;
> It was winter, and the frost
> Nipt his little chest, which was
> Most susceptible, because
> Bred so delicately, which
> Is not good for dogs and such.
>   Ah, they found him on the moor,
> Oil and wine in haste they pour,
> Wrap him safe as any man in
> Mother's best and warmest flannen,
> While to ease his racking cough he
> Has to suck the finest toffee;
> But in vain came comfort then;
> Poor Smut never smiled again."

This effusion is not signed. I cannot believe that my grandmother composed it; probably it is the work of some precisian of the schoolroom. To be really useful, however, the vowels should be represented by more accurate symbols. Are we meant, for example, to give the vowel in "toffee" the sound in *of* or in *off?* Probably the latter, for I was brought up to say *coff-ee*, and I so spoke the word without shame till my marriage, when the breadth of my vowel offended Sophia. A man who could exchange tobacco for snuff to please his mistress is not likely to stick at a vowel, and "cof-fee" it became; but alas! the very first day on which I aired my new accomplishment to a guest—it was the late Duke of ——, who honoured us by a call at the old Chobham camp—he replied to my "Will you have tea or cof-fee?" with "Thank you, a cup of coff-ee would be very pleasant;" and coff-ee it has remained for me. It is pitiful to remark what havoc the Board schoolmasters and railway porters are making among place names. Even at Lowestoft and Kelvedon, as I noticed in October, you hardly hear now the old-fashioned Lestoff and Keldon; and Edward Fitz-Gerald would turn in his grave to hear Boulge pronounced Bowlge instead of Bowidge.

December 1st.—*Punch* has struck a new vein this week in a comic armoury. Some of the charges are witty enough, but it is a pity not to make the thing a little more heraldically correct by mentioning in every case the tincture of the field, &c. Those persons who play pencil and paper games after dinner will find it an amusing pastime to concoct achievements of the sort. Having a family party last night we made an experiment at such a game, and led off with the Sultan of Turkey. Almost everybody gave him for crest "a Saracen's head couped at the neck proper," which showed good feeling. An alternative was: a savage from the middle gules holding in the dexter hand a scimitar gutté de sang, in the sinister a paper of reforms reversed. For supporters, dexter: a bear sejant affrontée imperially crowned or, holding in its paws a bezant; sinister: a bull counter rampant regardant, or. One of the suggested shields was: Purpure, a cross im-potent ermine, surmounted by a decrescent sable. In explanation of this it should be noted that Du Cange derives "ermine" from "Armenian." I may add that I was given for my own crest by a long-suffering family "a King Charles' head wreathed about the temples ermine."

At the curiosity shop in —— yesterday, among the highly-priced rubbishy books I came upon the autobiography of a last-century bookseller, and in turning the leaves found the following sentence on small causes leading to great results, which no one but a bookseller could have penned:—

"Sir Isaac Newton would probably never have studied the system of gravitation had he not been under an apple-tree when some of the fruit loosened from the branches and fell to the earth; it was the question of a simple gardener concerning a pump that led Galileo to study and discover the weight of the air; to the tones of a Welsh harp are we indebted for the bard of Gray; *and Gibbon formed the design of that truly great work, his 'History of the*

Decline of the Roman Empire,' while viewing the ruins of the Capitol."

An apple, a pump, a Welsh harp, and— Rome!

2nd.—A Devonshire district council has been mending its roads with Druidical remains, thereby proving itself as Christian and iconoclastic as any cathedral chapter. Still more far-reaching changes have been made in our own council by a mere stroke of the pen, and have excited no protest. In future no trees are to be planted in the hedges by the roadsides, and no cottages are to be roofed with thatch. The bicyclist will rejoice at the first of these orders, because undoubtedly the dripping from trees makes mire; but the lover of the picturesque may well wring his hands. The second order seems to be made in the interest of the infernal machines that snort down the roads scattering sparks and frightening your horses. But why should not motor-engines of the new type replace them? Berkshire (headed by Thatcham) should get up a monster petition against this piece of folly.

9th.—Village concerts have taken a new development hereabouts. The old-fashioned penny-reading, where the choir tenor used to warble " The Lass of Richmond 'Ill," and the vicar's son break down in " The Night before Waterloo," has gone " where Orpheus and where Homer are," and we have instead Christy Minstrels, with Bones, Tambo, and Mr. Johnson all complete, and all as black as your hat. Bones is Tom's groom, and no doubt the blacking helps to give him confidence. I believe he submits the joke-list beforehand, so that there may be no offence in it. The jokes, indeed, are quite inoffensive, very childlike and bland, and not a little vague; they would have delighted the soul of Hadrian, from whose time some of them perhaps date. I believe they derive immediately from those comic papers that one sees people buy at railway-stations and read in the train without a smile. But a few are home-made and topical. The vicar came in for a rap last evening for not lighting the churchyard lamp on week nights; and the parish council is a standing dish. A village Pasquin might find it worth while to get hold of some less dependent Bones, and write the jokes.

12th—Winter seems to have come at last—not "the weeping winter all whose flowers are tears," which has been here too long already, but the winter

> "When bicycles hang by the wall,
> And Dick the shepherd blows his nail"

instead of his tyre. I made a short experiment this morning, but the ruts were frozen hard, and the snow hid the flints, so that I had a rough journey, and once or twice I was near falling.

But anything is better than slush and south wind. A Berkshire poet (for we still have poets) has lately published an ode to this wind — perhaps really liking it, perhaps as a peace-offering, just as Kingsley tried to conciliate the north-easter, which, nevertheless, proved implacable and killed him. In this matter, as in others, I am content to be on the side of Shakespeare, who never alludes to the south wind but in disparaging terms. His characters curse by it. "All the contagion of the South light on you," says Coriolanus; "a south-west blow on ye," says Caliban, "and blister you all o'er;" and Thersites, who is less of a gentleman than these, and has less reticence, expands the curse into a dozen lines of diseases. The "sweet south" that many editors read in the famous opening lines of "Twelfth Night" is a quite impossible conjecture of Pope's for "the sweet *sound.*"

16th.—I read after dinner Dr. Birkbeck Hill's "Talks about Autographs," which the publisher *pro singulari sua humanitate* has lent me. Dr. Hill I knew for a vivacious talker when he lived at Burghfield, and I love an autograph but even too well, so that I turned the pages with lively expectation. The autograph letters here presented are naturally of very various degrees of interest, and collectors will contrast them, now with a smile, now with a sigh, with their own specimens. For example, I prefer my own letter from Miss Martineau, lamenting the death of her prophet, Mr. Atkinson, to the one here given about the slave trade; my Newman, too, is more characteristic.[1] But I grow gloomily covetous over the Sir Thomas Browne and the famous Cowper letter about Mr. Bull, the dissenting minister with every virtue and only one vice—tobacco. The Matthew Arnold on the deceased wife's sister question is interesting; it is an answer to a gentleman who complained that owing to the prohibition he had been married eight years only out of his eighty. The letter is dated from a Methodist training college where Arnold was examining. One wonders whether in a Socialist state—the Merry England of the future—a great poet will be relieved from such intolerable drudgery, or whether even in that millennium he will only be allowed to write his poetry and his essays if he can prove himself of substantial use to the community by making chairs and wall-papers.

[1] I print it *pro bono publico*:—

"THE ORATORY : *March* 29, 1879.

"MY DEAR SIR,—You must not think I have willingly delayed my answer to so kind a letter as yours. I thank you very much for it, and feel the value of such, though I should not myself allow that I was driven out of the Anglican Church, instead of leaving it because the Truth was elsewhere. But I know what your meaning was, and it was a kind meaning to me.

"Thank you also for your congratulations on my elevation. It has, as you may suppose, startled and even scared me, when I was of the age when men look out for death rather than any other change.—I am, my dear Sir, very truly yours, JOHN H. NEWMAN."

Arnold's reports are very good reading, but his methods of examination were sometimes highly poetical. I remember a tale told by a fellow inspector of a class of girl pupil-teachers that he asked Arnold to examine for him. Arnold gave them all the excellent mark. "But," said the other inspector, "surely they are not all as good as they can be; some must be better than others." "Perhaps that is so," replied Arnold; "but then, you see, they are all such *very* nice girls."

There is a letter from Mr. Ruskin, dated 1858, sending a message to Jones [Sir Edward Burne-Jones] that his stained-glass windows would not quite do, a message not delivered until nearly forty years after.

Dr. Hill's book is written for the American market, and therefore should not be judged by too English a standard. Moreover, it is professedly talk and not literature; but occasionally the talk is irritating. I do not refer to the irreverent squibs and crackers that are let off with boyish enjoyment at what are my own idols in Church and State; that is fair enough, and I am the last person to resent either a swingeing blow or a rapier thrust, administered in gentlemanlike fashion, by Radical or Nonconformist. It is Dr. Hill's irrelevant morality that distresses me. Why must poor Hartley Coleridge's weakness be dragged in by the head and ears? And why because Lamb is mentioned must gin be mentioned too? A furniture broker had recently for sale Lamb's spirit case; and if I could have afforded the sacrifice I would have bought it to burn.

18*th*.—I was roused from sleep last night about half-past five by hearing Sophia strike a match and address some one in a very excited tone, to the effect that she could see him, and he needn't hope to escape, and that her husband was a magistrate, with other threats. When I was fully awake, I gathered that she had heard a man walking up and down in the room. But if so he had disappeared, so I took a poker and went downstairs for further search. I have a great dislike to enter rooms before the evidences of the last night's occupation have been removed; everything looks uncanny; and this morning the curtains seemed to bulge a great deal as though they were hiding very substantial burglars. We had been warned once or twice lately by our blue-nosed policeman that a little party of old offenders had come into the neighbourhood, and yesterday the terrier disappeared, so that we were in a suspicious humour. However, I found no one, and imagined that Sophia had been dreaming, or that our friendly ghosts had been at their tricks again. For they have a queer habit occasionally of rushing across the drawing-room floor and flinging up the window

—at least that is what the noise sounds like. Later in the day we heard there had been a slight shock of earthquake, and several of our neighbours had imagined that the tremor, which ran east and west, was caused by a person hurrying across the room.

21st.—We came to London for a couple of days' shopping; that is to say, Sophia came for shopping and I for the pleasure of coming. Not that the country even in winter gives me the spleen, but after a few months in the wilderness of mid-Berkshire it is exhilarating to look in the faces of some apparently intelligent human beings. We started in a fog which promised fine weather in town, and we were not disappointed. London was as full as it could hold; the streets were full, the shops over-full; to buy a penny stamp at the Post Office it was necessary to take your place in a long *queue*. But everybody seemed in good spirits; matronly dames, puffing papas, tall serious sisters were letting themselves be tugged down every street by apple-cheeked schoolboys; nursemaids smiled as they pushed their perambulators through the thickest of the crowd; the poor tired shop-girls smiled under the fostering eye of the shop-walker; even the sombre pavement artist chose subjects that smacked of the season, high-coloured roast beef of Old England, plum pudding crowned with no mortal holly; and the mechanical people who touch their hats at street corners and give five sweeps if you drop in a penny were keeping holiday, and cheerfully overlooked the mud at their crossings. Having no business myself but that of Chremes in the old comedy, I took great interest in watching the crowds, and let my imagination work on the waifs and strays of conversation that floated by. I spent as usual a good deal of time in the bookshops, as much for the sake of the buyers as the books. It is pretty to observe ladies to whom a book is but a Christmas present make their way into the *terra incognita* of Bain or Hatchards or Bumpus, look vaguely round, make a despairing plunge or two, and then throw themselves on the mercy of the benevolent despot, who assigns them what will best suit Tom and Jack and Margaret. The great bulk of the new books seemed to be reprints of classic authors, which is a sign at least of healthy taste; but it seems the public will not buy them without a certificate prefixed from some modern critic. So Scott is patted on the back by Mr. Lang, Johnson by Mr. Birrell, the rest of the eighteenth century writers by Mr. Dobson, females in general by Mrs. Ritchie, Job by Mr. Jacobs, and the world at large by Professor Saintsbury. We were staying with our friend X., who is so good-natured that he does not resent our using his house as an hotel. He was civil enough to invite a few interesting people to meet us. He is master of the simple secret that a great dinner-party is a great evil unless all the company are bores. If there is a humorist at the upper end, and the table is long, and you are in your proper place below the salt, it is vexing, especially if you are as dull a dog as I am, to see the signs of merriment in which you cannot share. At home I have an old-fashioned round table, which holds no more than eight people, so that the talk must be general, and under these circumstances I find talk improves, because the wits have the stimulus of an audience, and the audience of the wits.

25th.—A bright day, which made the Christmas salutation more easy and natural. But why do some folks wish me "a happy" instead of "a merry Christmas"? Is it spiritual refinement? Do they think because they are virtuous there shall be no cakes and ale? Not being able to go to church, I read Stevenson's "Christmas Sermon," reprinted from Scribner in "Across the Plains." Most laymen could, I imagine, write one good sermon, into which they would put all their theology; but though good such homilies would not be gay. When laymen of literary genius mount the pulpit it is a different matter. Matthew Arnold's "Christmas Sermon" was excellent reading; and though too full of his pet heresies, it said a plain word for Christian morals. Stevenson preaches to us the lesson he had so successfully taught himself, the duty of cheerfulness. The older I grow, the greater value I set on this virtue, and, considering the increase in suicides, I should judge there was never more need for it. I have known a wife (to put the matter from a man's point of view) who by her resolute cheerfulness enabled her husband to keep heart and head when skirting the precipice of bankruptcy; and I have known a wife who by her curst[1] shrewishness made even a crumpled rose-leaf as agonising as a crown of thorns. Years ago I travelled many months together with a friend, who was the most cheerful companion in the world, and I had no suspicion that there was another side to his temperament until once at Lucerne we slept for a couple of nights in adjoining rooms with but a thin partition between. He is now dead, so I may tell the story. Both mornings I was amazed to hear a long soliloquy all the time he was dressing to this effect: "Oh, I am the most unhappy man alive! Oh dear! oh dear! what is the use of going on living? Oh, the wearisomeness of it! How I hate and despise myself! Wretch!" and so forth. It was just Carlyle's old wheezing clock: "Once I was hap-hap-happy, but now I am meeserable!" And each morning he came down to breakfast with his usual gaiety, so that I could but assume he had, perhaps unconsciously, come to

---

[1] I use the word in its Shakespearean sense.

adopt this remarkable means of purging his melancholy; and I felt a little ashamed of having penetrated his secret.

The post-bag, when at last it arrived, was full of letters for the servants' hall; Christmas cards, I presume. I hope this means that the custom of sending these picturesque souvenirs is sinking in the scale, prior to disappearing altogether, as valentines did. It may mean only that no cards come to us because we never send any to others. All such social habits soon become a tyranny, from which it is wise to keep as free as possible.

26th.—The "Feast of Stephen" has long been materialised into Boxing-day; and even the well-meant efforts of Dr. Neale and "Good King Wenceslas" have not restored it to the protomartyr. A measure of the poverty of taste in matters poetical is afforded by the popularity of that very tame carol. For weeks before Christmas we suffer it, and reward our persecutors with nuts and apples. I made an attempt one year to substitute the old Stephen carol printed by the Percy Society from a MS. of Henry VI.'s reign; but the old vicar objected. And perhaps from his point of view he was right; for the legend is entirely independent of the story in Acts. It opens unblushingly:

> "Saint Stephen was a clerk
>   In King Herodës hall,
> And served him of bread and cloth
>   As ever king befall.
> Stephen out of kitchen came
>   With boarës head on hand;
> He saw a star was fair and bright
>   Over Bethlehem stand.
> He cast adown the boarës head
>   And went into the hall:
> 'I forsake thee, King Herod,
>   And thy workës all.
> I forsake thee, King Herod,
>   And thy workës all;
> There is a child in Bethlehem born
>   Is better than we all.'"

King Herod naturally remonstrates, and asks Stephen if he has gone mad, or is striking for higher wages. Stephen replies shortly, and keeps to his point:

> "Lacketh me neither gold or fee
>   Ne none richë weed;
> There is a child in Bethlehem born
>   Shall helpen us at our need."

This is too much for Herod, who gives his retainer the lie symbolical:

> "That is all so sooth, Stephen,
>   All so sooth, I wis,
> As this capon crowë shall
>   That lieth here in my dish.'

Three vigorous verses complete the episode:

> "That word was not so soon said,
>   That word in that hall,
> The capon crew, *Christus natus est*,
>   Among the lordës all.

> 'Riseth up, my tormentors,
>   By two and all by one,
> And leadeth Stephen out of this town,
>   And stoneth him with stone.'
> Tooken they then Stephen
>   And stoned him in the way.
> And therefore is his even
>   On Christës own day."

"Therefore"! It is unblushing, as I said. But as a carol it takes the colour out of "Good King Wenceslas."

To-night the mummers came round. For old sake's sake one does not refuse to see them, but the glory has long ago departed. At least, I seem to remember that in my youth the performance was better; certainly it was the best of the village boys who used to act, now it is the tag, rag, and bobtail, and they do not take the trouble to learn all the verses. The principal characters are King George and a French officer, who fight, both get wounded, and are cured by a doctor; Molly, who acts as showman and chorus, and Beelzebub, who comes in at the end, dressed like Father Christmas, to collect the pennies. All the characters announce themselves in the manner of the old miracle plays, thus:

> " I be King Gaarge, a nawble knight,
> I lost some blood in English fight,
> I care not for Spaniard, French, or Turk,
> Where's the man as can do I hurt?
> And if before me he durs stan'
> I'll cut un down with this deadly han',
> I'll cut un and slash un as small as flies,
> And send un to the cookshop to make mince pies," &c. &c.

January 1st, 1897.—" And the new sun rose bringing the new year." The glass also has risen, and we may anticipate a couple of days of dry weather. But our new weathercock, in the exuberance of youthful spirits, is engaged in an endeavour, by more and more rapid gyrations, to hit that point of the compass which Feste calls the "south-north." Now for good resolutions. I find, as age creeps on, I spend too much time on the hearthrug with hands in pockets and coat-tails over arms, while letters remain to write and books to read. What is to be done? I knew an author once who printed a placard with BEGIN upon it in giant letters, and hung it in his study; but, not to speak of the disfigurement and the publicity, I doubt the effectiveness of any such memento. I can say "begin" to myself as often as I like without budging an inch. It is far more efficacious to set up an independent train of thought, and, by becoming interested in something else, leave the old attraction unconsciously. Mr. James (I mean Mr. William James the humorist, who writes on Psychology, not his brother the psychologist, who writes novels) has an amusing dissertation on the art of getting out of bed:

"We know what it is to get out of bed on a freezing morning in a room without a fire, and how the very vital principle within us protests against the ordeal. Probably most persons have lain on certain mornings for an hour at a time, unable to brace themselves to the resolve. We think how late we shall be, how the duties of the day will suffer; we say, 'I *must* get up; this is ignominious,' &c.; but still the warm couch feels too delicious, the cold outside too cruel, and resolution faints away and postpones itself again and again, just as it seemed on the verge of bursting the resistance and passing over into the decisive act. Now, how do we ever get up under such circumstances? If I may generalise from my own experience, we more often than not get up without any struggle or decision at all. We suddenly find that we *have* got up. A fortunate lapse of consciousness occurs; we forget both the warmth and the cold; we fall into some reverie connected with the day's life, in the course of which the idea flashes across us, 'Hullo! I must lie here no longer'—an idea which at that lucky instant awakens no contradictory or paralysing suggestions, and consequently produces immediately the appropriate motor effects."

The problem for me seems, then, to resolve into this—how to secure a "fortunate lapse of consciousness" soon after breakfast. I must engage Eugenia to come into the library every morning with an interesting piece of news; or I must have the post-bag placed on the writing-table away from the fire. And I will begin to-morrow.

On December 19th I made a note of having met a troop of six magpies, and wondered what it portended. A correspondent is good enough to send me a Cumbrian version of the old rhyme:—

> "One for sorrow,
> Two for mirth,
> Three for a wedding,
> Four for a birth;
> Five for Heaven,
> Six for Hell,
> Seven for the Divel's own sel'."

In Berkshire, not being theologically minded, we recognise only the first four lines.

2nd.—I went yesterday with Sophia on a new-year's visit to my aunt at Barchester. We had, as usual, much talk about dignitaries *au grand sérieux*, relieved by one or two anecdotes told by a clergyman more reverend than reverent. One was of the late Bishop ——, who lost his train through pacing sedately down the platform in the serene confidence that he would be waited for. Another was of the present Bishop of —— and his Conference. It seems that his lordship is a good chairman, in the sense that he keeps himself to his chair and leaves the meeting to manage itself. The whole business of wrangling over academic resolutions, which there is no power to make practical, is so transparently futile, that a bishop may be readily excused for treating a Diocesan Conference as a lesser Convocation and going to sleep—especially at the after-lunch sitting. When it came to votes of thanks, the proposer remarked that his lordship certainly deserved one, because the business he had been engaged in was so obviously distasteful. The Bishop rose twinkling with humour. He was at a loss to divine how the kind proposer of the vote of thanks could have come to such a conclusion. As a matter of fact it was quite true. It reminded him of an answer given in an examination to the question,

"Wherein lay the great sin of Moses at the striking of the rock?" The answer was, "I don't know; but I conclude it must have been something in the expression of his countenance." One repartee I will note because it told against me. An old-fashioned canon was inveighing against his lordship of —— for wearing a mitre. "But surely," I said, "there is more sense in putting a mitre on your head than on your notepaper and carriage panels!" "Then why don't you go about," said he, "on state occasions in a helmet with your crest atop?"

5*th*.—A second sleepless night, and there is, unhappily, no help for it. For I am cutting a wisdom tooth, and have been engaged in the business for more than a twelvemonth. The process is inoffensive enough, unless I catch cold, as I did yesterday, and then it becomes "tarrible tarrifying and pertickler 'nights," as we say here. One tooth came through a few months ago, and had to be at once extracted. So I imagine it will be with the other—

> "Ostendent terris hunc tantum fata, neque ultra
> Esse sinent."

11*th*.—During my convalescence I have been reading the early volumes of Miss Burney's diary. I found my old friends as diverting as ever. What company could be better than Daddy Crisp, or those excellent young men, Mr. Seward the vain and Mr. Crutchley the proud, or the S.S. who wept at will, or the Lady Say and Sele of that epoch, who went about quoting one sentence from her sister's unprinted novel, "The Mausoleum of Julia," or Mr. B———y, who "lost four years of the happiness of his life—let's see, '71, '72, '73, '74—ay, four years, sir, and all that kind of thing;" or Mrs. Vesey, who "thought it such a very disagreeable thing, when one has just made acquaintance with anybody and likes them, to have them die," not to speak of the greater names, Burke and Johnson, and Reynolds and Garrick; Carter, Chapone, Montague, and Thrale, and all the humours of the Court. Of course there are bores, too. The name of "sweet Mrs. Delany" is a signal for skipping, so is Colonel Fairly (*i.e.* Digby); whom F. B. somewhat affected, recording for hundreds of pages his talk about "longing to die," and how he read her a volume of "Love Letters," and elegant extracts from Akenside and Beattie, and who then accepted a fat sinecure and married a Miss Gunning. I thought it a good opportunity, while the book was fresh in memory, to look at Macaulay's essay, one of his latest, and see how far it would save his declining reputation. Its unfairness and inaccuracy struck me as extraordinary. Nor were they due solely to political prejudice. For instance, he has a very rhetorical paragraph suggesting and rejecting all sorts of impossible reasons why the Queen should have offered Miss Burney a post at court. The explanation is quite simple. Neither George III. nor his consort were such fools as Macaulay makes out; they were both—the Queen especially—much interested in literature, and wished to have so distinguished a literary lady about them. Moreover, Dr. Burney had just been refused the post of conductor of the King's Band, and this place for his daughter was meant as compensation. But it is too late in the day to review Macaulay's review. One particularly glaring mistake is perhaps worth noting. Macaulay says: "We have not the smallest doubt that Johnson revised 'Cecilia,' and that he retouched the style of many passages." Again, after quoting a passage, "We say with confidence either Sam Johnson or the devil." Now hear Miss Burney:—"Ay," cried Dr. Johnson, "some people want to make out some credit to me from the little rogue's book. I was told by a gentleman this morning that it was a very fine book, if it was all her own. 'It is all her own,' said I, 'for me, I am sure, *for I never saw one word of it before it was printed*'" (ii. 172, ed. 1842). Thus a categorical denial to his theory comes in the very book Macaulay was reviewing!

13th.—What is a gentleman? The question

has been raised in the *Morning Post* by a correspondent, who proposes to found a club open to none but gentlemen of coat-armour, or, as he prefers to say, "armigerous" persons. One would have thought a man's armigerous instincts hardly his most clubable side; it was his own page in Debrett that interested Sir Walter Kellynch, not the rest of the Baronetage. Probably if this bold gentleman founds his club he will find he has sown a crop of (heraldic) dragons' teeth—"*armigerâ prœlia sevit humo,*" to quote Propertius. For A, who is the tenth transmitter of a coat-of-arms, will look coldly upon B and C, who can only count five generations; C, who reckons twelve, will snub A; the vanquished will retire from the field, and soon the founder, who no doubt has the longest pedigree out of Wales, will be left alone in his glory. The correspondence called forth by the proposal is amusing. One person writes to expose it as a very palpable attempt of Heralds' College to raise the wind; surcoats, according to this testy witness, being on sale there, new or second-hand, surprisingly cheap, and not much in demand; being, in fact, reach-me-downs, "things which take the eye and have their price," as Browning says. Another writer follows him with the lament that this has been the sad case for four centuries. But why draw the line at four centuries? People have been dubbed knight "on carpet consideration" ever since dubbing was invented. Some coats-of-arms or augmentations really represent *achievements*, as they are all styled, and were won on the field of battle; but these are very few. All through the fourteenth century it was the custom for families to adopt what "achievements" they pleased, quite independently of any doughty deeds, though probably not without payment; and if one family happened to take a fancy to a coat that had already been adopted, there was a pretty row, as in the Scrope and Grosvenor controversy about *azure, a bend or*, in which Chaucer was a witness. But where in such cases is glorying? No, "these things must not be thought on after these ways." If Jones or I receive some distinction—a coat-of-arms, or an augmentation, or a V.C., or a Turkish Order, or a baronetcy—it is best to accept the fact for what it is worth, and be as proud as we can, without raising any question of why and wherefore, and the same wise maxim applies to ancestral distinctions. I am exceedingly proud of the fact (whenever I remember it) that an ancestor of mine sealed a thirteenth-century deed of gift with an *étoile* of six points; but the glory is simply "from its being far"; he *may* have been himself "some bright particular star," but the chances are he was not; and I have no doubt either he or his grandfather paid the Earl Marshal 2d. for the privilege. When there are no wars new families have no alternative but to buy their decorations. Elizabeth, for a consideration, made many hundreds of "armigeri," by no means most of them warriors; one was Shakespeare, who would have jumped at the chance, one feels sure, of joining an armigerous club for the sake of hob-nobbing with Sir Thomas Lucy. Of course, if besides being a new man, you had the luck to bear a common name, you could save your pocket and your countenance by hooking yourself on by imaginary links to some family already "gentle" (a Mr. Dawkins in 1597 lost his ears for concocting some hundred false pedigrees, for which see Debrett, *passim*); or, if you thought this course too risky, you might simply "convey" their shield, and trust to no questions being asked, as most new people seem to do now. I know of one gentleman who couldn't make up his mind between two very pretty coats borne by different families of his name, and so used them both, and the effect on his plate, which is the final cause of a coat-of-arms, was very magnificent. Persons in a lower rank of life are generally content with a crest and motto for their notepaper. But what is there in all this to enrage? No one worth deceiving is deceived. And why should any one be jealous of new men? Every family was new once, and they became new, then as now, by becoming wealthy. This is a commonplace of satire right back to the time of Euripides (see Frag. 20), and no doubt earlier.

But at bottom the question, "What is a gentleman?" is a serious one, and could not have been raised in a more pointed manner than by the proposal to found an armorial club. It comes to this: Is the word "gentleman" to be allowed to mean what in fact it has come to mean in England—a man of a certain type of education and manners—or is it to revert to its original sense of "gentilis homo," a man of a certain type of family? William of Wykeham answered the question deliberately in the former sense by his famous motto, "Manners makyth man," and the tradition of the English schools and universities has consistently set in the same direction.[1] The old story about the French Marquis, who opined that the Almighty would think twice before damning a gentleman of his quality, doubtless finds an echo in all genuinely "armigerous" bosoms; but there is another tale in Evelyn's Diary which puts what I believe to

---

[1] Contrast what Queen Charlotte told Miss Burney of a certain German Protestant nunnery, where the candidates' coats-of-arms were put up several weeks to be examined, and if any flaw was found they were not elected (ii. 402).

be the English position as pointedly as the other does that of the *ancien régime*: "March 10, 1682.—Vrats told a friend of mine who accompanied him to the gallows, and gave him some advice, that he did not value dying of a rush, and hoped and believed God would deale with him like a gentleman;" *i.e.* with courtesy and consideration. Everybody would admit that breeding has not a little to do with gentle instincts, but three generations may be trusted to do as much as thirty.

18*th*.—A perfect winter's day. The light thrown up from the snow makes all the indoor colour vividly brilliant. I went to help the Vicarage boys build a Grecian temple. With great foresight they had rolled enormous wheels of snow on Sunday afternoon while it was wet, from which to-day they carved glistening blocks. At —— I found a handsome piece of red morocco binding, lettered "Trial of Warren Hastings, Esq., 1788." I suppose it had been one of the notebooks supplied to the peers. But the person to whom it had fallen had given it for an album to his daughter, who had copied in "Paradise and the Peri!"

20*th*.—I find myself somewhat indisposed, and through my own fault. I make it a rule when dining out to drink no wine unless I am quite sure of the cellar, especially if my host is a clergyman; for the great fall in tythes has made economy in the port wine bill generally necessary, even among those who can still afford to dine. I find that not a few of my neighbours follow the same custom. Last night at ——, every one sat as if at a teetotal festival—νήφων ἀοίνοις— until the cloth was drawn. But something in my host's expression struck me as he helped himself to port and sipped it critically, so that at the second round I flung away discretion and helped myself and sipped. Then I understood. What I had taken for pride in his port was defiance in his eye; with just such a face Socrates sipped his hemlock. "Any port in a storm," says the proverb; but it is a proverb for young men. Even Tennyson, when he grew into years, became more cautious, and no longer bade the plump head-waiter at the "Cock," "Go fetch a pint of port," without specifying the vintage. Nay, the story goes that even at the tables of the wealthy he would not drink till his son had "tasted" for him. In that excellent book, Law's "Serious Call," there is some serious and excellent advice on this point:—

"*Octavius* is a learned, ingenious man, well vers'd in most parts of literature, and no stranger to any kingdom in *Europe*. The other day, being just recover'd from a lingering *fever*, he took upon him to talk thus to his friends:

"'My *glass*,' says he, 'is almost run out; and your eyes see how many marks of *age* and *death* I bear about me: But I plainly feel myself sinking away faster than any standers-by imagine. I fully believe one year more will conclude my reckoning.'

"The attention of his friends was much rais'd by such a declaration, expecting to hear something truly excellent from so learned a man, who had but a *year* longer to live. When *Octavius* proceeded in this manner: 'For these reasons,' says he, 'my friends, I have left off all *taverns*, the wine of those places is not good enough for me in this decay of nature. I must now be *nice* in what I drink; I can't pretend to do as I have done; and therefore am resolved to furnish my own *cellar* with a little of the very best, tho' it cost me ever so much'" (1st ed. p. 210).

24*th*.—Robert came to luncheon before going back to college, and we had a long chat about Oxford. I judge the prevailing philosophical tone there to be utilitarian, for the highest praise Robert gave to anything was that it was "useful," and the word seemed always in his mouth. Dr. ———, who is a young Cambridge graduate, happened to come in, and they must fall to abuse of each other's university. I endeavoured to mediate, quoting Q.'s ballad,[1] which neither knew; also Selden's grave judgment: "The best argument why Oxford should have precedence of Cambridge is the Act of Parliament by which Oxford is made what it is, and Cambridge is made what it is; and in the Act it takes place." I suppressed the last sentence, in which Selden shows himself a true son of Oxford: "Besides, Oxford has the best monu-

---

[1] "Green Bays: Anecdote for Fathers."

ments to show." At last the doctor said to Robert, "How strange it is that the only man in Oxford who does anything should be a Cambridge man." Upon this I resolutely closured the subject. It is a curious controversy. Some people profess to be able to tell at sight to which University a man owes his education. The old epigram says, "The Oxford man looks as if the world belonged to him; the Cambridge man as if he did not care to whom it belonged." I have myself seemed to remark a certain precision of outline and want of atmosphere about the Cambridge training, and perhaps a certain atmosphere and want of precision about the Cambridge toilet and manners; but I fear I take even less interest in the debate than I do in the annual boat-race. I own it is a defect. I remember that the only time Mr. Gladstone's eye brightened during his delivery of the Romanes lecture a few years ago was when he recited the old Caroline epigrams.

February 1st.—

"February fill dyke
With black or white,"

runs the rhyme, if it can be called a rhyme. It does not say that the dykes need be filled with both black and white on the first day of the month; but that is what has happened. We had a steady fall of snow the greater part of the night, and all day it has rained as steadily. I omitted to note at the beginning of last month, when we visited Barchester, that we had from my aunt less praise than usual of her own bishop, and I learned the reason from one of the canon's wives. The wave of Socialism had at last mounted to the Palace, which had been giving a number of dances to domestic servants, but none to the young people of the Close, who were a little indignant, but not so indignant as the servants in each household who had been passed over. They had clubbed together and hired the Assembly Rooms for a Twelfth-Night ball, and every house in Barchester was divided as to the policy of letting their servants go. What if a respectably-dressed burglar should get introduced to Caroline and learn all about the customs of the house, where the safe is, whether our diamonds only pretend to be paste, whether we dine off gold or electro-plate? In the first part of each day, as I heard, fathers of families were resolute against yielding to any such absurdity, but dinner brought more sombre thoughts. If cook should give notice! To lose a girl who could make soup like this! Was not Henri IV. politic who thought a kingdom worth a mass? After all, one might sit up oneself for a night to let the maids in, and get on with that Charge or that University sermon; and then morning again would bring more sober reflection. Herodotus tells of a wise race who debated all important questions both night and morning to give both reason and passion their due. One feels they must have found it difficult to come to conclusions. But whether the ball was held, and whether, in consequence, the Barchester cooks and housemaids have all moved on one place like the guests at the Mad Hatter's tea-party, I have not heard.

5*th*.—It is still raining, and does not seem to know how to stop, like crying children. All the ponds have overflowed, and in one or two places the roads have to be forded. It would take Mark Tapley to be cheerful under the circumstances, or Matthew Green; but that last-named worthy seems to have visited his farm

> "Twenty miles from town,
> Small, tight, salubrious, and his own,"

only in fine weather; for on wet days his prescription for the spleen is—

> "To some coffee-house I stray,
> For news, the manna of a day."

We have a coffee-house, but the villagers prefer the tap-room at the "Blue Boar"; and the news there is not to-day's manna.

8*th*.—The glass is going up at a great pace, but the wind has shifted from NW. to S. I went to look at the lambs, and the old shepherd, who has a whole meteorological department in his head, shook it at the weather. "We shall have a fall 'fore this time to-morrow." Aristotle bids us respect the opinions of the aged, even when unaccompanied by reasons; but their reasons are often very entertaining. So I pressed him: "Gentle shepherd, tell me why." "Well," said he, "did you see the moon last night lying on his back? I know'd he meant summat by that; he means a fall 'fore this time to-morrow, snow or rain however."

14*th.*—

> "Saint Valentinës day,
> When every fowl cometh to choose his mate."

And for once the day is worthy the occasion. One tastes in the air the first freshness of spring, and there rise in the memory forgotten scraps of the early poets, who seem somehow to have found the world fresher than we find it to-day; though even Chaucer complained that everything was used up. A few birds have been told off, as in *The Assembly of Foules,* to sing the canticle of Nature:—

> "Now welcome summer with thy sunnë softë
> That hast this winter weather overshaken."

I hope it may not prove a premature flourish. The unusual depression of this winter is signalised by the fact that our rooks, for the first time I can remember, made no attempt to build at Christmas.

The vicar is away to-day preaching at Cambridge before his University. Dr. Merry (*vero quem nomine dicunt*) has described the country parson's experience on such occasions at Oxford in a very humorous poem printed in "More Echoes from the Oxford Magazine;" and I suppose it is much the same at Cambridge. Meanwhile, we poor silly sheep are left "encombred in the myre," at the tender mercies of a "mercenarie." I must own I felt some curiosity as to whether the vicar would discover some new brand of *locum tenentes;* his predecessor's substitutes I used to suffer gladly, until he fell ill and they came too often. There was the gentleman who compared the Cross to a lightning-conductor, and recommended us to embrace it; there was another who preached from Jude on the contest for the body of Moses, and speculated in a very entertaining manner on the purpose for which Satan required it; and there was a third who made a substantial discourse of St. Peter's shadow, pointing out, first, that it was an *everyday* shadow, so that we ought never to despise the commonplace; secondly, that it was an *unemployed* shadow, and everything should have a use; with a whole hydra of heads besides, which I have forgotten. The young gentleman to-day was of a more modern school, a sort of Anglican dervish, who pirouetted in the pulpit, and occasionally nearly shut himself up like a clasp-knife. What impressed me most was his personification of Septuagesima, in this way: "Septuagesima comes to us, and lays a hand on our shoulder and insists with us, and is urgent and shrill and vehement, and intercedes and coaxes and persuades. She besets us and inveigles and adjures and implores," &c. He had, too, a disagreeable trick of emphasising *not*, against all idiom, in the Commandments, *e.g.* "Thou shalt *not* steal," as if we had said we should; and again in the Second Collect at Evening Prayer, "which the world can*not* give." Of course, the English negative is enclitic; the very form *cannot* proves this, as do such contractions as *doesn't, shouldn't, can't,* &c. To emphasise *not*, except in an antithesis, is to commit a vulgar error; or rather, it isn't, for ordinary folks would not dream of doing so; it is to fall a victim to that disease of pedants which the old physician of Norwich would have styled *Pseudodoxia Hieratica*. I have long wondered where *locum tenentes* are bred, for they are a distinct species of parson; the ordinary sort, one knows, hails from Oxford or Cambridge, and I remember hearing that a friend's gardener once gave as his reason for not going to church, "I've lived in Oxford where the parsons are made, and I don't think much of 'm." A catalogue from a Birmingham curiosity dealer this morning may throw some light on the problem, for an entry runs :—

"CLERGYMEN.—A fine collection of 200 clergymen, consisting of Protestant Ministers, Roman Catholics, Wesleyan Methodists, Unitarians, and Presbyterians, nice clean lot, 5s."

That sounds almost too cheap, even in this depressed state of the market. Perhaps it is a misprint for £5, 5s.

20th.—A long letter came this morning from Eugenia, who has reached Cairo, to her mother, from which I have leave to transcribe a few of the more general passages :—

All the family met us in the hall and welcomed us most heartily. They are most charming and delightful people, and they talk very good English, with plenty of idioms to make us feel at home, such as "the weather is briskish," "rather queerish for Cairo." The house is large, and we have a suite of rooms to ourselves, including a bath-room. The decorations are mostly Eastern, except a stuffed cotton cat which sits on the back of the sofa. The children of the house talk Arabic, French, Greek, German, and English, as occasion requires. At present I feel like a person in the "Arabian Nights"; the servants are Afreets, and we clap our hands for them to appear. The major-domo waits at dinner in white gloves, after first holding a magnificent basin and ewer for the

Pasha to wash his hands; and the things to eat are kabobs and pilafs. Of course, to break the spell we have only to go to tea on Shepheard's balcony on Saturday afternoon, when the English band plays. That is pure West, even transatlantic, as the other is pure East, but they are curiously mingled everywhere else: electric tramways and camels, bicycles and donkey boys, American heiresses and black bundles with two eyes near the top. We see Aladdin playing with his little friends, and hopeless-looking bronze babies sitting astride on one shoulder of their mothers, holding by the top of their head. It used to be the fashion to let them tumble, so as to disable them for military service, until we took over the army.[1] The blues and yellows are very fine; but the dirt beggars description, and the smells are overdone. There is occasionally a spicy, peppery, Eastern smell that is rather good, but some are pure typhus. Of the sights, I think I like the Sphinx best, then the running sais, then the camels, then the donkey-boys; the *Barrage*, too, is very wonderful. I will copy a few days from my diary.

Tuesday.—The Pasha took us to the big mosque, El Azhar, which is a university, the oldest in the

---

[1] I think Eugenia is mistaken about this; no doubt mothers occasionally let their babies fall, but to disable them for service they used to maim the trigger finger.

world. There are about 8000 students, and they do much the same work as when the university was founded. Each professor sits by his own column (the professorships are called columns instead of chairs) and addresses his class in a sing-song. Last year, in the cholera times, the students resisted the sanitary orders of the police, and some were shot. After lunch we went on an expedition to old Cairo with Mr. X——, in an electric tramcar full of natives. The *prix fixe* is a great mystery to them, as it is also on the railway, where they lose their tempers and sometimes their trains because the clerk will not bargain. There was a disturbance at one point because the guard gave a man rather less change than his due; one of the company said, "This guard is often short of farthings; it is a case for the police." Of course Mr. X—— was our interpreter; it is so much more amusing going about with him than with a dragoman, as he tells us what the people say. We saw, amongst other things, a Coptic church, full of beautiful inlaid work in ivory and mother-o'-pearl, and the mosque with 360 pillars of marble and porphyry. The sacristan was a potter, so we went afterwards to see him at work. His pace was four pots in five minutes. On the way back something went wrong with the electrical communication; a cord caught in one of the wires, so the guard stood on the roof and poked it with a piece of sugar-cane.

Friday.—Dervishes—we saw both the dancing ones and the howling ones. Crowds of people, mostly tourists, were looking on, and it was difficult to think of it as a religious service. The dancers were just like the pictures one sees; the howlers were more dreadful, as every trace of intelligence went out of their faces as they rocked themselves backwards and forwards, grunting " *La illáha il Allah.*" At Rhoda Island, where we went to see the ancient Nilometer, a little boy, who showed us the precise spot where Moses was found amongst the bulrushes, amused us by giving his own age as two days old. When we showed surprise, he raised it to three days. We suggested years, but he said it was all the same. And so it is in Egypt, at least as far as monuments and institutions are concerned. The Greek nurse went out to buy us some *helvas* (I think that is the word), a somewhat greasy sweetmeat made of butter and sugar in the shape of a Cheshire cheese, and the boy in the shop asking how he should cut it, his father replied with a frown, "As if you were cutting off the head of a Christian." This shows how high feeling runs. I wonder what people who talk about " Egypt for the Egyptians " really mean ! Who are the Egyptians—the Turks, or the Armenians, or the Greeks, or the Arabs, or the Copts ?

We dined with the —— at the Ghezireh Palace Hotel, a beautiful palace built by Ismail for the Empress Eugénie when she came to the opening of the Suez Canal, and in which she slept one night. At another table we saw the most interesting sight we have seen yet, Slatin Pacha. Afterwards we looked on at the " Petits Chevaux " in the Casino; no one may *stake* more than two shillings at a time, but you may *bet* what you please.

Wednesday.—Lady Cromer's ball, which I am told is the biggest thing in the year. The dancing-room was very full, so I only danced once, and came away very virtuously, like Cinderella, at twelve o'clock. The next event of importance is the Khedive's ball. It is usual for each Consul-General to send in a list of suitable visitors to the Khedive's Secretary. The American list this year was returned with the remark that the Khedive invited only the nobility, to which the Consul replied that all Americans were "kings in their own right," and, when no notice was taken, returned his own card. The end of the story is that they have all got their invitations—"*tout Shepheard.*"

Saturday.—This morning I went to the bazaars with an American lady who wanted to buy some Zouave jackets. She made a very good bargain with the man, and he said, " You want to buy a camel, an elephant, and you offer me a monkey, a sparrow;" finally, he took £4 instead of the £7, 10s. he had asked at first. What I like about shopping is the *backsheesh*. If you buy a hundred cigarettes, they give you one to smoke on the spot. Did it ever strike you that of the "Thousand and One Nights," the odd one was *backsheesh?* To-night there was a performance of "Our Boys" by English amateurs for the Armenian fund. Of course not a single Turk was present, but the house was quite full. You must excuse the disconnectedness of this letter, as I have been obeying father's commands to keep a diary. I fear it is not a very full one; in fact, the spirit of the Nile has quite possessed me, and I have adopted for a motto temporarily the word one hears forty times a day, "Mallesch," which means literally "Nothing on it," and practically "Never mind." I am sure the Pyramids have lasted so long because they do not worry. I know, so far, about fifty Arabic words altogether, most of them learnt while driving; for the coachman shouts all the time, "To the right; to the left; open your eye, O woman; listen, my uncle; mind your legs, O lady," and the people follow his instructions without looking round.

27th.—I came upon a passage a few days ago in Gower's *Confessio Amantis* (book iv.) describing the "happy warrior," which, though not amusing in itself—for Gower inherited none of his master's literary gifts—has a footnote that made me smile :—

> "He may not then himselvĕ spare
> Upon his travail for to serve
> (Whereof that he may thank deserve)
> Where as these men of armës be
> Sometime over the greatë sea,
> And makë many hasty rodes,"

and the note remarks, "rodes = raids."

March 1st.—I went up to town to see my dentist. By an odd chance Tom was also going to town, and by the same train, and we narrowly escaped meeting on the platform. Tom has a deeply-rooted distaste to travelling with people whom he can meet every day at home; on the rare occasions when he makes a journey he likes to pack as much novelty into the enterprise as possible, and I sympathise with the feeling. If you are a story-teller, and have a chance for an hour of an entirely new audience, it is heart-breaking to have it spoiled by the presence of some one who knows all your paradoxes and anecdotes, and sits bored. So when I saw the dog-cart approaching I retired to the waiting-room till the train came in, and then got into a smoking-carriage. I came back by an early train. Paddington was full of Eton boys, it being St. David's Day. Though the pavements in town were absolutely dry, I remarked that every young gentleman had his trousers tucked up some three inches. I must tell our yokels this, as they like to be in the fashion on Sunday. They have already discarded the walking-cane in deference to Oxford opinion.

I have heard in a roundabout way that Tom went to town to have his photograph taken. I am more than ever pleased we did not meet, as he has always expressed himself in good set terms against the vanity of being photographed, and I should not have liked to make him blush. I wonder how he stood the ordeal. Perhaps we shall hear; for if you have broken away from a principle there is nothing like making a complete *volte-face* and ignoring your old position. What is the explanation of the something ridiculous that attaches to the photographer's art? No one feels absurd in sitting to a painter. Is it the underbreeding of the presiding genius that gives one shame—his airs and graces, his injunctions to "look pleasant," or "moisten the lips," or "let the light flash in the eye," his twisting of one's elbow and spreading of one's fingers? I am inclined to think it is not altogether this, for even a Royal Academician must pose you; nor, again, is it the mere interposition of the mechanical camera, but rather the fact that everything depends upon the expression of a moment; and the attempt to choose a decent expression and maintain it on one's face, even for ten or twenty seconds, is disgusting. And then, too, the production of so many copies has the same *banal* effect as the hackneying of a phrase; so that a photograph is fitly styled a "counterfeit presentment."

2nd.—Mr. Birrell in one of his essays mentions the rareness of the works of our Berkshire laureate Pye. If he does not possess the "Summary of the Duties of a Justice of the Peace out of Sessions," I should like the opportunity of presenting him with it. It has a few poetical entries, *e.g.*, "Carrots, see Turnips." And this under Settlements: "It would be unpardonable in. *me* not to cite an authority on this case, reported in rhyme — I believe the only one in the books:

> "A woman having settlement
>   Married a man with none;
> The question was, he being dead,
>   If that she had was gone?
> Quoth Sir John Pratt, 'Her settlement
>   Suspended did remain
> Living the husband—but him dead
>   It doth revive again.'
>   *Chorus of Puisne Judges.*
> 'Living the husband—but him dead
>   It doth revive again.'"

Under the article "Pawning" comes this anecdote:—"A soldier in the Guards came to me in Queen's Square to swear to his having lost his duplicate. I looked at the affidavit to see if it were military accoutrements, &c., that he had pawned, when to my surprise I found that he had.

pawned a £2 bank-note for 10s. 6d. On asking an explanation of this odd circumstance, he said he received the £2 note, and was resolved to pass a jolly evening, but not to spend more than half a guinea; and to ensure this he pawned the note for that sum, and destroyed the duplicate afterwards, that he might not be able to raise the money on it in case his resolution should give way while he was drinking with his companions."

Let me note here a curious specimen of old-fashioned law jargon from one of the year-books: "Richardson Ch.Just. de C.B. al assizes at Salisbury in summer 1631 fuit assault per prisoner la condemne pur felony que puis son condemnation ject un brickbat a le dit Justice que narrowly mist & per ceo immediately fuit indictment drawn per Noy envers le prisoner & son dexter manus ampute & fix al gibbet sur que luy mesme immediatement hange in presence de Court."

3rd.—Yesterday's storm is still raging, a remarkable event on Ash Wednesday; Nature on that day doing her best as a rule to make Lent ridiculous by a prodigality of sunshine. The poets who speak of learning lessons from Nature, ought to warn us to pick and choose very carefully. Matthew Arnold in his "Discourses in America," having to praise Emerson, quoted with approval the following sentence:—" Nature does not like our benevolence or our learning much better than she likes our frauds and wars. When we come out of the caucus, or the bank, or the Abolition Convention, or the temperance meeting, or the Transcendental Club into the fields and woods, she says to us, 'So hot, my little sir!'" It must have been the list of monstrous illustrations, rather than benevolence and learning, that Matthew Arnold joined in condemning, for he has supplied the antidote to all such silly twaddle about conformity with Nature in his own sonnet, which begins, "'In harmony with nature?' Restless fool," and contains the fine lines:

> " Know, man hath all which Nature hath, but more,
> And in that *more* lie all his hopes of good."

I suppose when Wordsworth wrote the well-known verse in the "Tables Turned"—

> "One impulse from a vernal wood
> May teach you more of man,
> Of moral evil and of good
> Than all the sages can"—

he had in mind the impulse to aspiration, as in his poem about the Rainbow, "My heart leaps up," &c. But other impulses are not unknown in vernal woods, bird's-nesting, for instance. Certainly Eve's impulse from the famous apple-tree in the perpetual spring of Paradise, taught her more " of moral evil and of good" than her sage husband knew before, and according to South, " Aristotle was but the rubbish of an Adam." The only creatures that seem to enjoy the gale are the rooks, who make head against it for the pleasure of sailing back again.

8th.—Sophia seems to have taken an extraordinary fancy to Mrs. Vicar, who is certainly as sprightly as her *sposo* is the reverse. I overheard S. explaining, as we walked through the glasshouses to-day, that it was by a mere accident that my vines were not at the vicarage. I wish she would not wear her heart so very prominently on her sleeve before newcomers. "These violent delights have violent ends," and the time of grapes is not yet. Probably she has taken so decided an attachment because there is a slight coolness between her and my sister-in-law, whose personal motto is, "Dixi, custodiam," and who is apt to take into her custody things beyond her proper province. And it is a rule of the game in country villages not to be "out" with everybody at once, or there could be no gossip.

10th.—Another letter has come from Eugenia in Cairo, from which I make a few detached extracts :—

A curious misunderstanding occurred on one of our first days at dinner. I admired the dress of the footmen, who were waiting, and asked if it belonged to the occupation. My host replied, "Oh, no, they have always worn it." I found that he had taken "occupation" in its technical sense for the English occupation. Since then I am always hearing the word so used, and now, even if it comes in a book, it seems to jump out at me. In the "Tempest" to-day — for I still read my daily Shakespeare lection — Gonzalo says that in his ideal "Commonwealth" there should be "no occupation; all men idle, all." How many Turkish pashas wish the same![1] Another phrase one is always hearing is *Shughl Inglīzi*, which means "English work," or, as we should say, "just like an Englishman." It might be paraphrased by a phrase of Louis Stevenson's, "quite mad, but wonderfully decent." It is very comforting to find we have still left something of our old national reputation for honour. In the bazaar the other day, I protested I had spent all my money; but the Hindoo replied, "Take the things, and send me a cheque next year." I said, "Would you say that to a Greek?" He smiled and said, "You also, then, have had business with Greeks."[2] Our pasha, who is a great friend to the occupation, told us of a man who had some business to arrange between here and Constantinople.

---

[1] To cap Eugenia's quotation, the French may remember with satisfaction the phrase in "Henry IV.": "As odious as the word *occupy*, which was an excellent good word before it was ill-sorted."

[2] How different is this from the old Athenian character:

$$\ldots \quad τὸ\ γ'\ εὐσεβὲς$$
$$μόνοις\ παρ'\ ὑμῖν\ ηὗρον\ ἀνθρώπων\ ἐγὼ$$
$$καὶ\ τοὐπιεικὲς\ καὶ\ τὸ\ μὴ\ ψευδοστομεῖν.$$

[Among you above all other men I have found religion and *a temper of fairness and a habit of speaking the truth.*] The Greeks in Egypt are among other things village usurers, and sell all the drink and hasheesh. It is considered a good sign that, according to the latest census, they are not increasing. One wishes they would all emigrate to Crete!

Here it took him, to his amazement, only five days, and did not cost a penny; whereas, at the other end, he had spent three months and £200 besides in baksheesh to oil the machine. One hears plenty of stories concerning our national want of tact. A young soldier is said to have remarked to the Consul-General for Austria-Hungary, "Hungary isn't much of a place, is it?" and then, by way of plastering the sore, "I suppose Austria is better." Another young Englishman, who was in the street police, arrested the coachman of a Consul-General for not moving away from the front of Shepheard's Hotel when another carriage drove up (which, as you know, is the rule for ordinary folks), and had to be dismissed to a higher post in another department. I fear, therefore, that we are thought to be honest because we are not clever enough to be anything else; and the explanation of any voluntary surrender of profit or reputation is that stupidity in that case has risen to mania. A typical instance of *Shughl Inglīzī* was Sir Colin Scott Moncrieff's finding out Moughil Bey, the engineer who hadn't succeeded with the Barrage, and making the Government give him a pension. . . .

The pasha told us to-day a story of a judgment he gave, which reminded me of the Cadis in the "Arabian Nights." He had imported an English coachman and groom, and these did not agree with the Moslem servants, who complained that the Englishmen cursed their religion. "In what language did they curse?" "In Arabic." "How long have they been here?" "Six months." "Have they had lessons in Arabic?" "No." "Then they learned the phrase from you. I will tell them to curse you in English." "But we don't want to be cursed at all." "Then why do you curse them?" And so, having extracted a promise from each party to abstain from curses, he dismissed them. . . .

One must not expect too much from Orientals. In the East, as you will have noticed, the sheep and the goats are very much alike.

13*th*.—I went to Cherry Orchard to get some wild daffodils to take with me to town, "in their yellow petticoat and green gown." Everything about daffodils is interesting. The name is one of the prettiest corruptions possible; it ought to be "affodil," as it comes through the French from "asphodel"; but the parasitic *d* is a great improvement. For some time both forms were in use, affodil for what we now call "asphodel" or "king's spear," and "daffodil" for the narcissus. The poets have liked both the word and the flower. Amongst their encomiums, Autolycus's song and Perdita's few lines—

" Daffodils
That come before the swallow dares, and take
The winds of March with beauty "—

have never been equalled. I wonder how many of the people who have quoted this lately know what "take" means! Herrick's popular verses are a puzzle. Why does he say "we weep to see you haste away so soon"? The daffodil does not haste away before noon, and if it did, nobody, not even Rousseau, would drop the tear of sensibility. As usual, when there is a difficulty the oracles are dumb. Popular plant names were very vaguely and loosely applied in old days, and Herrick may have meant some other plant. Wordsworth's poem on the daffodils he saw dancing on the margin of Ullswater belong to his poetical prime. They were written in 1804, the same year as "The Affliction of Margaret," and "She was a Phantom of Delight." The most Wordsworthian lines in it, however—

> "They flash upon that inward eye
> Which is the bliss of solitude"—

were contributed by the poet's wife; and his sister celebrated the scene in a bit of prose no less beautiful: "They grew among the mossy stones: some rested their heads on these stones as on a pillow, the rest tossed and reeled and danced, and seemed as if they verily laughed with the wind, they looked so gay and glancing." I wonder how Tennyson came to think it legitimate to speak of March as a "roaring *moon* of daffodil and crocus;" probably he liked the sound of the broad vowels, and people quote it as a fine phrase instead of one of his failures.

15th.—Dentist. Then I took an omnibus down Oxford Street, and through the zeal of the authorities in repairing the asphalt we were compelled to make a *détour*, so that I was deposited at the very door of my destination, the British Museum, for which, considering the rain, I was grateful. It was what some people call an " almost providential " circumstance. I was much interested to notice on my way to the MSS. room how many people of the shabbier classes were reading the autograph letters of celebrated people exhibited in the show-cases. The spring fashions in the bonnet shops are very wonderful. One never sees men looking into hat shops—our peculiar vanity is boots.

20th.—I suppose the hunting season may be supposed at an end now, as the barber did not trim my eyebrows this morning. I noticed also the first adder sunning himself by —— copse. Larch rhymes with March, and the poets have noted the fact; but the larch is not careful, as a rule, to bud in March in our prosy gardens. There was, however, a rosy plumelet some ten days ago on the old tree at the bottom of the orchard, and to-day it is covered with them, thanks to the mild weather, and each streamer looks like a fibre of sea-weed stuck over with diminutive sea-anemones. But meanwhile the "peck of March dust worth a king's ransom" has not arrived, and the sowers are beginning to despair. I read "The Thackerays in India," an interesting account of many civil and military servants of John Company. Sir W. W. Hunter is an accomplished penman, with perhaps just a thought too much style and sentiment, so that he occasionally drops such a flower of pathos as the following: "On the first anniversary of his death she followed him to her own grave" (p. 177).

April 2nd.—Yesterday the lawn was mown for the first time this year. There is no such delightful smell as that of fresh grass. To-day the ivy has been cut on the house front, and the perfume is as eminently disgusting. I had shut myself up in the library with a book-catalogue, but was driven forth by Brown's putting his hook through a pane of glass and letting in the poison. So I went *bouquinant* in earnest.

My friend the bookseller at —— told me an amusing story about public spirit as it is understood by provincial ladies. The widow of a clergyman had sent for him to inspect her late husband's library. She wished it divided into two parts; the books of any value she would sell, the rest she would present to the free library. He showed me one of the books he had bought—an unopened copy of "Horace Walpole's Letters," the nine-volume edition. I had known the husband;

his conversation was far from lively, and for all those years he had dwelt by the side of this fountain of wit without tasting.

3rd.—Bob came to luncheon before departing on his first reading-party. He told me the only amusing contribution made by the undergraduates to the Nansen honorary degree festivity was the cry, "What, no soap!" I wonder if it was explained to the hero that the phrase is classical, and what he thought of the marvellous piece of improvisation from which it comes. Bob produced also some new nonsense verses. I have a great fondness for the Lear type of nonsense verse. One of the best I know is a little old-fashioned now, but it deserves recording :—

> "There was a young girl called Amanda,
> Whose novels were thoroughly *fin-de-Siècle*, but I deem
> 'Twas her *journal intime*
> That drove her papa to Uganda."

I say that to myself on fast-days, and I add this sentence from Renan by way of Antiphon: "The man who has time to keep a private diary has never understood the immensity of the universe" (*Feuilles Détachées*, 359). What interested me most in Bob's budget was the piece of news that the Magdalen authorities propose erecting a memorial chapel to Gibbon which is to eclipse the Shelley pantheon at University College opposite. There would seem from his story to have been considerable difference of opinion as to the form the memorial should take. Some of the more old-fashioned members of the committee advocated the classical tradition that a hero should be represented in his habit as he died (*cf.* the Dying Gladiator, all the St. Sebastians, &c.), especially as the University College people had put up a drowned Shelley. But a reference to the Biographical Dictionary showing that Gibbon had died of dropsy, their idea was overruled. The next suggestion was that the monument should be allegorical: Gibbon should be figured in Roman armour—the *lorica*, it was thought, would be excellently fitted to his somewhat gibbous person—and by a general slackness, or an appearance of unstable equilibrium, the statue might be made to indicate that it represented the historian of the Empire in its decline. An alternative proposal was that a model of the ruined Temple of Concord should be erected in the meadow encircled by Addison's Walk, in which should be placed a sitting statue of Gibbon at the moment when the idea of his great book occurred to him.[1] On every 15th October—which would naturally be the first day of term—the choir might go in procession round it to represent the friars, and if

[1] "It was at Rome, on the 15th of October 1764, as I sat musing amidst the ruins of the Capitol, while the barefooted fryars were saying vespers in the Temple of Jupiter, that the idea of writing the decline and fall of the city started to my mind." (Autobiography.)

thought advisable a little judicious clockwork might be introduced to help the illusion. Bob had not heard whether any decision had as yet been taken upon these various proposals.

5th.—The Diamond Jubilee Procession looms bigger than ever now that Parliament has risen, and all nature seems to have become infected. The hedgerow elms, the scarlet and yellow tulips along the garden walks, the park palings, all seem in procession. Where one used to meet one timber waggon or traction-engine one seems now to meet half-a-dozen. And the processions of sheep are endless! These last are like a nightmare. The first surprise at meeting your bicycle carries about a third of them past at a gallop. Then the leading dowagers forget you, and look over the hedge as though they were not the procession but the spectators; and if it were not for the sheep-dog you would be crushed into mutton by the block. Having escaped this fate to-day I got safe to ——, where I met a circus procession. It was exhibiting a masque of English queens, such of them at least as fall within the popular purview. There was Queen Elizabeth and Mary of Scots, and Queen Anne, and, high on a throne of royal state which far outshone the wealth of Ormuz and of Ind, her present gracious Majesty. The height served not only to enhance the dignity, but to get over the difficulty of the likeness.

6th.—In town to-day I was introduced to a very intelligent young French anthropologist, who is at work upon our manners and customs; he very good-naturedly showed me some proof-sheets of one of his chapters. The English, he considers, lack the genius for ceremonial, and are always trying to invest what ceremonial habits they inherit with a utilitarian meaning. He illustrated from washing, which as originally practised was purely ceremonial. This primitive use is still retained in baptism, though not without protest from a section even of the religious world (there followed here an account of the "Gotham" (? Gorham) controversy, and of the sect who insist on deferring baptism till it can be combined with a swimming lesson). Relics of the old ceremonial feeling he discovers in the phrase "to perform ablutions," which is a newspaper synonym for washing; in the Order of the Bath; and in the thence derived point of honour among English gentlemen to bathe; but he regards the frequency of this bathing as entirely due to the modern worship of Hygeia, and points to the annual dipping at Margate, still traditional among the lower classes, as a genuine survival from the more general practice. He notices incidentally as points elucidating his contention, that the theatre of so many affairs of honour in the last century was Cold Bath Fields, and that the sedans in which persons of quality used to be drawn to their annual immersion are still known as Bath-chairs, though they are now used only for invalids.

In Chelsea I came across a remarkable handbill, which I transcribe as a "document" for the historian of nineteenth-century morals :—

Night Tours through Whitechapel and Darkest London.

The West End Agency, in organising these tours through Whitechapel and the East End, has been careful to select men of well-known character and experience to conduct them, and under their guidance no danger need be apprehended if their advice is followed.

The party starts from the Agency's Offices at 8.30 P.M. and returns by 12 P.M.

The charges are One Guinea each, or for a party of five, Four Guineas. The party is limited to five in number.

Two clear days' notice is required of an intended visit, to avoid disappointment, and the fee must be paid on booking the tour.

Tall hats must not be worn.

Ladies who wish to see this neighbourhood can be conducted round in the day, but under no circumstances by night.

The places visited are varied—the resorts of the poorest of the poor—and in no city in the world can such sights be seen.

9th.—I called at the vicarage to take my good friend for a walk. We talked chiefly of Jowett, whose Life has just appeared, and the vicar promised to lend it me. He mentioned that he had at length summoned courage to dismiss his predecessor's "odd man," and taken a young fellow who showed at present more taste for gardening than stable-work. Returning from a few days' visit, he found a mushroom-bed in one of the stalls, and the coach-house doors quite blocked by a nursery of young cabbage plants. The odd man is a curious study: vicars may come and go, but as a rule he goes on for ever, getting crustier and crustier with age. If the parson stops many years in the same living, and the odd man stops with him, they grow to resemble each other. There may be some art in the process, but there is more nature. The odd man shaves or shapes his beard like his master, and acquires his expressions; but he also acquires his expression, his gait, his manner; and not only so, but his very features seem to reshape themselves to the parson's type, so that the odd man might often pass for a poor relation. Such growing likenesses are, of course, matters of common experience in people who live much together—in husbands and wives, for example. My own father and mother, when they travelled, were constantly taken for brother and sister: so that one need not be surprised that Abraham, from the longer life of patriarchs then, found it very easy to assume that relationship with Sarah when he visited Abimelech. One sees the same thing in young people: schoolboys catch more from their schoolmasters than their handwriting: and Eugenia used to astound us by the rapidity with which she became the "model" of the reigning nurse. But the odd man's resemblance to his master is an odder case than any of these. A mere creation of art is much less interesting. My barber, for instance, by virtue of an orange-tawny beard cut into a particular shape, has made himself a recognisable caricature of the Lord-Lieutenant; but the best specimen of the art-product I ever saw was in Sheffield, when I paid a visit years ago to Mr. Ruskin's museum at its old home. Inside the door I found a middle-aged man on a low stool—no, it was not Mr. Ruskin, but the generally *négligé* style of hair and dress was a very careful study after his pattern, and many of the superficial tricks of manner had been successfully caught. This worthy was sitting with the "Seven Lamps of Architecture" on his knees, following the lines with his finger, like the blind beggars who read the Bible at the corners of the streets to be seen of men. He looked up at me presently, by an apparent effort disengaging his attention from the book, and asked what I should like to see—for nothing was exposed to the casual eye—and I suggested missals. "Are you interested," said he, "in the subject-matter of them, or only in the decoration?" I thought that an excellent parody of not a little that Mr. Ruskin has written about Art.

19*th*.—The first brood of thrushes fledged in the garden. Yesterday, coming out of church, I overheard a lady remark to her neighbour about the Easter decorations: "How very appropriate all these primroses are to Lord Beaconsfield!" It recalled another *naïve* saying that fell in my hearing from the wife of an M.P., who, on going to church one Sunday morning during a visit to their borough for speech-making purposes, and finding it fairly full, exclaimed: "I declare they are giving us quite an ovation." Such is the dignity of statesmanship in a democracy. Is it not somewhat sinister that of all the Prime Ministers of the Queen's reign it should be the most un-English who is thus honoured with an annual commemoration; that the inventor of household suffrage should be accounted the champion of the Conservative cause; and the most flamboyant of personages be symbolised by the simple primrose? It is the most mysterious of cults, and perhaps serves the useful purpose of keeping one from taking party politics too seriously. Of course, Mr. Greenwood may be right, and Lord Beaconsfield be an entirely misunderstood genius in politics as in letters. "I write in irony," he is said to have sighed, "and they call it bombast;" so his politics, too, may have been ironical. Turning over the leaves of that remarkably clever day-book of Mr. Bowyer Nichols's, which, by a quip upon Hesiod, he has called "Words and Days," I find Primrose Day commemorated in the most appropriately ambiguous manner. There is a quotation from "Lothair," the only reference, I believe, to primroses in any of the novels :—

> "'These are for you, dear uncle,' said Clare Arundel, as she gave him a rich cluster of violets; 'just now the woods are more fragrant than the gardens, and these are the produce of our morning walk. I could have brought you some primroses, but I do not like to mix violets with anything.'
>
> "'They say primroses make a capital salad,' said Lord St. Jerome."

And this is followed by the very apposite lines from "Peter Bell" :—

> "A primrose by the river's brim
> A yellow primrose was to him,
> And it was nothing more."

The story is told—I know not on what authority—that the Queen, when she called the primrose "*his* favourite flower," meant not Lord B.'s, but Prince Albert's. If so, it would be but one absurdity the more. Has any Wordsworthian commentator analysed the attitude of Peter Bell in regard to primroses? If a primrose was a primrose to him, he must at least have taken note of it: primroses must have existed, so to say, in his world. For logicians are emphatic in asserting that no man ever yet made an identical proposition. To say A is A. (*e.g.* a primrose is a primrose) means far more than it seems to mean. There must be more in the predicate than in the subject, or the statement would not be worth making. And Mr. Bell went even further than this; he gave evidence of a definite, though not very exact, eye for colour. In short, there seems reason for regarding him as a misunderstood person, and in this respect also he sorts well with Lord Beaconsfield. Miss May Kendall, in her poem "Education's Martyr," has shown us what depths of inappreciation, far below Bell's, there may be in this matter of primroses:

> " Primroses by the river's brim,
> *Dicotyledons* were to him,
> And they were nothing more."

Shakespeare, who lived before æstheticism, seems to have considered the primrose an anæmic flower. See "Winter's Tale," iv. 4, 125.

20*th*.—I dined with ——, who invited me to meet a few literary people come from town for Easter, to see a primrose and hear the nightingale. There was much talk about books. I happened to say of Gibbon's style that he had a remarkable fondness for concluding sentences with a genitive case, when my *vis-à-vis* turned very red and addressed the company as follows:—" I made that remark twenty years ago, and" (with a glare at me) " I have made it in print; and" (with a bow) " I am delighted to have my observation confirmed by so much more distinguished a person." I fear this was the expression of a pungent irony, as I am not distinguished, and the speaker did not even know my name. Perhaps I showed annoyance, for our host hastened to interpose: "The remark was made long ago by Rogers." I took this at the time for a gentle Virgilian dust-throwing: "Hi motus animarum," &c. But on turning up the "Table Talk" I find this passage:—

"It is well known that Fox visited Gibbon at Lausanne; and he was much gratified by the visit. Gibbon, he said, talked a great deal, walking up and down the room, *and generally ending his sentences with a genitive case;* every now and then, too, casting a look of complacency on his own portrait by Sir Joshua Reynolds, which hung over the chimney-piece, that wonderful portrait in which, while the oddness and vulgarity of the features are refined away, the likeness is perfectly preserved" (p. 77).

Presently the talk fell upon Shakespeare's sonnets, and one of the company defended Malone's theory that the famous line—

"A man in hue, all hues in his controlling,"

must refer to a person called Hughes, and could not otherwise be paraphrased. I ventured to suggest that the imagined difficulty came from taking "controlling" as a verbal noun governed by *in*, instead of a participle agreeing with man; supply "hue" after "his," and the sense becomes—that the young gentleman's beauty controlled the complexion of all who were in his presence, making them blush, turn pale, &c.

The discussion continued for some time, and found no end, in wandering mazes lost.

21st.—From the hollow imitations of the school-children on every side I have no doubt that the voice of the cuckoo has been heard in our land; and Sophia tells me she heard it yesterday. Riding home last night with Eugenia I had reached the top of —— Hill about seven o'clock, when from the bushes on my right came two or three faint notes—faint, but unmistakably the nightingale's. "Listen, Eugenia," I cried, but the notes were not repeated. We have it on pseudo-Chaucerian authority, supported by a long tradition, that it is fortunate in love to hear the nightingale before the cuckoo.

> "And as I lay this other night waking
> I thought how lovers had a tokening,
> And among them it was a common tale
> That it were good to hear the nightingale
> Rather[1] than the lewdë cuckoo sing."

But if, as in this case, the lover hear the nightingale first and his lady the cuckoo, how then? Pseudo-Chaucer being dead, I must consult Professor Skeat, who is supposed to inherit something of his spirit. One cannot be thankful enough that the cuckoo has in these last days purged himself of his old Tudor associations. Perhaps Wordsworth attempted to carry the whitewashing a little far; a Berkshire poet comes nearer the mark with the epithet "ribald." For the cuckoo is not a

---

[1] *i.e.* earlier.

nice character; he always reminds me of Lord Byron bearing about ostentatiously the pageant of his bleeding heart, filling the air with clamorous self-pity, and occasionally dropping an egg into some one else's nest.

I went into school to hear the "general intelligence" lesson. Our master has a great idea of culture, and gives out questions on Monday in each week for the children to cut their wisdom teeth upon; on Thursday he hears what information they have gathered. Some of the questions I have, on chance visits, seen written up on the black-board have made me smile: Who is Grant Allen? who is Hall Caine? Others have made me weep: What is optimism? what is pessimism? This week the questions were not so far-fetched. We had an explanation of Eboracum, and were told that the other archbishop signed his name E. Cantab.; we learned that Sir Henry Irving was the greatest living actor, and Marie Corelli the greatest living novelist; that Lord Coleridge was the present Chief-Justice, and Mr. ——— a great "educationist." We heard, too, about Stonehenge and the White Horse, and what an M.P. is, and a Bart. (we keep a Bart. a few parishes off), and what the vicar wears round his neck in church, and how much her Majesty has a year to live on. Our schoolmaster is a perfect mine of information, conveyed in sesquipedalian words.

Tom has a story that he went into school one day at the Scripture hour, and heard the question put, "What are the divisions in the Litany?" To which a baby of six gave this spirited answer: "Invocations, convocations, comprecations, imprecations, and execrations." Tom would not swear to the *ipsissima verba*, but that was the general impression.

May 1st.—"I come to her and cry 'mum,' she cries 'budget,' and by that we know one another." A good many of us accost the Exchequer in the simple and hopeful temper of Master Slender, but not unfrequently that lady's "budget" does us as little good as sweet Anne Page's did him. This year, however, the Chancellor has really thought it worth while to pay us poor country folks a little attention. It is at last admitted on behalf of Government that we have as much right to letters and telegrams as people in town, and Jubilee Day is to inaugurate our new citizenship. People who are accustomed to the business-like promptitude of the young men and maidens in town offices have little idea of the casual way in which things are managed with us. A month or two since, having to register a letter containing a small present for the golden wedding of an old friend, which had reached me too late for our own despatch, I drove to a village on the railway where the mails leave two hours later. The following dialogue ensued :—Postmaster : " Do you know how old I am ? " I : " No ; are you seventy-five ? " P. : " Seventy-five ! I'm as old as Mr. Gladstone. Don't look it, don't I ? No, I mayn't look it, but I am. I've been postmaster here for fifty year and more. Yes, I ain't so young as I have a-been. Good day, sir." I : " But I want a letter registered." P. : " Registered ! Well, I hardly know. You see, I'm an old man now. Oh yes, I've registered 'em in my day ; but I don't somehow like the responsibility. No, I don't feel as if at my age I ought to take the responsibility. You see, I've been postmaster here, man and boy, for——" &c. &c. One sympathised with the old man's sense of irresponsibility, which certainly suited with his age and Mr. Gladstone's—but what was to be done with the letter ? In the end I had to take it home again. The promised reduction in porterage on telegrams will be welcome. Thoughtless friends make this a considerable item in the year's finance. Just lately I asked a man down to take pot-luck for the week-end. " Don't trouble to answer," I said, " but come if you can.' But his manners would not consent to this. Back came a telegram : " Delighted to come " (porterage, two shillings). In another hour came a second : "So sorry ; detained by important business " (porterage, two shillings). In another hour a third : " Can come after all " (porterage, two shillings).

2nd.—By sitting in shelter on the south side of the house it is possible to give a guess to-day at what spring was meant to be, but hardly ever is. The sun is lighting up the fresh green of the trees and grass :—

> " No white nor red was ever seen
> So amorous as this lovely green."

And the birds are singing after their kind. There is a spirit of youth in everything, and in the very air

> "Aetherium sensum atque aurai simplicis ignem."

Be tempted to go round a corner, and the northeast cuts like a knife; but be content not to do so, and you may exclaim with the poet :—

> " It were a most delightful thing
> To live in a perpetual spring."

The Elizabethan writer of this charming couplet, who, to use a vile phrase, "remains anonymous," was not brought up, as I was, on the "Looking-Glass of the Mind"—a series of highly-didactic stories borrowed from the French of Armand Berquin, and adorned with sculptures by John Bewick—or he would have known better. For there is a tale in that volume entitled "The Absurdity of Young People's Wishes Exposed," telling how Master Tommy exclaimed one day, when taking the air with his father, "Oh, that it were always spring!" and was at once desired to write that wish in his pocket-book. It chanced that when summer came, Thomas and his parent were abroad again in each other's company on one of the bright days that diversify an English summer. "Oh," cried Thomas, "that it were always summer!" "Write that wish, my dear boy," said his father, "in your pocket-book." The same circumstances recurred in both autumn and winter, the same wish that the present might last, and the same direction to make a note of it. And then the absurdity of young people's wishes was exposed. One does not know which to admire more—the far-sightedness and long memory of the parent, or the tidy habits of the son, who kept the same pocket-book going through four seasons. It was the latter fact that almost drove my infant mind into scepticism, and perhaps might have done so had I not liked to admire the piety of the child who would not spoil his parent's *bon mot* by stopping his exclamations with autumn.

Our nightingales have been more numerous and in better voice this spring than I ever remember them; probably they have liked the sun and not disliked the wind. It has been a pleasant object for an evening's walk to go from concert-brake to concert-brake—for each bird keeps his own station—and compare their voices; for they differ not unlike human singers and poets, one excelling in art, another in natural gifts, another in tenderness. By day, unless heard at a distance, their music has too much "execution," even something of the stridency of a mechanical pianoforte. Besides nightingale and blackbird, the chaffinch has been almost the only songster. The thrush seems to be growing rarer, and we have no linnets or goldfinches. Bullfinches there are in abundance; and if they could pipe, they might be tolerated; but then you must sacrifice your gooseberries. Hazlitt once described in *The Liberal* a visit he paid to Coleridge in 1798, in the course of which he says: "I got into a metaphysical argument with Wordsworth, while Coleridge was explaining the different notes of the nightingale to his sister, in which we neither of us succeeded in making ourselves perfectly clear and intelligible." There was so much of the nightingale about Coleridge's own music that we cannot but lament that Hazlitt wasted his time over Wordsworthian metaphysics, instead of listening to and reporting the other conversation. But it was not improbably the same conversation as that which formed the basis of the so-called "Conversation poem" on the nightingale, written in April 1798, and printed in "Lyrical Ballads"; for in it the poet addresses "my friend, and thou our sister." This is the poem in which Coleridge, first of our poets, departs from the Philomela convention (to which he himself had previously given in), allows the singer his true sex, and denies his melancholy :—

> " 'Tis the *merry* nightingale[1]
> That crowds, and hurries, and precipitates
> With fast thick warble his delicious notes,
> As he were fearful that an April night
> Would be too short for him to utter forth
> His love-chant, and disburthen his full soul
> Of all its music. . . . .
>
> Never elsewhere in one place I knew
> So many nightingales ; and far and near
> In wood and thicket, over the wide grove,
> They answer and provoke each other's songs,
> With skirmish and capricious passagings,
> And murmurs musical and swift jug-jug,
> And one low piping sound more sweet than all."

Let me note here (*à propos* of Wordsworth and Coleridge) a curious mistake that has been pointed out to me in Matthew Arnold's book of " Selections from Wordsworth." The " Stanzas written in Thomson's Castle of Indolence " are always understood to contain portraits first of the poet himself and then of his friend. But Arnold puts a footnote (S. T. Coleridge) to the first line of the poem, " Within our happy Castle there dwelt One," &c. Can this be anything but a slip or a printer's blunder ? Could Arnold have thought

---

[1] This description may not be so brilliant as the famous one of Crashaw's, but it is closer to nature. Compare the " one low piping sound more sweet than all," with Crashaw's " Trails her plain ditty in one long-spun note."

that Wordsworth must have meant Coleridge by the lines—

> "Ah, piteous sight it was to see this man
> When he came back to us, a withered flower—
> Or like a sinful creature, pale and wan?"

No doubt in "The Leech-gatherer," written a few days before, Wordsworth had his friend in mind when he said—

> "We poets in our youth begin in gladness;
> But thereof comes in the end despondency and madness,"

for Coleridge had just written his ode on "Dejection." But as Coleridge had drawn in that ode a flattering picture of Wordsworth (to whom it was first inscribed under the name of Edmund [1]) and an unflattering picture of himself, it is unlikely that Wordsworth, in returning the compliment, should not have tried to rouse his friend from his melancholy by putting his best side forward and dwelling

---

[1] How thankful we ought to be that poets have sometimes second thoughts! Edmund is a good name, but it lacks the ideality of "Lady." It would not be easy to wax tender over "O EDMUND, in this wan and heartless mood," or "O EDMUND, we receive but what we give," or "Joy, virtuous EDMUND!" and it might even, if the pseudonym were forgotten, lead to misconception, *e.g.*—

> "It tells another tale, with sounds less deep and loud!
> A tale of less affright
> And tempered with delight,
> As EDMUND's self had framed the tender lay," &c.

In short, the banishment of Edmund can only be paralleled in its miraculous effect on the poem with Wordsworth's banishment of "my brother Jim" from "We are Seven."

on Coleridge's natural joyousness, as Coleridge had dwelt upon his. The stanza, "Noisy he was and gamesome as a boy," &c., is borne out by such passages as this from Dorothy Wordsworth:— "Coleridge did not keep to the high road, but leapt over a gate and bounded down the pathless field." And then as to the portrait, "A noticeable man with large grey eyes," &c. It is not quite inconceivable that Wordsworth should have spoken of himself as "noticeable"; but the "large grey eye," "pale face," and "low-hung" lip are certainly Coleridge. The lines about the "withered flower" and the "sinful creature" seem to mean only that Wordsworth would sometimes go for very long walks, and come back exhausted.

4th.—These morning frosts are a little disconcerting, but, the weather being dry, no harm has yet been done to the fruit-trees. Dined at ——'s. I sat by a lady who talked not amiss about Spinoza, but by some mischance always called him "Spinola." I suppose one day's acquaintance with one book about him had left him still something of a stranger. I know no reason why ladies should not try to be philosophers, but I suspect that in most cases they find "cheerfulness is always breaking in." After all, it need only be for one season.[1] But for my own part, as I cannot go from house to house and pick up the phrases, but must dig in

[1] "Nec cultura placet longior annuâ."—Hor.

my mind for thoughts and recollections, I prefer to discuss my philosophy in the smoking- rather than the dining-room. Nature abhors a divided concoction. And so when my fair partner, after despatching Spinola with her *entrée*, turned on me with a "Tell me now, do you honestly think Green has added anything to Marsilio Ficino?" I replied, "Well, not more than Gray has added to Guido Cavalcanti, or Black to Jacopo Sannazzaro." How odd it is people will be pretentious! Perhaps it is as well, for, if all had the courage of their ignorance, the world would be a much duller place. The heavy plunger is a joy for ever; but ladies should be more cautious. There is a story I once heard in Oxford, that hot-bed of apocrypha, about a literary gentleman from town who was introduced to Professor ———, and fell on his neck with "I have *so* longed to know you ever since I read your *charming* edition of Heraclitus." Unfortunately, when Heraclitus was named, his father did not know he would have to run in double harness with Democritus; and the weeping philosopher himself did not anticipate so "charming" an Isis as the Oxford Professor to collect his scattered fragments, or he would have endeavoured to make them charming too. As it is, they consist of dark sayings which, when emendation has done its utmost, are conjectured to mean things like "Dry light is the best."

13th.—A fall of snow at breakfast; along the downs it lies an inch thick. This is cheerful for the farmers. The cause of my sudden retreat from my wife and daughter at the sea has worked itself off, and the bachelor feeling of emancipation which succeeded has gone too, and I must confess to feeling lonely. The true bachelor's solace is champagne. "When a button comes off," said my friend, "I open a bottle of champagne and fasten it on with the wire, which is both needle and thread in one." But my doctor will not let me drink champagne; so the buttons of my bachelordom cannot be so conveniently attached.

They say the Duchesse d'Alençon would not escape from the terrible fire at the Paris Charity Bazaar, on the ground that it was her duty and privilege to go last. Why is it always of French women, not of French men, that one hears these stories of high-bred heroism? ―― told me the other day of an ancestress of his, at a French convent school, who was saved from the guillotine during the Terror by her French companions insisting, though with most courteous apologies, upon preceding her to execution, so as to give her a chance of an expected reprieve, which at last came.

16th.—The Jowett biography, which I finished to-day, seems a capital piece of work, especially the second volume. It keeps the best side of its hero prominent, without obscuring the fact that there were other sides. Perhaps most readers will rise from its perusal with the conviction that Jowett was at once more kind, more pious, and more heterodox than they had imagined ; a man to love and revere and burn. Most great heretics have been persons of singular piety and charm. Jowett was not definite enough in his positions to have disciples ; or if he may be allowed one, still *he* has no disciple. But he cannot be acquitted of an influence upon his young men like that for which the wise Athenians got rid of Socrates. Whether Jowett believed any religious truth that was not held by Plato seems doubtful. When he was Vice-Chancellor he walked home one Sunday with the University preacher (who told me the story) and gave him many reasons against the doctrine of immortality, which the preacher had, in his poor Christian way, been urging in the pulpit. After luncheon the preacher started for his train to town, but, his conscience pricking him that he had been silent under Jowett's attack, he returned in haste to the Master's lodgings and delivered his soul : " Master, I ought to have said that I did not agree with the views you expressed this morning." To which the Master chirruped : " I know ; good-bye ; you'll lose your train." It is curious to observe that the *Quarterly*, once so savage and tartarly, vies in eulogy with the

Edinburgh, and spends its strength in hammering out thin Mr. Abbott's comparison between Jowett and Johnson. Jowett, who knew his Shakespeare, would have paralleled it in its *Quarterly* form with the comparison between Macedon and Monmouth; "for there is figures in all things." One point of comparison has escaped this reviewer. Boswell remarked of a casual visitor that he "thought him but a weak man." JOHNSON: "Why, yes, sir. Here is a man who has passed through life without experience; yet I would rather have him with me than a more sensible man who will not talk readily. This man is always willing to say what he has to say." "Yet," continues Boswell, "Dr. Johnson had himself by no means that willingness which he praised so much, and I think so justly; for who has not felt the painful effect of the dreary void, when there is a total silence in a company, for any length of time? Johnson once observed to me, 'Tom Tyers described me best. "Sir (said he), you are like a ghost; you never speak till you are spoken to."'[1] Johnson, however, was not shy, like Jowett, who attached an exaggerated importance to being able "to speak across a dinner-table" from the effort it cost himself. His other "moral malady," at which also he is always tilting, was sensitiveness; but, like most shy and sensitive people, he had very little realisation of these

[1] iii. 307, Hill's edition.

qualities in other people. Is it the publication of Jowett's sermons that has filled all the pulpits with attacks on "sensitiveness"? Wherever I go I hear nothing else: it seems the new sin. Jowett's biographers are generous of his letters, and more are to follow. This is right, for he was a writer far more than a talker—unlike Johnson again—and put his best things into his books and letters. Hence there are not many good things to be gleaned from his table-talk here recorded; the best is that the inscription over the gate of Hell may be "Ici on parle français." Moreover, he had more care for exact truth than to allow himself to slog like Magee. A criticism of his prose style would be interesting. Mr. Abbott well remarks that he excels in the phrase rather than in the paragraph. I should like to see a dissertation on his use of rhetorical figures—especially *meiosis* and *bathos*. To the first I should refer the charge often alleged against him of taking low views of things in his sermons; it was a trick to catch the undergraduate ear, and it succeeded. As an example of the second, I remember a sentence from a letter of congratulation: "Marriage not only doubles the joys of life, it quadruples them." Nobody but Jowett would have dared to write that. He was fond of taking well-known sentences and giving them a twist or an inversion. An authentic example does not at the moment occur to me; but I may illustrate by a parody. "It is often said, The child is father of the man; shall we not rather say, The man is father of the child?" His lectures were sure to contain good things. He delighted in the exact epithet. I recall a course of lectures on "Subjects connected with Thucydides" (which discussed incidentally the Homeric theory, the relations of the Synoptic Gospels, Herodotus, &c.), in one of which he gave each nation of antiquity an appropriate epithet, but had nothing ready (or so he feigned) for the Egyptians, and looked for several minutes out of the window. Then he gently smacked his lips once or twice, and continued: "That *ambiguous* people living on the shores of their ancient river." I can't say this taught us much political history, but it gave me a lifelong respect for style. Once, being by chance in Oxford when he was giving what proved to be his last lectures as Greek professor, I heard him turn his own reputation to good use. The matter of the lecture, if true, was not new, and the Greek dons who were there for politeness' sake had begun to whisper to each other. Jowett heard this, and laid a trap for them, which he baited with an expected epigram. "And now we come to Aristarchus, whom perhaps we may call ... (dead silence) ... the *great* Aristarchus." (Peals of laughter, in which Jowett joined as heartily as any one.)

The volumes contain several portraits. The Watts picture, stiff as a poker, with a head like an acidulated drop, and a most uncharacteristic sneer on its thin lips, is properly ignored. Lady Abercromby's portrait is not unlike him in the face, but the face does not fit the head. I do not remember Jowett in quite such cherubic youth as the Richmond drawing exhibits, but that probably does not much exaggerate his charm. For a true picture of him in later life we must go to the despised art of photography. The Cameron photograph printed in Vol. II. is excellent; it is not only a good likeness, but it gives the ideal man, "divinely through all hindrance." This cannot be said of Mr. Onslow Ford's cenotaph exhibited in the Academy. Jowett assisted at the opening of Mr. Ford's Shelley Memorial at University College—as he puts it himself, "I was one Sir Topas in this interlude;" and we may continue the quotation, "Thus the whirligig of time brings in his revenges;" now he is more personally interested in the question of Pythagoras's opinion concerning wild-fowl. For a fearful wild-fowl it is! First of all, why is it so tiny? It looks like a miniature model, but the precious materials prove it to be the thing itself. But why should Jowett be represented the size of a doll? Is it some conspiracy of the Pusey House? And what does the emblem mean on the sarcophagus? What is the significance of a winged cockle-shell? Is it an artistic rendering of High-cockalorum? It is no excuse that the artist has bagged it from the Carlo Marsuppini monument at Santa Croce in Florence, for symbolism was not the strong point of the fifteenth-century artists. I wonder what Jowett would have said? Perhaps only, being a kind man, that it was more appropriate to Shelley than to himself, and had better be sent across to University College with his compliments.

20*th*.—London has had not a few poets; and even politicians occasionally fall under the spell, and "in metaphor their feelings seek relief." Yesterday it was Lord Salisbury. "One of our most extraordinary delusions [as young men] was the imagination that the dominant opinion of London in all its parts was much more Radical than Conservative. It was the sort of delusion that a man might feel when looking upon a dry plain, and imagining that it is a waterless country, till he has pierced the surface, and finds that refreshing and abundant streams gush forth." To-day Sir William also is among the prophets, and takes up the burden of London: "There was a time when the metropolis was a fertile Liberal soil. By the accident of Nature (cheers) it has become covered with thorns and briers; but that is no reason why with intelligence and energy it should not be restored to its pristine fertility." Of all the ornaments of style, as Aristotle long ago pointed out, metaphor is by far the most valuable, being the product of original genius, and so having a creative influence.

21st.—There was some interesting evidence given yesterday before the Select Committee on Money Lending. One question and answer were vastly entertaining:

Chairman: Who is the money-lender?
Witness: Wilberforce.
Chairman: But what is his real name?
Witness: Pocket.

Brutus, it seems, will not start a spirit as soon as Cæsar.

From the advertisement-sheet I cull " Bull-dog for sale; will eat anything; very fond of children."

25th.—The ladies have been badly beaten at Cambridge, the unchivalrous undergraduates have made bonfires in honour of the event, and the question of feminine bachelors may now go to sleep—at least for a decade. The question is one that cannot be argued in the abstract, for abstraction is sure to be made of some very important element in the problem. My sister-in-law looks at the question from a matrimonial point of view. "I am told," she says, "that *some* first-class girls marry, *some* third-class, *no* second-class, and all the failures. You must consider, therefore, whether you wish to attract more frivolous girls to Cambridge, and so increase their chances of marriage by diminishing your son's chances of taking honours." To me it seems sufficient to say that when the Oxford or Cambridge degree comes to mean simply attending lectures and passing examinations, it will be time to put it on a level with that of London, and grant it to women. At present it means having lived in a certain society for a certain length of time, and having learnt certain things, the most important of which are not taught in lecture-rooms.

29th.—The house-martins have at last begun building.

June 1st.—We are now not only in the year, but in the month of Jubilee, and the word is on every one's lips. One squire reports unto another how he is going to celebrate the great event; by a dinner or a tea, by mugs round or medals, by fireworks, or by some new edifice. Though a little hesitating as to our own plans, we can each give a shrewd guess at our neighbours' duty. My own idea (for all whom it may concern) is that private possessors of property once public should take this opportunity of allowing it to revert to the original owners. This was assuredly the way they had of celebrating jubilees "down in Judee." Country gentlemen who have enclosed commons, lords who have impropriated tythe, antiquaries whose private museums are decorated with church fonts or registers or monumental brasses, should at once follow the excellent example of the Archbishop of Canterbury, who has just restored the log of the *Mayflower* to America, and purge themselves of ill-gotten gains. One case of spoliation I have greatly at heart. In Walpole's "Anecdotes of Painting" is figured by way of frontispiece a fine window which was presented to him by the then Earl of Ashburnham for the Gothic chapel at Strawberry, having been begged or bought or purloined from the church of Bexhill, in Sussex.[1] It was bought at the Strawberry sale by a Mr. Whitaker for £30. Where is it now? I love Horace Walpole, and should be glad if at last his ghost might obtain repose by the return of the glass. Happening to speak of the subject in a room where was a bust of this virtuoso, two drops of blood fell from its nostrils on to the pedestal;

---

[1] Horace Walpole writes to George Montagu (November 24, 1760):—"I have found in a MS. that in the church of Beckley, or Becksley, in Sussex, there are portraits on glass in a window of Henry the Third and his Queen. I have looked in the map, and find the first name between Bodiham and Rye, but I am not sure it is the place. [It was not. Bexeley was the old name of what is now Bexhill.] I will be much obliged if you will write directly to your Sir Whistler, and beg him to inform himself very exactly if there is any such thing in such a church near Bodiham. Pray state it minutely; because if there is I will have them drawn for the frontispiece to my work" (iii. 365). At first, then, it clear, Walpole did not contemplate sacrilege. On October 3, 1771, he writes to the Rev. William Cole: "I am building a small chapel in my garden to receive two valuable pieces of antiquity, and which have been presents singularly lucky for me. They are the window from Bexhill with the portraits of Henry III. and his Queen, *procured* for me by Lord Ashburnham; the other is," &c. (v. 346).

which confirms me in my belief that its restoration would be satisfactory to him. The excellent Sussex Antiquarian Society would have no difficulty in ascertaining the whereabouts of the window, and might start a subscription list for its repurchase.

2nd.—One of the most interesting social phenomena to watch is the retreat from a position taken up by some mistake or inadvertence. Ladies are often great adepts in such strategy; the art, I suppose, for ordinary mortals lies in a gradual retirement through a sufficient number of insensible degrees. This afternoon I was privileged to view a superb performance in my own drawing-room. We had a small party, and a writer of some celebrity was expected. At one point I overheard a leader of our local society pour out an effusion of civilities over the excellent and flattered but somewhat surprised doctor's lady of a neighbouring parish, who, from a certain similarity of name, was plainly being mistaken for the lioness. By the simple method of accosting her as I passed, and inquiring somewhat particularly after her husband, I exposed the error, and then retreated to watch the process of "drying up," which was magnificent, but quite indescribable. Men do these things with much less grace. The vicar and I were fellow guests, he being a complete stranger, at a house whose front door opened into an old-fashioned hall, where company was assembled; and when the hostess said to a young and rather well-set-up servant out of livery, "Sidney, will you take Mr. ——'s coat," the vicar understood this as an introduction to Sidney, presumed the son of the house, and wrung his hand with the heartiest *how d'ye do?* but not finding his greeting returned, subsided into a cough. A more awkward *contretemps* of the same sort happened once to myself. I was in ——, and saw my dear friend Mrs. B.'s pony-carriage outside a shop, with a very pretty girl holding the reins, whose face I knew perfectly, though I could not recollect her name. So I made my bow and some comments on the weather and the ponies, and while I stood chatting, out came Mrs. B. and seemed much surprised; and then I remembered the young damsel was her parlour-maid, whom, as I afterwards learned, she was driving in to the dentist. All which misadventures show that we live in a highly artificial society. I will conclude these reminiscences with one of a somewhat different nature. The scene was a drawing-room meeting convened by Mrs. Tom; our local dignitary, who is the modern Avatar of Menenius Agrippa, was bringing a very witty speech to an end with an anecdote which threw the meeting into a paroxysm of laughter, when it flashed across his mind (and his face) that he had been asked to dismiss the assembly with the benediction. Luckily he could on occasion produce a first-rate stammer, and this he at once summoned to his assistance. "I have ... been ... asked ... to conclude ... with the b-b-b-enediction ... which ... I ... will ... now ... endeavour ... to give." The time this sentence was made to occupy in delivery cannot be adequately represented by dots and dashes; it gave us ample leisure to compose our features. We all felt the "endeavour" to be a master-stroke.

3rd.—The rain came in the very nick of time to save the hay; and farmers are jubilant. "If I had had the sun in one hand and a watering-pot in the other," said old —— to me, "I could not have mixed 'em better." What a flight of imagination! The photographer from —— came over to take a picture of some fine old barns that have to be improved away. As there was no train back for several hours, I was compelled to put at his service a good deal of time and tobacco. Amongst other compliments he said, "I wonder, sir, you do not take to amateur photography." I replied modestly that I feared I had no skill that way. "Oh!" said he, "amateur photography is easy enough; it's a very different thing from professional photography. But what I was thinking was you have so much leisure for it." Such is the gratitude of men. They waste our time and then charge us with idleness!

I am glad to see that scholars like the Bishop of

Salisbury and Professor Skeat are protesting against the insipidity of the term "Diamond Jubilee." The right expression is "Great Jubilee."

Strawberries are very good this year. I agree with the Dr. Boteler whom Walton quotes that "doubtless God might have made a better berry, but doubtless He never did." For tarts, however, there is nothing to equal bilberries till damsons are ready.

5th.—A lady writes to me about Beaconsfield's affection for the primrose:—

"I see that doubt is again thrown on the late Lord Beaconsfield's love for primroses. However incongruous such an affection may appear, he certainly felt it. There is an old man in my little country town, a very, very commonplace old labourer, who once, long ago, did rough digging work at Hughenden, and he declares that from the earliest garden primrose to the latest to be found in the woods, Lord Beaconsfield was never to be seen without a primrose in his buttonhole—one blossom and no more—which struck the man who would have preferred a posy."

8th (Whit-Tuesday).—We should have begun cutting the big meadow to-day but for the return of rain. And yet I hardly resent the rain, as it will make the village clean and sweet after yesterday's revel. Our village is unluckily the rendezvous of the district benefit club; I say unluckily, for many of its members give us little pleasure from their company, and less advantage, unless it be on the doubtful principle of the "drunken helot." It is the ancient custom of the society to begin the festival with a church service, which is attended by the neigbouring clergy, with their wives and daughters, to whom a sermon is preached by some distinguished stranger upon the duty of brotherly love. Meanwhile the club-men are refreshing themselves after their dusty walk at the "Blue Boar," and by the time their vicarious devotions are over they are fresh enough for dinner, and when dinner is over lively enough to discuss the club balance-sheet. A Berkshire labourer's speech is a thing worth hearing. The action is that of a reaper. Tropes abound, borrowed for the most part from the meeting-house, and it is difficult to pierce through them to the point at issue. Yesterday a speaker began in biting accents: "I likes church an' chapel"—(long pause and dead silence) —" I say, I likes church an' chapel, 'cos I wants t' go t' 'eaven." (Slight expressions of assent and sympathy, after which the sentiment is repeated; then new ground is broken.) "Passon tells I to love one another; and so I does, 'cos why? I wants t' go t' 'eaven. I likes church an' chapel; an' I goes t' church an' chapel, and I 'ears passon tell I to love one another." But at this point several members, thinking it would be well to have " more matter and less art," interrupted with, "What be maunderin' about, Tom; what do 'ee want? Stop thee gab—'tain't a matin'," and the orator had to blurt out his grievance without more circumstance at all.

9th.—Cook has given warning, and I am not surprised, considering the provocation. She had become engaged to a young fellow in the —— Regiment, while he was on a visit home, but, bitterly disliking the service, had insisted upon devoting twenty guineas of her savings to buy him out. As soon as I heard of the arrangement I told the boy, whom I had known from his cradle, not to be a fool, and as his commanding-officer told him so too, he made up his mind to finish his seven years. But cook is not unnaturally exasperated, and is determined to cast off for ever both her ungrateful swain and her interfering master. I shall regret the cook, but not the interference. It is always worth while to try at making silk purses out of sows' ears; and with the cavalier the attempt has had some success. He has learned old Lovelace's lesson:—

> "I could not love thee, dear, so much,
> Loved I not honour more."

With the lady, of course, the attempt was foredoomed to failure. The occurrence throws a queer light on the love affairs of domestic servants.

10th.—My sister writes inviting us to stay with

her for the Jubilee week. She adds that even if we do not care to see the procession, we shall be glad to have seen it, which seems odd reasoning. However, I am not a superior person like Tom, who has begun to express himself in quite Miltonic fashion about not troubling to cross the road to see

> "The tedious pomp that waits
> On princes, when their rich retinue long
> Of horses led and grooms besmeared with gold
> Dazzles the crowd, and sets them all agape."

For my part I think few sights so splendid as the fluctuating movement of a body of well-drilled troops seen approaching down a gentle slope. Moreover, something must be conceded to loyalty. We reckon ourselves as a rule a very loyal family. My uncle Tom used to think it *lèse-majesté* to stick a "queen's head" upon a letter the wrong side up. But he was a sailor, and had romantic notions about many things; even considering it unchivalrous to profane with his feet the slippers fair hands had worked for him. I will write to Caroline accepting her invitation, and suggesting that the seats she secures shall not be on a stand in the eye of Phœbus, or at the back of a room with a view like that of the lady of Shalott, who

> "Through the mirror blue
> Saw knights come riding two and two."

A procession to be enjoyed must be seen in great reaches, if possible round a curve, and from not too great a height. We must be home again for the village celebration on the 24th.

12th.—I see in a catalogue this morning Lord Byron's copy of Horace advertised as "his lordship's favourite poet." The reference must be to the famous verse in "Childe Harold":—

"Then farewell, Horace, whom I hated so."

I have long dreamed of a collection of such "favourites" among contemporary poets, to include Byron's copies of Wordsworth's "Excursion" and Southey's "Vision of Judgment," Wordsworth's copy of "Peter Bell the Third," Coleridge's copy of the "Lay of the Last Minstrel" (with marginalia), and so on, down to our own day, and the Laureate's copy of "Pacchiarotto." My catalogue contains also a Bodoni folio Horace. Did any one ever read Horace in folio? The right Horace for reading is the Baskerville 12mo, a beautiful book. It was a true instinct that led Baskerville to publish his Bible in royal folio, his Virgil in 4to, and his Horace in 12mo. Later, he printed Horace in 4to, and proceeded with a series of the other Latin poets—the world of collectors loving sets— but his first instinct was the right one.

19th.—There has been a great discussion in the village as to whether "God save the Queen" shall be sung to-morrow in church; and if so whether it should be sung in its entirety, or in a selection, or in a revised version. We managed to convince the vicar that the revised versions were all intolerable, and as he objected on principle to confounding anybody's politics, it was an easy compromise to agree to sing the first and last stanzas. In time of peace the second may lie on the shelf; but if we have to go to war again, it will be through other people's politics, which will be all the better for a little confounding. I never thought so well of Henry Carey's verses as to-day when we compared them with their would-be substitutes. As we are to have a good deal of "Rule, Britannia," next week, I have asked the schoolmaster to see that the children sing the words correctly:

"Rule, Britannia—Britannia, *rule* the waves,"

not *rules* as one so often hears it.

22nd.—I need not labour a description of to-day's show. It will be enough to put away a copy of to-morrow's newspaper. It was interesting to observe the coolness of Lord Wolseley's reception as he passed along—

> "Without more train
> Accompanied than with his own complete
> Perfections"

—compared with the surprised shouts given when Lord Roberts appeared at the head of the colonial troops, for his name was not in the programme. But what can the crowd know of the merits of either commander? The spectators were as interesting, though not so picturesque, as the pageant. It was just such a crowd, though on a larger scale, as Shakespeare saw watching the progresses of Elizabeth, and described in "Coriolanus":

> All tongues speak of her, and the bleared sights
> Are spectacled to see her: your prattling nurse
> Into a rapture lets her baby cry
> While she chats her: the kitchen malkin pins
> Her richest lockram 'bout her reechy neck,
> Clambering the walls to eye her: stalls, bulks, windows,
> Are smothered up, leads fill'd, and ridges horsed
> With variable complexions, all agreeing
> In earnestness to see her: seld-shown flamens
> Do press among the popular throngs, and puff
> To win a vulgar station: our veil'd dames
> Commit the war of white and damask in
> Their nicely-gawded cheeks to the wanton spoil
> Of Phœbus' burning kisses."

The flamens were very conspicuous to-day, too; many of them had left home so early that they had to offer their morning incense as they stood in the press. Shakespeare's description makes no mention of the police who are so essential a part of our modern triumphs. They kept the crowd to-day in good humour as cleverly as if they had been supplied from Drury Lane. One interlude made us merry for a good half-hour. Two long-legged youngsters had climbed a lamp-post and were sitting "horsed" on the projecting bars. First one policeman, and then another, and then two together, tried to swarm up and pull the culprits down. Then we were regaled with "the lost child," "the dog on the course," "the imaginary pickpocket," and "the temptation of St. Robert" (with a pocket pistol) and all the good old pieces, which were received, as the phrase goes, "in the spirit in which they were offered." The sun most considerately kept out of the way till eleven o'clock, but the next three hours made it hard work for the troops lining the route, and not least for the officers in their dress uniforms. Henry Erskine used to say: "At the last day, when the secrets of all hearts shall be disclosed, it will be known why people wear tight boots." Some people have complained that the procession was not expressive of our great commercial enterprises. But why should it have been? It was a royal progress with an escort, not a Lord Mayor's Show. As long as we retain a monarchy, we must allow the monarch to be something more than our picturesque representative. But the fashionable Radical doctrine seems to be that the Royal family are merely puppets for the amusement of Hob and Dick, who may pull the strings at their pleasure. The *Daily Chronicle*, yesterday, was indignant with the Prince of Wales for staying in St. Paul's on Sunday till the service was over, whereas its reporter was anxious to get away after the sermon. "Some misunderstanding must have arisen as to the time of their Royal Highnesses' departure from the Cathedral. *Nobody could have expected them* to stay for the Holy Communion which *somewhat unnecessarily followed* the Thanksgiving Service. . . . The service was not over till a quarter-past one, and *the royal party might well have been out of the cathedral an hour sooner."* What delicious impertinence!

23rd.—To-day we were taken to the Victorian Era Exhibition in order that we might gauge the immense improvements that had characterised the reign. In many cases, however, models had been erected of things as they used to be, and this spoiled the pleasant dream; for they looked so much finer in every way than what had taken their place. "The spinsters and the knitters in the sun" were specially charming, and I lingered for quite a long time in their neighbourhood, hoping to hear them sing "Come away, death;" but I was not fortunate. In the tea-room, whose walls were completely covered with advertisements, I overheard a girl remark to her companion, "Why, you could think you were in a picture-gallery, if you shut your eyes." At night we chartered an omnibus to view the illuminations. I sat by the driver, who good-naturedly pointed out the objects of interest. His talk was very vivacious, and he made use of many remarkable expressions; but I could not well jot them down at the time, and I have forgotten most of them since. Of some rather brilliant transparencies in the West End, which I praised, he said, "Oh, they're only *paraphernalia;* wait till we get to the City." And certainly the City was very splendid. The marble above St. Paul's dome looked richer than I have ever seen it, with the search-light upon it. My driver was frequently indignant at the inefficient driving of vehicles that got in his way, and though he plainly was holding himself in, he could not restrain an occasional "Other hand, matey," or "Now then, gardener." He said the average of driving was much lower since the cab strike.

24*th*— "Sir Walter Vivian all a summer's day," &c.

The village is very gay with flags; it would be still gayer if last night's rain had not made some of them "run." This jest in many forms, with or without reference to "fast" colours, or to the flags that run having been "made in Germany," has served the village wits the whole day. The Caterpillars have done their best to festoon all the oaks; the "Blue Boar" has got a new coat of paint; the roadsides have been cleared of grass; a triumphal arch has been erected in front of the park gate; and we are all feeling very loyal and happy—except such of us as have still to get rid of our after-dinner speeches. A thunderstorm has threatened for several hours, and it seems doubtful if we shall be able to let off the fireworks.

P

11 P.M.—The storm has passed down the valley without interfering with us. The fireworks were superb, especially the rockets. With what alacrity they rise, and with what dignity they fall!

26th.—I saw to-day, at our small garden-party, a sight too rarely seen—a girl walking quite beautifully. Her motion was the perfection of natural movement, and breathed for me a new meaning into the old classical poetry that speaks of goddesses being recognisable by their walk—*vera incessu patuit dea.* English girls do not as a rule walk finely, and so English poetry takes no heed of walking except when it copies the antique as Shakespeare does in the "Tempest" Masque: "Great Juno comes, I know her by her gait," and Milton, speaking of Eve—

> " Soft she withdrew, and like a wood-nymph light,
> Oread, or Dryad, or of Delia's train,
> Betook her to the groves; but Delia's self
> In gait surpass'd and goddess-like deport."

It is a pure pleasure to have one's eyes opened to a new grace, but then its withdrawal is a pure pain, and Miss A.'s departure filled me with regret.

July 3rd.—I am spending a few days in Surrey, at my old friend K.'s, for bicycling. The roads are far better than ours in Berkshire, and the scenery is more diversified. I have visited Norbury, and Juniper Hill, and Chesington, and the other spots made interesting by Fanny Burney. At Leatherhead I looked in vain for the old glass which an old vicar, the celebrated antiquary, Dallaway, had brought from France. It must have been removed lately, as Murray still speaks of it. I am a friend to the clergy on their sacerdotal side, but I think them as a rule but careless custodians of Church property. To give a curious instance. I wished some years ago to verify the date of a marriage, and called upon the rector of the church where the marriage had taken place. He assured me that the register I wanted was lost, but I might see the others. It was cold comfort; but my good genius led me to assent, and I was taken to the vestry, the chest was unlocked, and the books exhibited. "Is there nothing else in the box?" I asked. "No," said the rector, somewhat nettled; "I have been here forty years, and I should know what registers there are." "Of course," said I, "but one side of the chest looks a different colour from the other." "Nonsense!" said he. "Well," I said, "you must forgive my presumption, but will you allow me to feel?" And without waiting for leave I felt, and flat against one side of the chest was the missing register.

That is an instance of oversight rather than neglect. But look at our own church! What has it not suffered from fashion and from heedlessness! It was fashion that made my great-grandfather put in the beautiful panelled ceiling, and fashion that made my father pull it down, the vicar acquiescing.

It was fashion that sent our old plate to the melting-pot, and our old font goodness knows whither, perhaps to some pigsty; and then ignorant indifference came in to devour what fashion had spared, blocked up the old rood-loft staircase, pulled up the old tombstones and cut them into lengths for flagging, turned out the old helmets and hatchments, and made itself generally busy with axes and hammers. Of course, occasionally you do get a vicar who is a bit of an antiquary, and takes an interest in his treasures. I knew one once who used to skip up his chancel like a priest of Dagon, for fear of treading on the precious brasses that were inlaid in the floor. This was, perhaps, carrying caution to an extreme.

5th.—There is such a large family of children here that one grows young again oneself. Dorothy came to me this morning, and asked if I knew the words she liked best. They were "lack" and "Mazawattee." She will, I suppose, be the poet of the family. Sybil (a Sybil of the second generation, for Lord B.'s novel appeared so long ago as 1845) is the eldest, and the censor of morals. "I shouldn't call her a *beast*, Rosalind," she was heard say to her sister; "it is a vulgar word; I should call her a *devil*." How well that illustrates the discrepancy of the two ideals, between which even their elders are tossed! You get it again in that story of the Highland and Lowland servants of one of the Hamiltons. Said the latter, " I wuss I had an assurance that Mr. Hamilton was a converted Christian." To which his indignant fellow: "Mr. Hamilton a converted Christian! Mr. Hamilton is a pair-r-fet gentleman!"

7th.—It is worth while at this moment to look at the past history of Phil-Hellenism. Mommsen has an interesting sketch of Greek history under the Empire in his "Roman Provinces," in which he shows how Greece was always the spoilt child of the Powers. For instance, after the battle of Pharsalia, in which the Athenians had taken the side of Pompey, Cæsar contented himself with asking them "how often they would still ruin themselves, and trust to be saved by the renown of their ancestors."[1] Mommsen inclines to the opinion that "the considerate treatment of the Greeks in general, and the special kindness shown by the Government to Hellas proper, did not redound to the true benefit either of the Government or of the country." But Mommsen's a German.

9th.—To-day is the centenary of Burke's death, but I hear of no commemorative speeches. And yet it was only the death of his son that prevented Burke's being Lord Beaconsfield! In that case I

---

[1] *Cf.* also what Plutarch relates of Sulla after the capture of Athens. When he was entreated to stay the slaughter, "after that he had somewhat said in praise of the ancient Athenians, he concluded in the end to give the greater number unto the smaller, and the living to the dead." (North's *Translation*, p. 474.)

should certainly have joined the Primrose League. I do not care much for the "Reflections on the French Revolution," but the "American Speeches" and the "Present Discontents" are full of the first principles of politics. On every page one meets a phrase or a paragraph that applies itself to modern times. How wise he is about the Colonies: "I look upon the imperial rights of Great Britain, and the privileges which the colonists ought to enjoy under these rights, to be just the most reconcilable things in the world. The Parliament of Great Britain sits at the head of her extensive empire in two capacities: one, as the local legislature of this island; the other, and I think her nobler capacity, is what I call her *imperial character*." (Surely Burke must have been Lord Beaconsfield after all!) "My hold of the Colonies is in the close affection which grows from common names, from kindred blood, from similar privileges, and equal protection. These are ties which, though light as air, are as strong as links of iron."

What a pity it was that the element of τὸ περιττόν so often marred his practical effectiveness! The best example I know (though in that case we cannot regret the ineffectiveness) will be found in Miss Burney's diary, where she describes her emotions during the speech against Warren Hastings: "His opening had struck me with the highest admiration of his powers, from the eloquence, the imagination, the fire, the diversity of expression, and the ready flow of language with which he seemed gifted in a most superior manner for any and every purpose to which rhetoric could lead. And when he came to his two narratives, when he related the particulars of those dreadful murders, he interested, he engaged, he at last overpowered me; I felt my cause lost. I could hardly keep on my seat. My eyes dreaded a single glance towards a man so accused as Mr. Hastings; I wanted to sink on the floor, that they might be saved so painful a sight. I had no hope he could clear himself; not another wish in his favour remained. But when from this narration Mr. Burke proceeded to his own comments and declamation—when the charges of rapacity, cruelty, tyranny were general, and made with all the violence of personal detestation, and continued and aggravated without any further fact or illustration, then there appeared more of study than of truth, more of invective than of justice; and, in short, so little of proof to so much of passion, that in a very short time I began to lift up my head, my seat was no longer uneasy, my eyes were indifferent which way they looked or what object caught them, and before I was myself aware of the declension of Mr. Burke's powers over my feelings, I found myself a mere spectator in a public place, and looking all around it with my opera-glass in my hand" (iv. 119).

11*th*.—A slight bicycling accident kept me from church, and I took down the third volume of "Donne's Sermons." I went by preference to the third volume, not because it contains my favourite sermon, for that is the seventy-sixth of vol. i., with its magnificent close, but (let me confess) because my copy is printed on large paper to match the first two volumes, and is, so far as I know, in that state unique. My choice to-day justified itself by coming upon a State Sermon with which one's new-tuned loyalty proved to be in key; a sermon, moreover, containing a panegyric on the Great Queen; a fact sufficiently remarkable considering the sermon was preached at St. Paul's Cross before the Council on the anniversary of James's accession. For James did not love Elizabeth, or love her praises.

"We need not that *Edict* of the Senate of *Rome*, *Ut sub titulo gratiarum agendarum;* That upon pretence of thanking our Princes for that which, we say, they had done, *Boni principes quæ facerent recognoscerent*, good Princes should take knowledge what they were bound to do, though they had not done so yet. We need not this *Circuit*, nor this *disguise;* for Gods hand hath been abundant towards us in raising Ministers of State, so qualified, and so endowed: and such Princes as have fastned their friendships, and conferred their favors, upon such persons. We celebrate, seasonably, opportunely, the thankful acknowledgment of these mercies this day: This day, which God made for us, according to the pattern of his *first days* in the Creation; where *Vesper et mane dies unus*, the evening first and then the morning made up the day; for here the saddest night and the joyfullest morning, that ever the daughters of this Island saw, made up this day. Consider the tears of *Richmond* this night, and the joys of *London* at this place, at this time, in the morning; and we shall find *Prophecy* even in that saying of the *Poet*, *Nocte pluit tota*, showers of rain all night, of weeping for our Soveraign; and we would not be comforted, because she was not: And yet, *redeunt spectacula mane*, the same hearts, the same eyes, the same hands, were all directed upon recognitions, and acclamations of her successor, in the morning: And when every one of you in the City were running up and down like Ants, with their eggs bigger than themselves, every man with his bags to seek where to hide them safely, Almighty God shed down His *Spirit of Unity*, and recollecting, and reposedness, and acquiescence, upon you all. In the death of that Queen, unmatchable, inimitable in her sex; that Queen, worthy, I will not say of *Nestors years*, I will not say of *Methusalems*, but worthy of *Adams* years if Adam had never faln; in her death we were all under one common flood and depth of tears. But the *Spirit of God moved upon the face of that depth:* God took pleasure, and found a savor of rest in our peaceful chearfulness, and in our joyful and confident apprehension of blessed days in His Government, whom he had prepared at first and preserved so often for us.

"As the Rule is true, *Cum de Malo principe posteri tacent, manifestum est vilem facere præsentem,* when men dare not speak of the vices of a Prince that is dead, it is certain that the Prince that is alive proceeds in the same vices; so the inversion of the Rule is true too, *Cum de bono principe loquuntur,* when men may speak freely of the virtues of a dead Prince, it is an evident argument that the present Prince practises the same vertues; for, if he did not, he would not love to hear of them. Of *her*, we may say (that which was well said, and therefore it were pity it should not be once truly said, for so it was not when it was first said to the Emperor *Julian*), *nihil humile aut abjectum cogitavit, quia novit de se semper loquendum;* she knew the world would talk of her after her death, and therefore she did such things all her life were worthy to be talked of" (p. 351).

There have been three deans who stand out from the decanal multitude as ideal occupiers of the metropolitan stall, men at once of broad culture, fine eloquence, and passionate piety—Colet, Donne, and Church. They had much in common, despite the differences proper to their different periods, and one point especially, that though living in the heart of the great city, they pursued the *fallentis semita vitæ*. It was a maxim of Colet, and may well have been the maxim of his like-minded successors, *Si vis divinus esse, late ut Deus.* I was glad to see on my last visit to St. Paul's that Donne's monument, in which he is figured in his shroud, had been restored to the south aisle. (See Walton's Life.)

By the way, I observe an appeal to men of wealth in the newspapers, bidding them come forward with subscriptions to decorate in St. Paul's what still needs decorating. The appeal is feathered with the promise to find room in the scheme of decoration for the donor's coat-of-arms. Certainly heraldic shields are highly decorative, but except on monuments they seem a little out of place in a cathedral. But the custom is, of course, ancient and well established. Savonarola records it in one of his Lenten sermons just four centuries ago. "How is it that if I were to say, Give me ten ducats to one in need, thou wouldst not give them? but if I tell thee, Spend a hundred for a chapel here in St. Mark, wouldst thou do it? Yes! in order to have thy coat-of-arms placed there. Look through all convent buildings, and thou wilt find them full of their founders' armorial bearings. I raise my head to look above a door, thinking to see a crucifix, and behold there is a shield; I raise my head again a little further on, and behold there is another shield. I don a vestment, thinking that a crucifix is painted on it; but arms have been painted even there, the better to be seen by the people."

14*th*.—I dined yesterday with —— to meet a few of his Irish friends. They had all been, as it turned out, at Trinity College together, and there is no such college for *camaraderie*. "I am so glad you think so," one would say, "for your opinion on a point like that is worth having." "I have never forgotten," the other would presently take occasion to remark, "the admirable way you put that objection in *Kottabos*." To the mere outsider, who had been bred but at an English university, the utmost compliment they would allow was, "I see your meaning." We had many anecdotes. One was of Dr. Henry, the eccentric physician and Virgilian commentator, who in his former capacity refused to charge more than a five-shilling fee, and wrote "Strictures on the Autobiography of Dr. Cheyne," the fashionable practitioner of the day; and in the latter wandered over Europe on foot, crossing the Alps seventeen times, in search of illustrative matter for his "Æneidea." On his deathbed, what troubled him was the view he had previously expressed about Dido; with his last gasp he said, "Dido was never married to Sichæus."

Another anecdote with the right Irish flavour

was of a Roman deacon sent to baptize a baby. In the cabin he could find no water, but there was a pot of tea. "Tea," he reasoned, "contains water, the rest is but accident," and proceeded to pour out a cup. But it was strong, even to blackness, so he went in search of water, and having found some watered the tea down to a more reasonable colour, christened the baby with it, and reported the circumstance, as a case of conscience, to his superior. It had not occurred to him, having found the water, to use it by itself. Other stories were donnish. One was of an undergraduate's telegram: "I have missed my train; what shall I do? I will come by the next." Another, of a tutor's letter of condolence sent to a bereaved parent. This was unkindly attributed to Oxford. The tutor wrote: "I am sincerely grieved to hear the sad news of your son's death. But I must inform you he would have had to go down in any case, as he had failed to satisfy the examiners in classical Moderations."

23rd.—Bob is anxious to collect something that no one else collects, and I have suggested "dictionaries." It will last him a year, cost only a trifle, and give him a good deal of amusement into the bargain. Cotgrave will enlarge his vocabulary of slang. I should like to have known Cotgrave; his conversation must have been highly nervous and picturesque. Open the book anywhere. Take, for instance, his explanation of *niais*. "A neastling; hence, a youngling, novice, cunnie, ninnie, fop, noddie, cockney, dotterell, peagoose; a simple, witlesse, and unexperienced gull." What a man to quarrel with! I wonder what Mrs. Cotgrave was like! Under so tame a word as *journée* you find an entry like this: "*Journée des Esperons.* The battell of Spurres, woon in the year 1513 by the English upon the French, possessed with a sudden feare, and preferring one paire of heeles before two paire of hands." That in a French-English dictionary! And history is not the only subject in which he shows himself proficient. This is what he has to say s. v. *Haricot:* "Mutton sod with little turneps, some wine, and tosts of bread crumbled among; 'tis also made otherwise, of small peeces of mutton first a little sodden then fried in seam, with sliced onions, and lastly boiled in beefe broath with Parsley, Isop, and Sage: And in another fashion, of livers boyled in a pipkin with sliced onions and lard, verjuice, red wine, and vinegar, and served up with tosts, small spices, and (sometimes) chopped hearbs." Perhaps the most racy of all are his versions of French proverbs. For *vogue la gallere* he gives: "Let the world wag, slide, goe how it will; let goe, a God's name: not a pin matter whether we sinke or swimme." Occasionally he offers a metrical version.

Then there is Bullokar, who, as befits a Doctor of Physick, devotes himself chiefly to scientific terms, as science was then understood; that is to say, he gives elaborate descriptions of the Phenix and Scolopendra, &c., and of such famous trees as the Sethim, "which never rotteth," from which the Ark was made. Cockeram is even more interesting, for he supplies not only easy words for hard, but hard words for easy; so that a would-be gallant like Sir Andrew Aguecheek could garnish his speech with picked phrases. Thus, for "to vex" is given *perasperate;* for "to spurn" *apolactise;* for to "put off your hat," *vail your bonnet.* Occasionally our gallant might be misled, as when he is told that the fine word for "false witness" is *pseudo-martyr.* Then there are Palsgrave and Minsheu, whose "Guide into Tongues" contains the first known list of subscribers, and a very interesting list it is. And from the Stuarts one can go back to the *Promptorium Parvulorum, Catholicon Anglicum,* &c., or on to Johnson and his successors.

Bob also asks for a motto for his book-plate. I have suggested *Optimi Consiliarii Mortui,* as appropriate to a collector of old books. It might not be amiss for the bulk of new books as well.

30*th.*—We have had Lord Mayors who quoted Latin, and Lord Mayors who talked French; now comes a Lord Mayor who lectures upon English.

You should not say "Where do you come from?" "Where are you going to?" his lordship is reported as urging upon the boys of the City of London School. "Such phrases are a misuse of your magnificent English. Above all, you should never say *It's awfully jolly*. What is awful is not jolly, and that which is jolly is never awful." The *that which* of the last sentence looks like a desperate effort of the Lord Mayor to bring himself up to his own magnificent standard of seventeenth-century idiom. But do people in the City really talk Old English, or is it confined to the Mansion House? There is an alderman approaching the chair for whose prelections on history I wait with an awful joy,[1] if the Lord Mayor will allow the expression. For the alderman's history, like the Lord Mayor's English, is seventeenth century, as the following veracious anecdote will show. He was exhibiting to a gentleman some famous pictures in the Hall of his Company, portraits of George I. and his consort, which had been mysteriously lost, and which he by good luck had found in a *bric-à-brac* shop. "But how," said my friend, "could such treasures—a royal gift—have been taken so slight care of?" "Ah," said the alderman, "I have a theory about that, and I give it you for what it is worth: I think they must have disappeared in the confusion caused by the Great Fire!"

[1] "And snatch a fearful joy."—*Gray.*

August 1st.—To Cambridge through Oxford and Bletchley—a most tedious journey. I travelled third-class, not because there is no fourth, as the wits say, but hoping the unstuffed carriages would be cooler, as they proved. Besides, I enjoy in certain moods, the humours of "the masses"; and to-day I was not disappointed. A woman got in presently with two children, the skin of all three being concealed beneath a mask of dirt. But though filthy, she knew her manners. When one of the children sniffed, she sharply reprimanded her and bade her use her handkerchief; and the dear child produced from her pocket a rag as black as my hat. A party of workmen who entered later extinguished their pipes with complimentary references to this good woman, and laid themselves out to amuse the children; one who had red hair putting it out of window for a danger signal, &c.

6th.—Bal———. We are to spend three weeks here with ———, who still shoots over his ancestral moor instead of selling the privilege to some wealthy Saxon. We travelled by the night train, Tom and Bob and I in a corridor compartment, the ladies in the *wagon-lit*. I fear I was but poor company. I had just been reading " Les Aveugles," for culture comes slowly up this way; and the portentous gloom of that work of imagination " garr'd me grue," as folk say up here. So completely had it hypnotised me that I found it impossible to contribute anything to the conversation but a repetition of the most insignificant of my neighbours' remarks, as though they were full of profound meaning. With growing sleepiness the conversation became still more Maeterlinckian, till it altogether dropped into silence. When we were roused at Carlisle by the official coming to examine tickets, the sight of my neighbours fumbling hopelessly about them, and the strange, impassive face of the collector between the two rows of us so startled my dazed senses, that for a moment I thought with horror that we were all ourselves in the play. We had a ten-mile drive from the railway terminus, and I sat on the box by the coachman, who gave me the names, with more or less scorn, of the owners or occupiers of the *châteaux* we passed.

9th.—Among some tea-party guests to-day we were presented to a lady who credits herself with "second sight." Though Southron-bred, and not prone to this particular superstition, I confess to having felt some uneasiness in her presence, as part of her quality is to see people's faces more or less covered with a grey veil, according as their death is nearer or further off. Sophia kept her own veil resolutely down, and I did not happen to interest her. Tom did, and though he avoided the good lady to the best of his power, and even at last took refuge in the smoking-room, she tracked him thither; and from what I could afterwards glean amongst his frequent exclamations of "Fudge!" the sibyl had given him a date on which he would be in peril of a watery grave. It will be interesting to see if he will give up his cruise to Norway. Another odd power possessed by this lady is that of seeing one's head in an aura of other heads, these being the people who have most influenced one. I was delighted to learn that my own cloud of witnesses was so nebulous as to be indistinguishable. Others may lay this to my bad memory; I prefer to impute it to original genius. Eugenia's most prominent ghostly companion was a young person with what seemed to be a halo. Him she claimed as St. Aldate, the saint for whom she has peculiar devotion. But I tell her St. Aldate has been exploded by the young Oxford historians; and the wraith is probably the new curate at ——— in his soft felt hat. We were greatly pleased at the sibyl's success with Tom. "Only one head," said she, "is very plainly marked; and that is furnished with a stubby chin-beard; and has something odd about the eyes, not a cast, nor a squint. . . ." "It is a glass eye, ma'am," said Tom, "if, as I infer, you are describing my gamekeeper." Surely this is a new thing even in ghosts, the ghost with a glass eye!

In the evening we sat round the fire in the hall

and told ghost stories, beginning with the ghost of the house, of whom I then learned for the first time. It haunts the corridor, which is perhaps considerate; though if I were a ghost I should haunt the dining- or smoking-room, not of course for the creature comforts, but for the society. Scotland has this great advantage over England, that in any company there are sure to be one or two persons who have seen a ghost themselves. One lady had seen several, but the particulars were not especially remarkable, except in the case of one which she saw in a street in Dresden pointing to a scaffolded house, which fell the next day, killing several persons. Another lady was more sensitive with the ear than the eye. She was sleeping in a room at a girls' school opening into a large dormitory; at the door came several raps, and opening it suddenly, she found nothing at the other side. By the post she heard that her aged father had been picked up fainting outside her bedroom door at home, at which he had knocked, forgetting her absence. In another house, the lower part of which had once formed part of a monastery, she was nursing her mother who was ill with heart disease; and hearing suddenly the cellar doors being unbarred, and suspecting burglars, she hurried downstairs with the plate that was brought to her mother's room every night, to bribe the thieves to depart, fearing that the shock of their appearance would kill the old lady. But the doors were all fast.

12th.—A fine day in every sense. But, admiring Goldsmith's art in leaving his famous "Grouse in the gun-room" story to the imagination, I shall follow his example.

15th.—Now that the first fierce zest of slaughter has been satiated, I have begun to explore the beauties of this romantic neighbourhood. The brown-watered river flows through the strath, and there is fascination enough in hanging upon the bridge or walking along the side to watch the water swirling under. We came this morning upon a little dell with a cascade dashing down through it, and on the banks here and there among ferns and thistles a rich poisonous-looking plant, which, not being botanists, we named "Aglavaine." It was a picture out of the "Faëry Queene," and if Una had appeared with her lion we should hardly have been surprised. A little higher, we found ourselves in Beulah, with the Delectable Mountains full in view.

In the afternoon we made an excursion to —— in a waggonette, indulging by the way in a form of reciprocal torture, each side calling the attention of the other to the beauties at its back. At the best of times one resents having the obvious beauties of the landscape pointed out to one; even the transports of the judicious are somewhat boring.

Coleridge tells a story of how at the Falls of Clyde he was unable to find a word to express his feelings. At last a stranger at his side said, "How majestic!" It was the precise term, and Coleridge turned round and was saying, "Thank you, sir; that is the exact word for it," when the stranger added in the same breath, "Yes, how very *pretty!*" One sight much impressed me. As we were nearing a bridge with a single span, arching considerably, a flock of Highland sheep with black twisting horns appeared suddenly crowding the ridge in face of us. It was quite beautiful.

17th.—This duel between the French and Italian princes is a godsend to the newspapers, and, taking tale and moral together, fills many columns. The moral of the matter is really very simple. Selden in the *Table Talk* is reported as having said: "War is lawful, because God is the only Judge betwixt two that are supreme. Now, if a difference happen betwixt two subjects, and it cannot be decided by human testimony, why may they not put it to God to judge between them by the permission of the prince? Nay, why should we not bring it down, for argument's sake, to the swordmen? One gives me the lie; 'tis a great disgrace to take it, *the law has made no provision to give remedy for the injury*, why am I not in this case supreme, and may therefore right myself?" We have only to remember that modern law *has* made provision to remedy such injuries to see that duelling is therefore as indefensible in these days as the old "wager of battle," of which indeed it is a survival.

18th.—A misty morning; what we English in our violent idiom call "raining cats and dogs." The books of the house did not, at the first blush, look alluring. "Saurin's Sermons" (who was Saurin?), "The Scottish Biographical Dictionary," *The Edinburgh Review* from the commencement, Boswell's "Tour in the Hebrides"—I noted that for use if better books failed—and then my eye lighted on "Sir Charles Grandison." It was just the book for the situation. At noon it cleared suddenly, and we ventured out to the Highland sports at ———. Of the party was a French professor, a member of the Franco-Scottish League, who considered it necessary to pay Eugenia compliments, the very elaborateness of which would have rendered them innocuous, even if they had not been addressed to the company at large. He compared the colour of the heather to her hair, at which she did not look enchanted. I fancy the compliment was a classical reminiscence, and I fancy too they were not both looking at the same patch; for the colour varies greatly under so cloudy a sky. The smoke from a cottage chimney which showed blue against the firs gave him a better opportunity. "To think, Mademoiselle Eugénie, that so much beauty—the exquisite blue of that smoke—should depend upon the turbidity of the medium. Is it unnatural that the blue of so beautiful eyes should in their turn mediate a turbidity?" I don't think Eugenia quite understood the theory of turbid media or the point of the application. But the professor proceeded. "It is a grand pity our poets know so little. I am full of ideas, but the expression I can give them does not satisfy. You know our poet Sully Prudhomme. He asks a question which draws tears.

> ' Partout scintillent les couleurs,
> Mais d'où vient cette force en elles?
> Il existe un bleu dont je meurs
> Parce qu'il est dans les prunelles.'

How much more tears should he draw, if like me he knew the answer!" At this point we reached the field. The sports did not differ from those of other places in the Highlands. Our professor grew very eloquent over "tossing the caber." He had no doubt that the sport, like the word, was originally Norman, and had come to Scotland with other essentials of civilisation, such as "napery" and "carafes," in the days when French and Scotch were brothers-in-arms. I confess I have my doubts about this.[1] We Southerners very much resented the intrusion of hornpipes into the dancing com-

---

[1] I quote the description of "Tossing the Caber" from the "Voces Populi" of Mr. Anstey, a gentleman whose pen is as accurate as it is facile. "The caber—a rough fir-trunk twenty-one feet long—is tossed, that is, is lifted by six men, set on end, and placed in the hands of the

petitions. But on reflection I don't see why Highlanders should not be sailors as well as soldiers.

25th.—Our party, leaving the Toms behind, returned by Edinburgh and York. Sophia left the hospitable roof, according to her custom, with a monstrous bunch of heather, a root or two of tropæolum, a basket of ferns, and a recipe for scones, begged from the cook.

On our way to Perth, whom should we meet but our young friend H. and his bride honeymooning. They were occupied, when we took them by storm, in reading Maeterlinck's " Aglavaine and Selysette." I could not help congratulating H. on finding his Aglavaine, without first declining upon any Selysette with a range of lower feelings. I confess I forgot at the moment that he had been engaged before; but as he seemed to have forgotten it too, no harm was done. Sophia, when his present engagement was announced, had been overjoyed, because, as she said, " now neither of them can spoil another pair." I am afraid they both have just a touch of the prig in their constitution. When they had left the train at the little station where they are fleeting the time carelessly, Sophia, always tender-hearted, upbraided me with my unkindness in comparing them to " those horrid

athlete, who after looking at it doubtfully for a time, poises it, raises it a foot or two, and runs several yards with it, after which he jerks it forward by a mighty effort, so as to pitch on the thicker end, and fall over in the direction furthest from him."

creatures." But it was plain they took my speech for a compliment, as I knew they must. And I protested I had said nothing nearly so unkind as a remark that fell from her. I was saying to the bride, "I suppose, when you get home, you will be setting up a *salon?*" And when she blushed and bridled, Sophia put in, "Take my advice, my dear, and set up a *salle à manger.*" Sophia undervalues Maeterlinck's play through a feminine distaste for irony, which does not allow her to recognise that the author of the prigs knows how priggish they are, even better than the reader. When the book came from Mudie's we had quite a warm discussion over it. "Now," Sophia began, "in the first scene of all; look at this description of Aglavaine: 'Her hair is very strange ... you will see ... it seems to take part in every one of her thoughts ... as she is happy or sad, so does her hair smile or weep; and this even at times when she herself scarcely knows whether she should be happy or whether she should be sad.' What twaddle is that!" "My dear," I said, "a most unfortunate place to choose for censure. Living here in the retirement of the country you have never chanced to meet a case of emotional hair, that is all. Now I have. At school there was a boy whose hair used to play all sorts of pranks. We used to make him eat marmalade, which he hated but his hair liked, just to make it sit up.

That is what the poet means here; both were cases of uncertainty between conflicting emotions." "Well, then," said Sophia, "what does this mean? 'So long as we know not what it opens, nothing can be more beautiful than a key.'" "My love," I replied, "it means just what it says. I have always admired your chatelaine, and I have not the most distant idea which key fits the jam cupboard. In fact," I continued, "you must accept an author's remarks in the spirit in which they are offered, and if he likes talking about hair and keys, he is not to be blamed because you think these subjects beneath mention. And as to the play, you, my dear, *must* like Meligraine, and you, Eugenia, cannot help loving Selysette; and, for my part, I can find a sentiment to echo even in that prince of prigs Meleander: 'I wonder what it is that Heaven will exact in return for having allowed two such women to be near me.'" "And I, too," said Sophia, "can find something to echo even from Aglavaine: 'How beautiful of you! you grow more beautiful every day; but do you think it is *right* to be so beautiful?'"

At Perth, Sophia started the idea that the luggage had not arrived, although these eyes had seen it labelled and put into the van. So after debating the question we started in search. Certainly it was not to be seen, and the guards knew nothing of it. At last a porter advised us to look if it had not already been transferred to the train for Edinburgh, where we found it. What guerdon Sophia gave to that porter is between themselves. From having been brought up by her grandmother, who flourished in the time of "vails"—a word which, curiously enough, still survives in Berkshire for any kind of gratuity—Sophia has an idea that every servant who is reasonably civil to her should be lavishly fee'd; and, despite the injunctions of the railway companies, she saps the altruistic instincts of every guard and porter by the most extravagant tips. At Edinburgh we paraded Princes Street and saw the usual sights. By a wise provision the bonnet shops and book shops are arranged so that husbands and wives may stare at what best pleases them without losing each other. In one shop I had the pleasure of hearing a lady with an American accent ask for a portrait of Charles III.; but the bookseller was no Jacobite, and did not know whom she might be meaning. At the corner of a street we came upon a young prophet preaching to about thirty people. He was good-looking and carefully dressed, his camel's hair being shaped into the frock coat of ordinary civilisation. When we came up, he was proving from the Apocalypse that it was foretold the whole Church would lapse into error as a prelude to his re-discovery of the truth. But Sophia does not like standing, and the prophet took so long over the preliminaries that we were forced to pass on without hearing the new revelation.

I cannot leave the train at York without remembering the ancient tale of a sleepy traveller going North, who, knowing his weakness, begged the guard to see that he was put out at this station, willy-nilly; but to his disgust found himself at Edinburgh, and "swore consumedly." "Well, sir," said the guard, "you can swear a bit, but nothing to the gentleman I put out at York." Some publisher might do a good turn to himself and to an impoverished order if he would commission a few clergymen in each county to collect the humorous tales of their district before they lose all their original brightness. Yorkshire is especially rich in such stories, the prevailing quality being dry. The following was given me recently by a Yorkshireman as an example of "red-tape." A man is lying *in extremis,* while his daughter takes from the pot a fine ham. The old man asks for a slice, and is met by the rebuff: "Thee get on with thy deeing; t' ham's for t' funeral."

27th.—Home. We left summer behind and find autumn here; for raspberries, blackberries. Bicycles have once more to take heed to their ways, for the hedges are being clipped, and the stone walls of Scotland had encouraged us to ride carelessly.

30th.—The value of local tradition was well

illustrated this morning by a speech of my neighbour, old John Brown. I was showing a visitor what few traces are left us of antiquity, and especially a field called "England's piece," which I have no doubt, from its neighbourhood to an old camp called —— Castle, was the scene of some battle or skirmish between the English and Danes. Old Brown was leaning over the fence at the time, and I asked him if he had heard about any battle fought there. "It were the battle of Waterloo, sir," said he, "so they say, 'wever; and I thinks they're right, becos ye can see the bullut marks in the fence." Speaking of —— Castle reminds me of another curious piece of antiquarian intelligence. The gentleman whose property it is has built a keeper's lodge there in the castellated style; and once, when putting up for a picnic, I asked the keeper by way of pleasantry whether that were the castle, and was thunderstruck and delighted to hear his answer: "Well, sir, some says it is, some says it ain't: for myself, I rather think it must be, and I'll tell you why: *there's so much more room inside than you'd think from looking at it.*"

31st.—*A propos* of my remarks on the sometimes conflicting ideals of religion and gentlemanliness, a lady sends me an amusing anecdote of a friend who bewailed to her the loss of a somewhat ill-bred but extremely wealthy neighbour, who had been very liberal in his help to her country charities. "Mr. X. is dead," said she; "he was so good and kind and helpful to me in all sorts of ways; he was so vulgar, poor dear fellow, we could not know him in London; but we shall meet in heaven."

September 3rd.—Birds are plentiful, so are hares. There was once a Major Cartwright, a friend of H. C. Robinson's, who used to give his friends an invaluable piece of advice: "Always roast your hare with the skin on." The Doctor told me a tale this morning of a young novice in his profession who was also somewhat of a novice with the gun, and, after he had missed several coveys, the old keeper said to him, "Let me have a shot. I'll *doctor* 'em." This is the best story so far this season.

Eugenia has been bringing a little colour into the drab complexion of our village life by driving her donkeys *tandem*. The result has justified the experiment, for both donkeys go better together than apart. The reason is simple. The leader trots his best because he thinks he is not in the cart, and the wheeler always goes well when there is a horse or another donkey on ahead.

I had an odd dream last night. For some reason I was attending a law lecture, and when I first woke I could remember a good deal of it. All I can now recall is one sentence. "This is known as Statellion's case. He was servant to Robert Burns, and was stabbed by him at a Highland wedding. In this case it was ruled that *esse* in law is to be understood to mean *esse ni fallor*. Thus 'I am stiff' is to be construed, 'If I mistake not, I am stiff.'" Sophia used to keep a book of my bed-talk, but she once showed it me, and I entreated her to destroy it. I may not be a brilliant converser at the best of times, but I am not such a fool as my sub-liminal personality, nor am I such a humbug. For my s. l. p. has, it seems, a way of pulling up and feigning sleep just when its remarks should begin to get interesting. Thus, a few weeks since, according to Sophia, I roused the darkness with the following important observation :—"The exact difference between Whistler's etching and Seymour Haden's is . . ." (snore). On another occasion—this was on a Sunday night—I recited an original hymn, becoming inaudible at the end of the lines, where the rhymes ought to have been. The only scrap Sophia got hold of was—

> "Do thy duty without works ;
> It gives thee grace beyond thy will"—

which is sufficiently mystical, not to say Antinomian.

4*th* (*Saturday*).—I was on my way to the christening of T.'s child at ———. The day was cold, and the rector's wife is a motherly person. As we stood round the font, the rector took up the ewer and poured in the water. It was boiling, and the steam ascended to the roof. As the rector is tall and dignified, the action had a very solemn air, and reminded me of the pictures of patriarchal sacrifice in the old family Bible. There was no cold water to be had, so there was nothing for it but to sit down and wait. I noticed that the village inn is called the "Angel," but exhibits on its signboard an infant Bacchus wreathed with grapes and sitting on a cask. I suppose he has been christened.

A few friends to dinner. Talk fell on Tennyson. Some one mentioned that one of his best poems, the ode "To a Mourner," was very little known, because it had been slipped in amongst the 1842 poems in a late edition. As an artist everybody was disposed to rank him very high. I mentioned that one of the most convincing proofs of his consummate skill was the leaving one line unrhymed in the "Break, break, break," and "Oh that 'twere possible!"—to gain the effect of spontaneity. S. had a fling at "In Memoriam," but I defended it, and especially the metre, which always seems to me excellently chosen. The best proof of that is the fact that Whewell accidentally fell into it in writing a very emphatic sentence:

> "And so no force however great,
>   Can strain a cord, however fine,
>   Into a horizontal line
> That shall be [absolutely] straight.

R

I have seen the passage, and the word is not "absolutely," but I cannot remember what it is. Talking of sonnets, some one praised E. C. Lefroy's as the best written of late years, and I should agree. There is an interesting memoir of him just appeared, with a collected edition of his poems. Old General X. was very anxious to show us how the great Duke of Wellington used to eat figs. But it turned out to be the ordinary way—quadrisection down to the stalk, and then four licks.

7th.—I was amused by receiving through the post a curious request from a blushing bridegroom, whose father is a very old family friend, for advice as to taming a shrew. He had read Shakespeare's play in his secret chamber, but thought the method rather violent, and not easy to put in practice. In reply I have told him that I am happily without experience, but as pure matter of theory I think Shakespeare's principle excellent, though its application in these days would have to be Victorian, and not Tudor. The principle is to have the worse temper of the two, and if an occasion of dispute presents itself, to begin first and finish last. People of original genius would no doubt be able to devise methods of their own proper to the special case. Thus, I have heard of a literary man who let it be understood he was preparing an essay on the Unreasonableness of Women, and whenever his *cara sposa* became shrewish, he would pull out his pocket-book and make notes with an affectation of absorbed interest; which was not without effect—his wife having brains and some humour—upon the volume and brackishness of the stream. But it is, as a rule, your unreasoning and unhumorous woman who makes your shrew, and, notwithstanding the spread of education, few women care to reason, and still fewer have imagination enough to see things from any point of view but their own. And yet men, forgetting this elementary fact of psychology, go on putting things to their wives in a clear and convincing light, which is like pouring oil on a fire. The only safety for those who feel the method of Petruchio beyond them lies in flight to some coward's castle, club, or billiard-room, or library. Sophia, to whom I have communicated these sentiments for criticism, thinks them unworthy of me, and insists that all shrewishness comes either from bad health or confined interests. If a young husband, she says, would choose his house with some reference to his wife's neuralgia as well as his own fishing, and would play chess or piquet, or read Dante with her in the evenings, and not be always praising his sisters, there would be no shrews to be tamed. But Sophia was always an optimist.

The local paper contains once more the advertisement of a secluded residence in a "remote part of the county," that unmistakably means ——. We welcome every change, but every change so far has been for the worse. Within the last ten years the house has been occupied by a fraudulent bankrupt; a major who had a sunstroke in India, and if you crossed him would bite—not his thumb at you, but your thumb at him; a gentleman "with no visible means of subsistence," except a very rough pony that he rode about, and a piece of wood that he carved as he went; a widow with seven virgin orphans, who would talk nothing but peerage; a chicken farmer whose chickens were impounded by the Cruelty to Animals Society; and at present by a person who eloped with his neighbour's wife. Who will succeed? The house is so near that it is next to impossible not to be affected by its occupants. It is that word "secluded" that does all the mischief. I wish Tom would buy the place and let it to a decent tenant.

10th.—A cold in the head has confined me to the house for two days. These days indoors ought to be so profitable, but are so useless. What could one not read if only one's eyes and spirits would permit one to read at all! I have found it impossible to do anything more intellectual than paste book-plates into recent purchases, and sort through letters. The last task is penitential. I have so great a reverence for the written word that I find it hard to destroy any but the most trivial notes. And then the accumulation "cries on havoc." Some day I must sort the old piles, but from such an heroical adventure nature shrinks. "Sometimes the friend is dead, sometimes the friendship." And one must let sleeping friendships lie.

People are disposed to blame the penny post for the decay of letter-writing, but they forget that there was a penny post last century for letters in London, while for others there were franks. So that cheapness has little to do with it. I suspect the fact that letters were known to be preserved had not a little to do with the pains taken about writing them. Other people besides Miss Jenkyns experimented on a slate before seizing the last half-hour before post time to put their mature thoughts on paper. I remember still, though it was a good many years ago, the shock I received from seeing a friend crunch up a letter of mine and throw it into his waste-paper basket. He did it mechanically, and the epistle deserved no better fate. But since that time, though all my letters are too careless, those to him have been mere scribble. Were I ever to write the one sermon which all good laymen yearn to write, it should be on the power of faith, or expectation, to create the qualities, good or bad, with which it credits people. *Possunt quia posse videntur;* but also *non possunt, quia non posse videntur.*

19th.—At the Harvest Festival to-day the Vicar was badly stung by a wasp, attracted to him by the ripe fruits with which the pulpit had been lavishly decorated. It chose his leg for attack. I have not yet received my annual sting, and feel like Damocles whenever I think of it. What happens is this. A wasp comes in at the window, and gets warm and sleepy. When the lamps are lit it wakes up, crawls along the bright edge of a piece of furniture or the under side of a door-handle, and you press it with unsuspecting hand. Or else it crawls up your coat on to your neck; your collar squeezes it, and it "sits down."

20th.—I called at the Vicarage this afternoon to inquire, and found the wasp forgotten in a more serious sting. "One fire drives out one fire." It is an odd thing about the Vicar that his nose swells and reddens when he is angry. He ought to be told this, as the knowledge would make for peace. I found he had been discussing with Tom a proposal to cut down a tree on the glebe, to open a view, as the Vicarage is pretty much shut in; to which Tom would by no means consent, on the ground that the next vicar might prefer not to have a view, and that it was easier to take trees down than put them up again. The Vicar was feeling righteously indignant, and spoke of appealing to the Archdeacon; but I dissuaded him, as the lay and clerical authorities are at present sufficiently embroiled. "Why not," I said, "if you want a view, walk over every morning and enjoy Tom's; or, better still, cut your tree up instead of cutting it down?" On our walk the Vicar described to me Mr. Caine's new story, which he had felt bound to read in the interest of his profession. "He proposes to us," said he, "a homicidal maniac, and worse, for a typical Christian, and shows his intimate knowledge of Church affairs by blundering over so simple a matter as the Marriage Service." He went on to suggest getting some rich member of the House of Laymen to endow a lectureship to literary men and women on the clerical office and character. "Just look," he said, "at the parson of fiction; he is a priest *pour rire*. Whether he is dressed up as a Cowley father, or sits in his rectory garden cracking up his creed 'into nuts and shells mere,' did you ever meet anything like him in real life? Look at Mr. Hope's 'Father Stafford'! Look at the young gentleman in Stevenson, who, though he had been in orders several years, had not yet obtained his first curacy." I thought the idea of the lectureship a good one, especially if an occasional lecture were given to poets and pressmen on clerical vestments and ritual. Poets think a stole a sufficient covering for anybody in all sorts of weather. Milton even sends out Morning in nothing but an amice, which is the priest's neckcloth to keep his macassar from soiling the chasuble; it survives also (if it does survive) in what are called "bands."

> "Thus passed the night so foul, till morning fair
> Came forth with pilgrim steps in amice grey."

The Press is improving, but is still capable of much, as any one may see from the *Times'* account of the recent doings at Ebbsfleet—Roman, I regret to say, but still deserving a skilled reporter.[1]

Later in the day I came across Tom, who was very amusing about the Vicar's view. "He says to live in a ring-fence suffocates him, and he thinks to fell a tree would relieve his oppression. It reminds me of the man at an inn who woke up in the night and thought he couldn't sleep till he had opened the window; but he couldn't find the fastening, so he smashed a pane, and then went to sleep again like a top. In the morning he found he had broken a pane in the bookcase. Besides, I know this mania for views and cutting grows on a man: in ten years there wouldn't be a stick on the glebe." "Speaking of stories," I said, "do you remember the amusing old woman who, when her servants overslept themselves half-an-hour on Monday morning, called upstairs, 'Girls, it is six o'clock; to-morrow's Tuesday, and the next day's Wednes-

---

[1] Lord Beaconsfield in "Endymion" speaks of "an aggregation of lands *baptized* by protocols and *christened* by treaties." I wonder what he took the difference to be.

day; here's half the week gone, and no work done'?"

For my own part I sympathise with both Tom and the Vicar: with Tom because I inherit my father's distaste for the axe, and with the Vicar from an experience of our early married life. When we came to our present home, which was then a farmhouse, there was on the lawn a gigantic horse-chestnut tree. For the first year we let it stand, and pointed out to all our guests what a magnificent creature it was, as we drank our tea beneath its "spreading" branches. And then Sophia said one day: "My dear, this is a very beautiful tree—it always reminds me of Longfellow, and makes me feel poetical; but wouldn't it be well to make a few windows in it to let in a little air? And perhaps it would be nice now and then to see what the sun was doing. I sometimes think it may have something to do with the maids' anæmia." So after a little more talking the colossal vegetable was doomed, and as limb after limb was severed we felt very miserable and wicked. Eugenia, who was just four years old, burst into tears, and said, "I shall sit down on the grass;" —I suppose in self-abasement, but I never quite understood what she meant;—and then suddenly a gust from the north-west came through. It was a sparkling September day, much like this, and to have real wind in our own garden was so intoxicating an experience that we laughed and played idiotic gambols. The tree, in fact, was a fiend; it had for years absorbed all the fresh air like a mammoth sponge, and left the garden stagnant.

21st.—We are having a St. Matthew's summer. To Oxford. We took the new guide-book, and explored some of the colleges we less frequently visit. Coming out of the lovely chapel at Trinity, I glanced at a notice on the door in a familiar hand, when an American remarked, "It is in Latin," as who should say, "You're bit." I thanked him for his information, and then he asked whether, as he supposed this was the chief college in the University, his son might try to enter, and if he failed, whether he might try somewhere else; on which points I satisfied him as well as I could. We peeped into Balliol, but the modern spirit was too much for us. Time being money at this college, the grass-plot in the front quad had been cut up into triangles by gravel paths seeking the shortest distance between every two doors. Wadham gave us a great deal of pleasure, especially the garden front, but the paths would be all the better for a little of the Balliol gravel. The porter at All Souls' was very sympathetic, and after sending us into the chapel, which was open, while he finished his newspaper, took us round, and showed us many things of which guide-books make no mention. For example, in the magnificent Codrington Library he aroused a curious echo by clapping his hands at a particular spot, rapped a marble table till it rang like metal, and pointed out a peculiar expression on the face of the great Blackstone statue, which on the hither side smiled and on the further frowned—true emblem of the law, from the point of view of us litigants. If I were a bachelor, and had the necessary qualifications, and could live in the physical and spiritual atmosphere of Oxford, I should choose to be a Fellow of All Souls', as was an ancestor of mine in Henry VIII.'s time. There nothing can disturb the mind bent on study, and there are no undergraduates to vex the spirit; and if the cook, as may happen in any earthly paradise, is unequal to himself at any meal, why one's

> "Choler would be overblown
> By walking once about the quadrangle,"

as Shakespeare says.

24th.—I have received a letter from a young lady at Wycombe who is kind enough to say she dotes on my Diary, but asks, why don't I write a "day-book" instead, like Bethia H. (name illegible), because then I could bring in the dear old-fashioned names of flowers, and give funny recipes from old cookery-books, and mix some original poetry in with it about morality and hellebore, and so on, in those lovely Herricky verses, don't I know? (I fear I don't). And I am not to forget some astronomy, because they are doing astronomy at school, and the names of the constellations are so delightfully poetical. I fear neither cookery nor morals are much in my way; but I put the matter to Eugenia, and though she disavowed any deep knowledge of botany, she promised to do what she could, and brought me the following verses on a dandelion:—

> "The peeping botanist, with glee,
> Murmured 'perfection,' eyeing me;
> 'Nature,' he said, 'devise ne'er shall
> A finer ligulifloral.'
> The smug physician, for a sum,
> Prescribed me as taraxacum
> When Giles and Norman, seeking cherries,
> Had surfeited of arum-berries.
> Bethia, who in ancient books
> Hunts quaint receipts to tease her cooks,
> While meditating some new ballad,
> Pulled my fresh leaves to make a salad.
> The garden-boy, whose soul is mud,
> Hath dug me up with ruthless spud,
> And on his tumbril borne, I come
> To slow and smoky martyrdom."

I told Eugenia that the verses could not, with the widest construction of the term, be considered "Herricky"; I thought, too, they lacked freedom of movement, and so advised her to try again. Take, I said, something you remember from any conversation we have had about flowers, in the garden or on a walk, and put it into a six-line stanza. This was the result:—

"To Bethia, who had called attention to a remarkably fine Plant of Chicory or Succory.

"'How rarely,' quoth Bethia, 'doth one see
  The chic- or succory with flowers so many!
Too often sprawleth it right lazily
  By the wayside, with too few flowers, if any!
For once the plant hath soared to his ideal.'
Quoth I, 'Some chance hath sent it a full meal.'"

I was uncertain whether my correspondent wished the morality to be mixed with the botany, or kept separate. However, I lent Eugenia the "Œuvres morales de M. le duc de la Rochefoucault," and this is what she brought me:—

"A Question Resolved.

"*What is youth?* you bid me guess.
'Tis a natural drunkenness.
'Tis a fever, slow to cure,
Yet without distemperature.
'Tis the folly of the reason,
'Tis a constitutional treason;
Or, if this Bethia shocks,
'Tis any other paradox."

"Another Question.

'Twixt pride and *amour propre* the difference say?
Pride hates to owe, and *amour propre* to pay."

"To Memory, Mother of the Muses.

"Blest Memory! thy sacred nine
  Could ne'er have babbled half a line
If thou, their mother, from thy lore,
  Had not said much the same before."

Eugenia says she finds the morality easier to do than the botany; but she will try again at the latter if my correspondent will state a little more circumstantially what she wants, or, better still, send a pattern. The astronomy she fears is beyond her; but then, most of the poetical names have already been used up.

October 4th.—The old debate between the advantages of a town and country life could not but incline, one must think, to the latter when the season comes round for planting and replanting. And yet I do not know that those who have handled the question in poem or essay have made anything of this most important factor in it; which helps to persuade one that the whole problem is academic, and that the writers on both sides have composed their eclogues in Fleet Street. The only reference I recollect even in Marvell comes in the couplet—

> "Transplanting flowers from the green hill
> To crown her head and bosom fill"—

which looks as if the word "transplanting" bore no real significance to him. I suppose the old "formal" garden when once made left little scope for improvement. Cowley would have sung these joys in Pindaric strain had he but known them, but he sadly confesses in dedicating his great garden poem to Evelyn, "I stick still in the inn of a hired house and garden, among weeds and rubbish, and without the pleasantest work of human industry, the improvement of something which we call (not very properly, but yet we call) our own." And in the next century Gray takes up the same lament, writing to Norton Nicholls: "And so you have a garden of your own, and you plant and transplant, and are dirty and amused; are not you ashamed of yourself? Why, I have no such thing, you monster; nor ever shall be either dirty or amused as long as I live! My gardens are in the window like those of a lodger up three pair of stairs in Petticoat Lane or Camomile Street, and they go to bed regularly under the same roof that I do: dear, how charming it must be to walk out in one's own garden, and sit on a bench in the open air with a fountain, and a leaden statue, and a rolling stone, and an arbour!" (June 24, 1769).

That is so often what happens: the singers, the Cowleys and Grays, lack experience, and those who have experience cannot sing. This year the rage for improvement has set in with more than common severity, owing to the publication of a very delightful book on gardening, by Mrs. Earle, called "Pot-pourri from a Surrey Garden." I first heard of it one day at breakfast in the following manner. Eugenia began, "Wouldn't it be nice to make a Dutch garden in the middle of our lawn?" I was so much taken aback by this outlandish proposal that I forbore to deprecate the slang use of the word "nice," and could only repeat "a Dutch garden?" "Yes," said Eugenia; "you sink a wall four or five feet all round it, and lay it out with beds and nice tiled walks, and have steps down on each side, and a fountain in the middle and a few statues, and plant tea-roses against the wall——" "Stop," I cried, "for mercy's sake; may I ask if you have made an estimate of the probable cost of this Dutch paradise? *Imprimis*, bricklayer; shall we make the enclosure twenty yards square and six feet high? That will come, with bricks at 30s. a thousand, to about £25, and then time at 6½d. an hour—— But dare I ask, first, whence this Batavian inspiration?" And then I heard of Mrs. Earle, and how she had pronounced against lawns. Nothing more was heard for a week, and I hoped the infection would pass, but it had bitten too deep; and seeing the book lying in every house I visited, and seeing, too, the furrowed brows of most fathers of families, I had serious thoughts of becoming a second Lord George Gordon and starting a "No Pot-pourri riot." Then I, too, had an inspiration. "Why," I said, "copy the Dutch? If the lawn is too large for croquet under new rules, why not make at the end of it a bowling-green, or rather a *boulingrin*, as it used to be called? You will save your bricklayer's bill, as the sides are sloped and turfed; and you will have the satisfaction of doing something a trifle more original than your neighbours. The fountain must wait till water will run uphill; but I know of a noseless stone bust in a curiosity shop that will do for a garden god just as well as for Marcus Aurelius, whose name it now bears." So it was agreed, and I lent Eugenia from the library James's translation of le Blond's book,[1] which is full of the most elaborate plates of formal gardens. I took the opportunity last night, when the ladies had retired, to borrow Mrs. E.'s precious volume, and I have found much in it that seems to me true, much that is arguable, and much that,

---

[1] "The Theory and Practice of Gardening: wherein is fully handled all that relates to fine gardens, commonly called pleasure gardens, consisting of Parterres, Groves, Bowling-Greens, &c.; containing several plans and general dispositions of gardens, new designs of parterres, groves, grass-plots, mazes, banqueting-rooms, galleries, porticos, and summer-houses of arbour-work, terrasses, stairs, fountains, cascades, and other ornaments of use in the decoration and embellishment of Gardens, &c. &c., by Le Sieur Alexander Le Blond. Done from the late edition printed at Paris by John James of Greenwich. 1728." Amongst the advertisements at the end of the book is one worth copying: "England's newest way in all sorts of Cookery, Pastry, and all Pickles that are fit to be used. Adorned with Copper Plates. Setting forth the Manner of placing Dishes upon Tables. And the newest Fashion of Mince Pies. By *Henry Howard*, Free-Cook of *London*, and late Cook to his Grace the Duke of *Ormond*, and since to the Earl of *Salisbury*, and Earl of *Winchilsea*. To which are added the best Receipts for making Cakes, Mackroons, Biskets, Gingerbread, *French*-Bread; as also for preserving, conserving, candying and drying Fruits; Confectioning and making of Creams, Syllabubs, and Marmalades of several Sorts. Likewise Additions of Beautifying Waters and other Curiosities; as also above fifty new Receipts are added. Which renders the whole Work compleat. Price 2*s*. 6*d*."

though true, I hold it not discreet to have thus set down, such as the advice to buy second-hand furniture. Why drive good taste into a mere fashion, and so quadruple the price of pretty things for those who can appreciate them? There was a time when silver of a good pattern could be bought cheap because it was old; now it is dear for the same reason, just because old silver has become fashionable. So with old Sheffield plate. So with old furniture. I deeply offended some young friends the other day by saying of a very beautiful piece of Chippendale in their new-furnished house, "Why, that must have cost ten pounds," when it had cost twenty; so much have prices risen since I furnished. How well I recollect the horror of the new domestics when what little furniture we had arrived after our marriage! The Persian rugs were sent up to the servants' bedrooms; and the housemaid at once gave warning, on the ground, as she told a fellow-servant, that "there was not a stick in the house that wasn't second-hand." I remember also, though it is nothing to the point, my old aunt's paying her first call, and saying to Sophia, "Now, my dear, I am sure there are many things you must want in coming to a new house, so I will give you—a list of reliable charwomen."

I discovered further in Mrs. E.'s book the authority for a dish that has suddenly made its appearance on all tables about here—green tomatoes. Most outdoor tomato plants at this season have many fruits that there is not heat enough to ripen, and, it seems, Mrs. Earle has discovered a way to treat them. Cooked according to her prescription, they taste something like an artichoke. In the receipt for brandy cherries, I should substitute sugar-candy for sugar—a decided improvement. It is very generous of this good lady to give jaded housekeepers the benefit of her experience, instead of amusing herself, like some literary ladies, with rummaging impossible receipts out of ancient tomes. I shall never forget how once, in early days of literary enthusiasm, I had a carp dressed after Walton's recipe for chub. I believe it was relished in the kitchen, where taste is about a couple of centuries behind the dining-room. And that reflection recalls the memory of an amusing anecdote of travel. Some friends while staying at a Swiss hotel were given a pudding with rum sauce. One mouthful was more than enough for them, but the servants ate heartily and were very ill. That is the first act. The second act, which synchronises with the first, is the rage and grief of the male of the party for the disappearance from his chamber of a new and large bottle of bay rum. The solution of the plot is obvious. The bottle found its way mysteriously back again nearly empty.

5*th.*—An autograph list, come by post, advertises

a letter of G. H. Lewes's, written in 1871, proposing to have texts from the works of George Eliot hung up in schoolrooms and railway-stations "in lieu of the often preposterous Bible texts thus hung up and neglected." Oh, those ages of simple faith, the early seventies! The same list, with a fine tolerance, catalogues a sermon by White of Selborne on "Repentance," which is marked as having been preached thirty-one times. There is also what is styled a "telegram sent by Tennyson" to his publisher; but surely this must mean the telegram received by the publisher, which would be in the clerk's autograph. A repulsive item in the catalogue, which at best cannot help being somewhat ghoulish, is a collection of letters by Mr. Ruskin. Surely Mr. Ruskin should not yet be sold as mummy.

6th.—I have been roaming the countryside in search of a suitable house for ———. How few have answered the agents' description! Even when I have been assured that the house had certain conveniences, I have found them lacking. "Has it a south aspect?" I would inquire; and would find that what looked south was the larder! One beautiful old house attracted me greatly, and I wondered it had been so long without a tenant, till on reaching the basement, in the room beneath the dining-room, the venerable housekeeper lifted up a board and said with pride, "And here is the cesspool; it must be hundreds of years old." I was much struck with the excellence of the roads about Culham and Abingdon, an excellence due in the main to the piety of the district in keeping up toll-gates. Our fathers thought it right that those who used the roads should pay for them in some sort of proportion to their use; the modern notion is to let the squires and parsons pay for everything. "Tax, tax tergo meo erit," cries the modern ratepayer; he cannot add "non curo." I have taken what opportunities offered on my journey of seeing any famous houses in the neighbourhood. Shaw House, by Newbury, where King Charles was shot at while making his toilet, has exquisite gables. With Ufton Court I was a little disappointed; the middle part of the house, including the hall with its beautiful ceiling, is occupied by the forester to the estate, and only one of the wings is a dwelling-house; but its present tenant has deserved well of lovers of antiquity by an admirable book upon the house and manor. Its interest for literature is that Pope describes it in his letters, and that it was the home of his Belinda, Arabella Fermor. Bramshill is a beautiful and perfect example of a Jacobean mansion. In the descriptive volume put together by the father of the present owner is a dunning letter from the contractor to the Lord Zouch who built it, which shows that human nature, both in Lords and Commons, keeps to its types. It is written with bated breath and whispering humbleness, not without a shrewd sting in the tail:—

"To the R^t Honble the Lord Zouch Lord Warden
"of the Cinq Ports & one of his Maties Privie
"Councell.

"The humble peticion of Thomas Selby.

"Humblie shewinge to your Lordshipp that your peticioner hath wrought dyv^{res} peeces of work for your Lordshipp & the last peece of worke held your peticioner on worke 16 weekes, during which tyme your Peticioner borded himself. The stuffe belonging to the worke cost 20 markes for which your honor yet oweth your peticioner and for which your peticioner is yet indebted to dyvers men who seek daylie to arrest your said peticioner for the same, soe that for feare he cannot perform any busynes whereby to get his livinge beeing restrayned of libertie to his utter undoinge. The stuffe with your peticioner's labor came to xxij^{li} as by a particular noate on the other side, which your peticioner (for your better satisfaccion) haith sent your Lordshipp, which specifieth all the moneyes that your peticioner haith receaved, the last receapt was ten pounds, six pounds whereof was for dyvers other workes done about the house, as by a bill appeareth, and the four pounds was taken in part of your peticioner's bill of xxij pounds.

"Maie it thirfore please your good Lordshipp in comiserating your poore servaunt for that xviij^{li} that remaynes of your peticioners bill due to your saide peticioner three yeares and half. That it would please your good Lordshipp to give order for your peticioner's satisfaccion, & your peticioner shall be ever bound to pray for your honors prosperous health & happines longe to continew.

"From the Ould Jury in London
"the xxiiij Januarii 1619."

Then follows:

"My Lord . . . I humblie beseech your good Lordshipp not to be offended with mee in taking of this course, for this three years I have weighted with peticions after your Lordshipp for my money, and none of your gentlemen would take my peticion to your Lordshipp nor suffer my admittance unto you & for want of my mony I am utterly undone. Therefore I humblie beseech your honor that I may have my money or that your Lordshipp will send unto my Mr Mr Thomas Capp in the old Jury and let him understand your Lordshipp's pleasure; if your Lordshipp should not paie me my necessitie is such that I must peticion to the Kinge, and send your Lordshipp a Privie Seale; beseeching your Lordshipp to render my needes, and be noe way offended wth me for seekinge of my owne."

11th.—Dinner conversation in October has a way of repeating itself from year to year. There is the discussion as to which birds taste the better, wild or maize-fed; there is the various descant on the lamentation " up goes a guinea and down comes half a crown ;" and there is the speculation whence the local butcher procures his excellent supply of game. To the last discussion those who stand and wait could contribute a few interesting particulars, for every local poacher is thoroughly well known. My man William, for example, tells me he saw a rag and bone man heavily laden with fattish rabbit-skins about 4.30 this morning, as he was meditating at his window, " but it was none of his business." As a rule, the local ne'er-do-wells do no more than act as guides to the gangs that come over from the county town. I was much struck to-day by a sharp contrast between the manners of East and West in regard to hospitality. When my friend —— was in Turkey, he saw a man feeding his turkeys; and while he was so engaged, a flock of wild turkeys came down to feed too. The man drove them into a shed. "What shall you do with them?" asked my friend; "kill them?" "Kill them?" said the man; "they are my guests. In the morning I shall feed them and let them go." To-day a hunted hare took refuge in a cottage here, where it was presently jugged. I am far from blaming the cottager; I wish but to note the contrast. The Western word "guest," philologers tell us, is connected with "hostis."

Cf. Bacon: "The inclination to goodness is imprinted deeply in the nature of man; insomuch that if it issue not towards men it will take unto other living creatures; as it is seen in the Turks, a cruel people, who nevertheless are kind to beasts, and give alms to dogs and birds; insomuch as, Busbechius reporteth, a Christian boy in Constantinople had like to have been stoned for gagging in a waggishness a long-billed fowl."[1] (*Of Goodness and Goodness of Nature.*)

13*th.*—X., an old college friend of mine, came down a fortnight since from Saturday to Monday, and we found him a very pleasant companion. He had a way of conversing easily on most subjects, and (what is even more interesting) of making one converse easily oneself. In the small hours, over a pipe, I found myself telling him many anecdotes of my past life—adventures by sea and land, money losses, bereavements, and what not. But since that day I am nervous of opening a journal. I find my anecdotes in the evening papers, my spiritual experience distilled into sonnets for the *Weekly Observer*, my political reflections clothed in thunder in the *Daily Phonograph*. My friend's friends should be

[1] Mr. Harrison Weir writes to the papers to-day suggesting "in a waggishness" that the cock that crows in the morn should be gagged. Perhaps Mr. Long might be induced to make a muzzle order (16th August 1898).

worth to him not less than five hundred pounds a year; but he must be continually enlarging his circle, to allow for shrinkage.

The newspapers are full of the Church Congress. I once went to a congress before the heyday in the blood was tame and waited upon the judgment, but I have never repeated the experiment, as I wish to think well of the clergy. Is it or is it not an argument against Socialism that people show badly in groups, especially professional groups? "The merriment of parsons" is certainly, as Dr. Johnson found it, "mighty offensive"; but so is a meeting of county gentlemen to protest against sacerdotal tyranny. I suppose, too, between a syndicate of employers and a trades union there is not a pennyweight to choose for the nasty things they will do and say. And we all know "the poor *in a lump* is bad." Hear the modern mystic: "Ils sont là, rassemblés n'importe où; et lorsqu'ils se trouvent réunis, sans qu'on sache pourquoi, il semble que leur premier soin soit de fermer d'abord les grandes portes de la vie. Chacun d'eux cependant, lorsqu'il était seul, a vécu plus d'une fois selon son âme. . . . Quand ils sont ensemble ils aiment à s'enivrer de choses basses. Ils ont je ne sais quelle peur étrange de la beauté; et plus ils sont nombreux, plus ils en ont peur."

My sister has gone to the Women's Conference. I do not know how ladies bear the test of union, though I have heard tales of merciful individuals becoming members of a Sweating Committee. Charlotte tells me the platform is a fine revealer of character. Your merely pretty and attractive person dwindles there into insignificance, while your really great woman doffs her cloak of commonplace and shines in her true brightness.

16th.—More " Pot-pourri." While "doing" my Michaelmas accounts this morning, I found that the butter book (for we use Tom's dairy) was half as much again as last quarter, and the reason given by the responsible Eugenia is that Mrs. Earle protests against economy in butter. On referring to the passage, I find that she suggests instead an economy in meat, and I pointed this out to E.; but the butcher's book shows no proportionate diminution. This has led me to reflect how much more infectious extravagance is than economy. I can recollect some half-dozen pronouncements of various people in favour of expansion in this or that direction, and not one in favour of retrenchment. I suppose we shamefacedly keep our economies to ourselves. An intimate and impecunious friend told me he said to his wife on their wedding-day, "Now, however closely we have to cut things, we will not try to save in the washing-bill." Another friend cautioned me seriously as a young man against reading penny papers instead of the *Times.* A pious old clergyman once said to me, "I have noticed that some people spend much brain power before every journey in making up their minds whether to travel by first or second class. The best rule is always to go first." My aunt warned me, when I began to collect, never to buy cracked china or imperfect books. And it was one of my father's commonplaces that one must drink sound wine and smoke good cigars. Now, I have found all these counsels fruitful in my own experience. On the other hand, one has to invent one's own economies, and I have not got much further than to use a wax taper instead of matches, to buy my coals in the summer and stack them for winter, never to be photographed, and to take in the three-penny edition of Bradshaw instead of the sixpenny.

My father's dictum about sound wine comes the more readily to memory as I was dining last evening with a teetotaler who regards wine as poison, and, I am bound to say, acts up to his theory. He should at least dispense it in medicine glasses. I have no prejudice against teetotalers. We have a very flourishing (so-called) "temperance society" in the village, and the result is seen in the increased comfort of the cottagers. I used sometimes to show my interest in the cause by taking the chair at a meeting now and then, but I have given it up since ladies have begun to appear on platforms; for ladies recognise no rules of the game. In the middle of a passionate address they think it not indecent to appeal to the chairman to set a good example by taking the pledge. At the last meeting I attended, a lady speaker, the wife of a clergyman, told how her husband used always before his evening service to eat an egg beaten up with brandy, which made him bilious; but since he had left off this drunken habit, he had also left off his bilious attacks. This was more than old B. could stand, for he roared out, "'Twere the egg, marm, what made he bilious. You tell your mister to take t' brandy wi'out un." One of the villagers at this meeting made a mysterious speech, in which he gave as his reason for taking the pledge, that there was only in a pint of beer as much goodness as would lie on a shilling. I have one story that I used to keep in lavender for these occasions; I had it of the doctor. When he was walking the hospitals, there was a brewer's drayman who had broken his leg, and in six weeks the bone had not set. So they questioned him about his diet. "Was he accustomed to drink beer?" "Yes, a little." "About how much?" "Oh, not more than three gallons a day." So they allowed him a couple of quarts, and the leg began to mend at once.

22nd.—The new Professor of Geology at Oxford found some kind words to say in his inaugural lecture about Dr. Plot, who wrote the natural histories of Oxfordshire and Staffordshire. The latter is sought by collectors for the beautiful plans of the great houses in the county, but the work itself is far above contempt. It proves the good doctor to have been a curious observer. He has recorded, for example, instances of the now common practice of lip-reading by deaf people:

"But I have more wonderful passages relating to *women* than any of these yet to declare, whereof the first and strangest is of one *Mary Woodward* of *Hardwick* in the parish of *Sandon*, who loosing her hearing at about 6 years of age, by her extraordinary ingenuity and strickt observation of the peoples *lipps* that convers't with her, could perfectly understand what any person said, though they spake so low that the *bystanders* could not hear it: as has been frequently experimented by the right Honorable the Lady *Gerard*, and divers others of her *neighbours* now living, with whom she would go to *Church*, and bring away as much of the sermon as the most attentive *hearer* there; all which she did, not with difficulty but so much ease and satisfaction that if one turned aside and spake, that she could not see his *lipps*, she thought herself much disobliged. Nay so very well skill'd was she in this *Art* (which we may call *Labiomancy*) as 'tis generally beleived (though I could get no personall testimony of it, some persons being dead, and others removed into *Ireland* who sometimes lay with her) that in the night time when in *bed*, if she might lay but her hand on their *lipps* so as to feel the motions of them, she could perfectly understand what her *bedfellows* said, though it were never so dark. For confirmation of the possibility and truth whereof, there are many parallel *Histories* sent us from abroad, of *persons* that have done the same in all particulars . . . ;" and then follows a string of cases from Borellus, Job a Meek'ren, Petrus a Castro, Tulpius, and Casaubon (p. 289).

25*th*.—

> " This day is called the feast of Crispian,
> And Crispin Crispian shall ne'er go by
> From this day to the ending of the world
> But we in it shall be remembered."

I wonder if any one but me keeps the feast of Crispian. Good Navy Leaguers have difficulty enough in getting people to remember Trafalgar. The awkward thing is that you can't have a victory without some one else having a defeat, and too loud a flourish of trumpets might hurt sensitive feelings across the water. Still, it is possible to be too considerate ; our first business lies in educating our own people, and not the least part of education consists in praising famous men and our fathers who begat us. The other side can always persuade themselves that they were betrayed, or that it was their tyrant who was defeated, not themselves. And we shall not grudge them the celebration of their own victories, such as Waterloo. I wonder if Shakespeare kept the feast of Crispian. I can imagine some soldier, a matter-of-fact person like myself, calling at New Place on 25th October, two years after "Henry V." was written, and being greatly shocked to find that Shakespeare did not even know it was Agincourt day. I suppose if persons of genius stimulate the rest of us, we must not be too curious as to their practising what they preach. I remember such a one expatiating to me upon the titles of Scott's novels, and saying of "Peveril of the Peak": "Now I call that a perfect name for a romantic novel; no one could hear it without being bitten with an instant wish to know all about Peveril;" and he rhapsodised for several minutes on all that the name suggested to him—hairbreadth escapes, conspirators in gloomy caverns, &c. &c. "Tell me the story," I said, "for I am ashamed to say I have never read it." "Nor have I," said my friend.

I was dozing to-night in my chair towards eleven o'clock, when the cook rushed in, with hair up-staring and the tongs in her hand, and begged me to go to the back door, which was bewitched. I took up a poker and a candle and went to inspect. It was sufficiently curious. The door was shaking as if it had the palsy, and the yard-dog outside was yelping most uncomfortably. When I drew the bolt the shaking at once stopped, and there was a slight scuffling noise. The candle cleared up the mystery by showing a small heap of *débris* where a rat had been gnawing the sill to make a way into the house. Its body must have pressed against the door as it worked, and so caused the shaking. But to which of us the rat had a message we are yet in ignorance.

27th.—We are all in woe to-day, as the great beech has been felled. For months we had shut our eyes to the ominous cracks and more than ominous rot, but at last it would not do. Its brother was blown down two years ago, and, as the newspapers are now prophesying a gale, it seemed good policy to choose the direction in which the tree should fall. Our neighbours think us a little doting in our fondness, for the beech did not conform to the regular type. As the two trees had stood very close together, each had branches only on one side; and when the first tree was down, the other looked wild and horrid (in the classical sense), like a tree of Salvator Rosa's. But it was beautiful in a way of its own, and had never looked so beautiful as to-day in the sunlight, all on fire with crimson and orange and brown and green; as it fell the leaves shot away from it like flames. Eugenia sketched it in water-colours just before execution, and is going to have a frame made for the portrait from one of the branches—a true relic. The rest will serve, perhaps, no less well to keep it in memory, as it should supply fuel to a pyre for many weeks. By what looks to us at the moment like an odd attempt at compensation, I hear that my kinsman Beaufoy

("foy" is *fagus*) was presented to-day with a son and heir.

The first sod of the new bowling-green [1] was cut this morning with due formality. I have had good luck in my search for ornaments to decorate it. An old house in the neighbourhood has just changed hands; and the new master, being a Nabob lately returned, as the poet says,

"Home from the rule of Oriental races,"

with a taste for fine art not unnaturally Orientalised, has banished from the garden some very beautiful Italian stone urns, carved with subjects in relief, and these I have rescued from an adjoining farm. They are delicately discoloured, which reminds me that yesterday I met the vicar in a coat green with

[1] The French writer, Le Blond, already referred to, who was a pupil of the great gardener, Le Nôtre, is much exercised about this term bowling-green. He says of it in Mr. James's translation, "The invention and original of the word *bowling-green* [boulingrin] comes to us from England. Many authors derive it from the English words; namely, from *bowl*, which signifies a round body, and *green*, which denotes a meadow, or field of grass; probably because of the figure in which it is sunk, which is commonly round, and covered with grass. Others will have it, that the word takes its name from the large green-plots, on which they are wont to play at bowls in England, and for which purpose the English take care to keep their grass very short, and extremely smooth and even. A *boulingrin* in France differs from all this," &c., and he goes on to explain that it is only the sinking that makes it a *boulingrin*, together with the turf that covers it; the fact, of course, being that bowling-greens in England were usually sunk. After this desperate effort in philology it is not surprising to find our author deriving the *ha-ha*, or sunk hedge, from the exclamation of surprise, *ah-ah*, that breaks from the traveller at the vista beyond.

age hurrying along on his bicycle at scorching speed; whereas to-day I met him as neat and spruce as a new pin. He told me he was off to town to lunch with his publisher. "And where," I said, "were you posting to yesterday in such break-neck haste?" "Oh, I had to appear before the Schools' Association to plead for a share in the grant to necessitous schools." Dear vicar! how good-natured of him to dress for the part! I see he too has fallen a victim to the motto mania, and has inscribed over his door, "Ut migraturus habita" —the text which so charmed Mrs. Ewing. I wonder if the Crown or the Bishop will take the hint. I fear neither is a frequent visitor.

28th.—The splendid weather seems at last to be drawing to an end; each day is "miskier" than the last. But the few hours when the mist clears are still glorious. As Henry Vaughan says, " Mists make but triumphs for the day."

November 5th.—The memory of Guy Faux seems likely to outlive that of many saints in the calendar, whether Catholic or Positivist—a consideration which should supply a hint to the conservators of the old religion or the inventors of new ones. Let them celebrate their heroes with a bonfire! Bonfire, say the philologers, is bone-fire. What could be more appropriate to the feasts of martyrs? Such fires, moreover, would be very useful for burning up refuse, which in our villages has a way of festering in heaps and breeding disease. It would seem that such fires were the custom on at least one festival in old England: "In vigilia beati Johannis colligunt pueri in quibusdam regionibus ossa et quædam alia immunda, et insimul cremant" (Brand's "Antiquities," i. 298). The "Guy" in our village varies from year to year. When the Liberal party is in office it is apt to be the Premier, or some other prominent Minister; this year it was a local personage. The pyre burned splendidly, and had the usual maddening effect on the spectators. The bigger boys leaped through the flames like the old Moloch worshippers, and once two of them, jumping from opposite sides, met in the middle and nearly made a bone-fire of it in grim earnest. The younger imps had furnished themselves with besom stumps dipped in tar, which they flourished like male Mænads. Indeed, one could almost have imagined oneself in a college quadrangle at Oxford.

6th.—A magnificent day for colour. Walking eastwards about four o'clock I met a regiment of some thousand lapwings at drill. Their evolutions were very skilful, from line to column, and from column to line. The level rays of the sun, as the birds circled overhead, struck on their cuirasses and made them shine like gold.

When the elements were mixed in me, the ingredients were omitted that go to make a partisan.

I feel my deficiency whenever G. pays me a visit, for his friends are always in the right, his foes always in the wrong, any deed being but a colourless abstraction apart from the doer. Words follow much the same law, especially if they are humorous. We had the vicar and a few of our more literate neighbours to meet him. At dinner I defended some paradox, no matter what, and was rather severely handled; but G. afterwards congratulated me on the admirable manner in which, as host, I left the advantage to my guests. The compliment was quite undeserved, but I liked it all the same.

There seems to be a movement afoot just now for preserving wild creatures of all sorts by making paradises for them, but I hear of no paradise for insects. And yet they too tend to extinction. The ivy round our old houses does, of course, a great deal towards preserving certain species, such as wasps and spiders, but these are still plentiful. The hornet, however, is growing quite scarce in Berkshire. When I was a child they were common enough. I remember my father's old gardener suffering severely from a sting. He brushed a bevy away from a jargonelle pear tree with his hat, but unhappily one stayed inside for purposes of revenge, and as old Northway's head was bald, the creature had a walk over. The hornet also used to figure in a moral poem I was taught when a youngster, as quite the natural playmate of childhood. It ran something like this:

> "O mother, I told him the hornet would sting him,
> Which he in his hand from the garden was bringing."

Perhaps it comes in a poem by the Misses Taylor. I have searched for it in vain in Mr. Lucas's "Book of Verses for Children"; a charming collection, in which I am glad to see a return to the old-fashioned strait-laced children's poems. Parents had grown too shy of Struwelpeter, and the prompt and awful fate of the wicked in the "Cautionary Stories" of Elizabeth Turner, forgetting that children can purge their passions by these, as their elders by "Hamlet" or "Macbeth." Here, for instance, is a couple of stanzas on "Repentance," not in Mr. Lucas, which do more for a baby's morals than calling upon him to hear sermons:

> "'Tis not enough to say
> 'I'm sorry and repent,'
> And then go on from day to day
> Just as you always went.
>
> Repentance is to leave
> The sins you did before,
> And show that you in earnest grieve
> By doing them no more."

How clean and incisive it is—"Just as you always went"!

10th.—I have been giving my household lately an address now and again upon patriotism, taking occasion by any stimulating report from India. This morning I learn that the garden-boy has walked into Reading to enlist. Of course I am willing to spare his services to the country, but I should have preferred his giving me warning in the ordinary way, so that I might look out for a substitute. But that, I know, would have been contrary to local etiquette, which directs that when a boy takes his hand from the plough, he should go off to the depôt without looking back. No doubt, if young men spoke of their intention beforehand, fathers and mothers would in most cases exert pressure to keep them at home. This secret enlisting presents a curious parallel to the usual mode of joining the Church of Rome—a resemblance of which I can imagine the late Cardinal Newman making very effective use.

I have been reading lately the poems of that forgotten worthy and patriot, Edmund Waller, whose name is known to young ladies as the author of "Go, lovely rose." His patriotism was of that finer sort which is above party. He was the cousin of Hampden and related to Cromwell, and was employed by Parliament to negotiate with Charles; the negotiation became known as "Waller's plot to seize London for the King," for which adventure he was fined £10,000 and banished. His panegyric on Cromwell is a fine piece of writing, finer than his welcome to Charles II., as that monarch did not fail to point out to him. He comes to mind now as the writer of some spirited verses to the King on the English Navy:

> "We are most happy who can fear no force
> But wingèd troops or Pegasean horse.
> 'Tis not so hard for greedy foes to spoil
> Another nation as to touch our soil.
> Should Nature's self invade the world again
> And o'er the centre spread the liquid main,
> Thy power were safe, and her destructive hand
> Would but enlarge the bounds of thy command ;
> Thy dreadful fleet would style thee lord of all
> And ride in triumph o'er the drownèd ball."

Dr. Johnson called these lines "so noble, that it were almost criminal to remark the mistake of 'centre' for 'surface,' or to say that the empire of the sea would be worth little if it were not that the waters terminate in land." By "centre" Waller means the earth as centre of the universe.

I came on a curious passage in a letter of Mrs. Waller's to her banished son about the marriage of his daughter. She wishes to know what dowry he is prepared to give. "I am not in hast to mary hir, she is yong enough to stay, but the danger is if she should catch the small poxe or hir beauty should change, it would be a great lose to hir." Everybody is familiar with the frequent references to smallpox in the letters and memoirs of the seventeenth century. Pepys is full of it ; but I have never met a passage that brings so keenly home to one the nearness of the risk.[1]

11*th*.—I went up to town to see my tailor, and called in at my hatter's to have a mourning band removed. The shopman remonstrated: "Hatbands are fashionable just now, sir." "Oh," I said, "you refer to Court mourning." "Oh dear no, sir; hatbands have been fashionable all this season." So it seems young gentlemen still, as in Shakespeare's time, can be sad as night only for wantonness!

My sister Charlotte was in distress at having to change her butler, and she fancied the new man had already begun to take liberties. "So," said she, "I gave him a lesson last night. He did not offer me cheese at dinner; so I said, 'John, where is the cheese?' 'I thought you did not take cheese, ma'am.' 'Bring it.' And when he brought it, I said, 'No, thank you.' I don't think he will forget." Charlotte told me she was glad to observe that more attention was being paid to heraldry. "I hate to see widows prancing about with their husbands' crests on their harness."

I searched for a wedding present for K. I saw a lovely Sheffield-plated urn, which I would have

---

[1] Would it not be possible for an Anti-anti-Vaccination Society to issue a small pamphlet containing select passages from our older literature about small-pox as it used to be? Copies might be sent to all magistrates for free presentation to the conscientious, who come before them to swear under the new Act (21st August 1898).

bought if I were not certain she would confuse it with electro-plate. If I were only a little older I could be eccentric, like the lady who, according to the papers, gave a brooch with "Granny" in diamonds. There would be some fun in that; the expectant grandchild would be in such a delicious quandary. *Odi et amo.* My own dear grandmother was almost *too* eccentric at the time of our marriage; she had promised us our house linen, and talked so much about it beforehand that she came to think she had given it, and would not be undeceived.

12th.—I walked with the vicar, who told me some anecdotes of an ordination examination. The best was this: The question was, "State what you know of Christianity in Britain before Augustine?" and the answer, "Before the coming of Julius Cæsar, B.C. 55, there was practically no Christianity in Britain." The "practically" is good. On our walk we met the stationmaster of a neighbouring village, who gave me a military salute with his right hand and raised his left three inches to the vicar. "Why does he treat you to such maimed rites?" I asked. "It puzzles me," said the vicar, "as it is neither Saturday nor Monday. On these days he is full of the sermon he has delivered or is to deliver at Bethel, and smiles on me as a fellow-augur. But on other days he gives me his full courtesy as one of his masters, the general public."

At the station we heard that the good man had resigned his position on the railway to devote himself to the cure of souls.

We talked of the "Golden Treasury." I thought Mr. Palgrave's "Lectures on Landscape in Poetry" a much better book; but it did not hit an especially happy moment, like the "Golden Treasury," and would never be popular, as the public does not care for criticism. The changes in the various editions of the "Treasury" are an interesting study. It was originally issued in 1861. Sidney was not recognised until 1883, nor was Cowper's "Castaway," his finest poem. In 1891 appeared for the first time Coleridge's "Kubla Khan," Vaughan's "They are all gone into the world of light," Marvell's "Picture of little T. C.," and "Nymph and Fawn," and ten poems of Campion, besides Habington, Lord Essex, Greene, Lord Rochester, Norris of Bemerton, and Lyte, all hitherto unrepresented, and all unnecessary. The defect of the book as a selection is that beginning with an aversion to anything eccentric, which justifiably excluded Donne, it lapsed too often into a tolerance of the commonplace. There is an extravagant over-proportion of matter from Wordsworth (who has forty-three poems), Campbell, Scott, Moore, and the minor Scotch poets. To point the moral more clearly, additions to the long tale of Wordsworth were made room for by excisions from

Shelley. "A Widow Bird" and "Life of Life" disappeared in 1891. The representation of several poets—notably Blake, Keats, Campion, Carew—is really misrepresentation. But when all deductions are made, the book must be reckoned to have thoroughly deserved its success.

15th.—Curiosity is a well-marked trait in most of the higher mammals. The new trees I have planted this season, some red oaks and a maple (Schwedleri), have been objects of careful investigation to the cows and horses, and our new bowling-green is exciting just as much interest among our own species. Some of the neighbours make a circuit, as they can, to the front door, by way of the garden, in order to inspect it; some indeed, having inspected, forget to proceed to the front door. In the village it is spoken of as ———'s new pond. I have a tenderness for curiosity, holding with Coleridge that it is at the root of all philosophy and all science. I remark, however, that the persons most curious about my affairs are the most reticent about their own. I suppose this is only a particular example of the general law that a habit of spending rarely coexists with a habit of getting.

Three weeks of fine weather have finished the excavation; the turf has been rolled down the sides, and we are now waiting for the brick paths to be made before putting in the bulbs. And we shall probably have to wait till spring. For the big house that is building at —— for the gentleman from town, in addition to spoiling all our roads by the daily passage of traction engines, has engrossed all the local bricklayers. This is excellent sport for them, but hard on the casual employer. As a rule, in our part of the country such contracts are liberally construed, and we borrow workmen from each other for an hour or a day; but the gentleman from town has no knowledge of our primitive ways, and sticks to his pound of flesh. Nor would I blame him, for sometimes a bricklayer will have half-a-dozen jobs going at once. He will half unroof the church, and then go and half buttress the meeting-house; from this he will be called off to make a pit at the manor or new steyne a well at the vicarage. While he is busy there Tom's bailiff, who is "the Master," will fetch him off to lath and plaster a cottage wall; and when that is done he will work gently round the other jobs, with an occasional new one interspersed. Perhaps I may be able to get my friend X., who is an amateur bricklayer, to put in a day with the trowel when he is tired of the gun.

Eugenia, who suddenly perverted from Mrs. Earle to Mr. Inigo Thomas, has been insisting of late that we must have peacocks on the terrace, like those in his drawing of Risley Hall.[1] I do not like peafowl as gardeners, nor does Brown; but I

---

[1] See "The Formal Garden in England." By Blomfield and Thomas.

must allow that those Eugenia has begged from her grandmother have given us little trouble so far. Not that they have remained on the terrace in the graceful attitudes illustrated in Mr. Thomas's picture, but that they have taken themselves off altogether to Tom's farm, where they adorn the great central midden. Once a day Brown fetches them home, one under each arm, and at once they begin a stately march back again. I think after this I shall believe, what people often tell one, that no quality is so mistakenly imputed as pride.

The fall of the leaf has revealed on many trees the encroachments of ivy, and I have been walking round the place with a knife. It is curious that, notwithstanding all the home truths that foresters and poets tell of the ivy, it should be still allowed in so many parks to hurt and disfigure the elms. Tom unkindly says that when on an estate you see ivy having its own way, it is at once a sign and a symbol that the lady rules the manor.

16th.—Sophia overheard the following dialogue at a registry office :—

Lady. Are you Church of England?
Maid. No, ma'am.
Lady. Roman Catholic?
Maid. No, ma'am.
Lady. Wesleyan, perhaps?
Maid. No, ma'am.

Lady. May I ask, then, what you are?

Maid. Please, ma'am, I belong to the church at Caversham.

This individualising tendency is an English instinct, and accounts not only for the existence of the Church of England, but also for the two hundred and odd sects tabulated in Whitaker. The last time Disestablishment was in the air, I was told by an old fellow that he would like the church disestablished at P——, but not at S——.

18*th.*—"Conventions are the rudimentary organs of duties. The duty of brotherly love dwindles into the convention of leaving one's visiting-card at a neighbour's house, just as the old-fashioned duty of burning one's enemy dwindled into burning his name on a piece of paper. In particular, the duty of 'visiting the sick' survives in the convention of 'calling to inquire,' and, if the sick are persons of importance, writing your name in a book for the press to copy." These sombre reflections, which I have written in my "Pilgrim's Scrip," were suggested by a visit I have just paid to my sister, who is recovering from a slight illness. I found at the house a young and fashionable lady, engaged in making apologies for her mother, who was a near neighbour, and "had been so much occupied all the week with her housekeeping, and to-day was so busy arranging her flowers, that she had really found no time to call." I was greatly tickled. It was plain the maternal conscience was so far instructed as to have heard of the duty of visiting the sick, but not so far as to understand that if a thing was a duty at all, time must be found for it. As to any useful object that a visit might serve, it was out of her horizon. The duty, in short, was merely a convention. In the course of conversation with the elegant daughter, I assured her that not visiting the sick, so far from needing any apology, was the only rational course to pursue. The phrase "to visit," I explained, does not mean "to make a call," but "to take care of;" and I pointed out how opposed it is to the principles of medical science to go into the same room with a person suffering from any infectious disease, such as a cold. "In our village," I said, "we reconcile religion and science by leaving little vessels of *tisane* at each other's doors, and hurrying away as fast as possible." As a matter of fact I am myself a little old-fashioned, both in my science and my religion, and I continue to pay visits even to people who have colds; only I make a point of not doing it as a duty; because, so far as I can see, the only object of such a visit is to cheer the spirits of your patient, which it fails to do so soon as it is perceived you are calling from conscientious motives. I find that the best way to raise a person's cheerfulness, if the ailment be only slight, is to take a gloomy view of it. People hate to have it assumed that they are better, or even to be asked if they are better; they hate, if they have broken a tendon in a bicycling accident, to be told how easily it might have been a bone; or if on the top of this they have taken influenza, to be congratulated on the rest in bed, which is just what the leg required. And indeed to play the superior person with an invalid is really to steal from him the moral advantage of his situation. He knows what bright side there may be to the case better than you do, but he is feeling the dark side, and what he asks is a little sympathy; and when, having enjoyed that, it is time to waive it away and erect himself above the calamity, why, the moral advantage lies with him, as it should.

20*th*.—I was looking this morning at the fine colour everywhere, bright in the foreground, and fading into a fairy-like distance; and I was groping round my mind for some fit expression of that fairy world, when there leapt to memory the familiar line—

"'Tis distance lends enchantment to the view."

I believe this is the first time I have realised what the poet meant by "enchantment." At this rate, before I die I may be able to appreciate "To be or not to be." I have been reading "Hamlet" lately, and trying to recover the sharpness of first impressions. How strange and unlike anything else in literature is the "*Ghost beneath*, Swear!" Shakespeare must have enjoyed it as a new thrill; and Hamlet's queer speeches and hysteria in that scene must have been more puzzling to his audience then than now. They must have been set down purely for the self-indulgence of Shakespeare himself—indeed, like half Hamlet says. One of the best things said yet about "Hamlet" is to be found in a back number of the *Pall Mall Gazette*, by "An Old Playgoer," who was Matthew Arnold. "Shakespeare created 'Hamlet' with his mind running on Montaigne, and placed its action and its hero in Montaigne's atmosphere and world. What is that world? It is the world of man viewed as a being *ondoyant et divers,* balancing and indeterminate, the plaything of cross-motives and shifting impulses, swayed by a thousand subtle influences, physiological and pathological. Certainly the action and the hero of the original 'Hamlet' story are not such as to compel the poet to place them in this world and no other; but they admit of being placed there; Shakespeare resolved to place them there, and they lent themselves to his resolve. The resolve once taken to place the action in the world of problem, the problem became brightened by all the force of Shakespeare's faculties, of Shakespeare's subtlety. 'Hamlet' thus comes at last to be not a drama followed with perfect comprehension and profoundest emotion, which is the ideal for tragedy, but a problem soliciting interpretation and solution" (October 23, 1884).

Let me jot down here a question proposed to be set in a college examination: "From the characters of Polonius, Laertes, and Ophelia, deduce that of Mrs. Polonius."

24*th*.—Middle-aged men like myself are often haunted by the notion that in some factitious way they can raise the value of the libraries they leave behind them. The most childlike method I ever heard of was that of my neighbour at ——, who wrote across the title-page of every volume, "This is a scarce and valuable work." But his device did not take in the local tradesmen who assisted at the auction. If a man is a poet or painter, and is sure of dying before his boom is over, let him write his name in every book. Else "the eftest way" is to buy a book-plate of Mr. Sherborn. Annotation tends to depreciation; I know it well; but no bad habit so grows upon a man. To-day I made two entries in my copy of Bacon's "Essays" to No. xlix., *Of Suitors*. On the words "Timing of suits is the principal," I say: "If you know a great person to have something against you, of which in consideration of your services he is loth to speak, make your request then, as he will probably grant it as a cover to his complaint." On the rule *iniquum petas ut æquum feras*, which might be rendered, "Ask more than your due to get your own," I note that an Oxford scholar of my acquaintance, if he wished a valuable book to be taken from the Bodleian Library into the Radcliffe Reading-room that he might continue reading it after the library was closed, used to begin by asking leave for some unique manuscript, and when that was refused, a book somewhat less valuable, coming gradually down a scale and being refused with less emphasis, until he reached the book which alone he wanted, when he would say, "At least you can have no objection to my taking this."

In Lamb's essay which he entitles "Detached Thoughts on Books," he makes several strictures as to the form, folio or octavo, in which certain works should be read. On this I comment: "I knew a clergyman once ('tis true he was also a baronet), who used to read his Thomas à Kempis in a Bodoni folio, and a vellum paper copy at that; a truly magnificent way of despising the world." One notices that Lamb cares nothing for first editions as such; he even pooh-poohs the first folio of Shakespeare, a copy of which my fingers still tingle from handling. What would he have thought of a young lad whom I heard ask at a bookseller's for "Three Men in a Boat" (or some such title), adding, "I should prefer it in a first edition!" What would he have said, too, of the folk who put handsome volumes into handsome book-cases, and leave them there for a quarter of a century without removing the auction tickets!

26th.—I heard to-day a story from the Education Office. An inspector was asked why he had charged so much for his fare between two places when as the crow flies it was only so many miles. He replied, "I do not ride a crow."

29th.—The sale at Sotheby's of some letters written by Sir Philip Francis has revived an ancient controversy. I once knew an old gentleman living at Windsor, who thought he had discovered a satisfactory proof of the Franciscan authorship of the "Letters of Junius." He would take his victim with great solicitude into St. George's Chapel and point to a tablet erected to the memory of the Anglo-Saxon scholar Francis Junius; and then would proceed to a demonstration how on certain days Francis *must* have been in the chapel, and *must* have seen the tablet, and so doubtless adopted the name. "But why," I once protested, "need he have gone so far in search of his pseudonym as Windsor? Why could he not have borrowed it from the address on his own letters—Philip Francis, *Junior*, Esq.? He could always have alleged, if the point were brought home to him, that the name must refer to Junius Brutus."

December 3rd.—I have had another letter from my young journalist friend asking for advice in his matrimonial difficulties. His wife comes of a stock not much given to the contemplative life, but full of practical energy, which in her case has not large resources of physical strength to draw upon. The consequence is that when she herself is weary with much coming and going, the sight of her husband calmly driving a quill irritates her nerves and is apt to cause a discharge. I have ventured to suggest a homœopathic remedy: that a writing-table be provided for the dear lady—as handsome a one as means will afford—and that she be persuaded to attempt a novel. This should act as a counter-irritant for overworked feelings, and might at the same time tend to create a respect for the labour of literature. The servants might be encouraged, for the first few days, to burst into the room with messages from the butcher and baker and candlestick-maker, whenever she was quietly settled to work, and in this way create an understanding of the conditions necessary for the practice of letters. The other symptoms were, I fear, beyond my skill to prescribe for. "What can I do when dear X., after an outburst which reduces me to pulp, wonders why I am so glum; or, if I am a little silent at meals, stimulates me by a 'Why don't you say something?' a question which at once makes my mind a blank." The only thing to do in this case, I feel sure, would be to put the matter as delicately as possible before the lady herself. I suggested making her a present of an album, in which from time to time some ideal Chloris or Lalage might be blamed for similar *bêtises*, or, better, praised for their absence. To open the volume, I sent the following pieces, the first in the manner of Waller, the second in that of Donne:—

"TO CŒLIA.

"Cœlia, I wonder and admire
    That though a short hour since you frowned,
    Chiding, as Boreas were your sire,
    So chill the gust, so fierce the sound;

Now bright as sunshine and as fair
    Your halcyon [1] face does soothe and bless,
As with a mild engaging air
    You question of my pensiveness.

So the other Heaven, her anger spent,
Emerges from the cloudy tent
Suddenly splendid and serene,
As no disfiguring storm had been.
For her 'tis past, for men not so;
Whose ways long weeks are choked with snow."

The second piece might be entitled "To his contrarious mistress, who bade him talk."

"If our souls are the hemispheres
    Of one vast world, our love, it is but fate
    That the same sun should light and dark create,
Thy smiles accompany my tears;
    And if to bright
    Night turn at last, day cannot but turn night,
While the earth's revolution makes the years.

---

[1] I am aware that Waller would have accented "halcyon" on the penultimate.

>   As the same vocable 'Let be'
>   Both 'fiat' is and 'finis'; both the call
>   That wakes the spring and hush that shuts up all;
>   So fares it, Love, with thee and me!
>   So thy meant *yea*
>   Sounds in my willing heart a chilling *nay;*
>   Thoughts bud not out, shake not their petals free.

15*th*.—The judgment of the House of Lords in Allen *v.* Flood has been rapturously welcomed by all trades unions, and not least by the honourable order of baronets, now on strike. It is believed in well-informed circles that many will now resign their positions if any further increase is made in their number. Every one must allow that the baronets have been in some respects hardly used; but as ancient philologers derive their title from the Greek βαρύς (heavy), and more modern ones from the root of the verb *to bear*, it would look as if they were born to sorrow. They complain that King James, to whom they owe their foundation, promised for himself and his heirs that the whole number of baronets should never exceed two hundred, and should gradually decrease as the first creations became extinct; whereas there are now no less than eight hundred. If a sufficient number take advantage of the new decision to throw up their patents, this grievance would at once be remedied. But that, of course, would not bind the future action of the Crown. Might not a petition be presented urging the Queen to follow her ancestor's example and create a new order, leaving the baronets to the distinction and extinction they desire? It is true that King James pledged himself and his successors to create no new dignity below a baron, but very little regard has been paid to his other pledges, and this deserves no more respect; or, if it does, it would be possible to create a degree equal to baronet with a somewhat different title, such as *baruncle*, allowing it the same honourable particle *Sir* for prefix.

Another complaint made is, that many of the recent creations are of people who have risen to fortune in commerce, whereas English etiquette allows no trading for gentlefolk below the rank of marquis. But such a complaint rests upon a misconception of the original purpose of the order. The first instructions to the commissioners do certainly require candidates to have had at least a grandfather, but they lay much more stress on the amount of their incomes; and in the original patent hardly a word is said about blood, and a good deal about wealth. This is how it runs:

"James, by the grace of God, &c., greeting. Whereas among the other cares of sovereignty with which our mind is constantly exercised, that neither is the least nor of least moment, the plantation of our kingdom in Ireland, and chiefly of Ulster, a large and famous province of the same kingdom, which now under our government and by our arms being happily subdued, we endeavour so to establish that so great a province should more and more flourish not only in the true practice of religion, civil humanity, and probity of manners, *but also in an affluence of riches* and abundance of all things which contribute either to the ornament or happiness of the commonweal; . . . and whereas it is intimated unto us, on the part of certain of our faithful subjects, *that they are most ready as well with their persons as their fortunes to promote this our royal undertaking,* WE moved with a desire of accomplishing so holy and wholesome a work, and fondly regarding such generous inclinations and minds so addicted to our service and the public good, have resolved with ourselves to be wanting in nothing which may reward the aforesaid good will of our subjects, or excite a spirit and alacrity in others to perform their parts, and *furnish their expenses upon this occasion;* therefore, weighing and considering with ourselves that virtue and industry are cherished and supported by nothing more than by honour, and that all the splendour and amplitude of honour and dignity take their rise from a King, as from a fountain, to whose high prerogative it properly belongs to erect and institute new titles of honour and dignity, as he from whom the old ones flowed; we have thought proper (the service of the commonwealth and the exigence of the times so requiring) to reward *new merits* with new ensigns of dignity; and therefore of our certain knowledge and mere motion we have ordained, erected, constituted, and created a certain state, degree, dignity, name, and title of Baronet within this our kingdom of England, for ever to endure," &c. The patent then goes on to say that A. B., "who with a generous and liberal mind gave and yielded to us a relief and supply ample enough to maintain and support thirty men in our foot forces in our said kingdom of Ireland for three entire years," shall "by these presents" be raised, appointed, and created a Baronet.

The price, that is to say, of the first baronetcies was £1095. Application was to be made any Wednesday or Friday afternoon at Whitehall, and the sooner the better, as there were only a limited number to be disposed of; and to quiet scoffers, "because there is nothing of honour, or of value, which is known to be sought or desired, be the motives never so good, but may receive scandal from some, who wanting the same good affection to the public, or being in other considerations incapable, can be contented, out of envy to those that are so preferred, to cast aspersions and imputations upon them, as if they came by this dignity for any other consideration but that which concerneth this so public and memorable a work," the commissioners were to allow the new baronet to take an oath that he had not paid for his dignity more than the market price.

It is interesting, in view of the recent agitation, to notice that within a year of the establishment of the order, the baronets were out on strike, owing to precedence being accorded over them to the younger sons of viscounts and barons.

The present list of complaints is a long one. Besides those I have noticed, one of the most interesting is the protest of the Home Rule baronets against being compelled to bear the " bloody hand " of Ulster.

20*th.*—I notice in the magazines that there has been a discussion about the reality of " dowsing " or discovering water by the divining rod. One wonders how the fact can be in debate when it is a lucrative profession. Mr. M., who is the only " dowser " I have seen, is generally accurate in his estimate of the depth at which water will be found, so much so that he is ready to contract for the required well on the simple understanding " no water, no money." I have a friend, not in the " dowsing " line of business, who experiences very curious sensations when he crosses water—I do not mean in a boat—even in the dark when the water is not visible. And everybody knows how averse those sensitive creatures donkeys are to crossing a stream.

A lady who " has read with interest my remarks on the need of comforting the sick by taking a gloomy view of their condition," writes to tell me that it was her invariable custom when her late husband was at all seriously indisposed to read the Burial Service to him! I confess I was thinking of minor ailments.

21st.—There is no contagion so inevitable as that of ideas; and therefore when an idea once—which is seldom—gets into our village it spreads. The current idea at the present moment is garden improvement. The vicar is anxious to formalise the vicarage garden, and as it was made about two centuries ago, it would not be difficult to reduce it to its old lines. But one thing is indispensable, and that is time; and I warn the vicar that before the yew hedges are grown the Church will be disestablished. Being a man of faith, he will probably reject my advice, which is to plant privet instead. Privet is as susceptible to the knife as yew, and if my memory serves me it was the material, according to Du Bartas, of the hedges in the Garden of Eden. They were clipped, too, according to the same authority, in the extreme of the fashion—

"In satyrs, centaurs, whales, and half-men-horses."

There is, however, an even chance that nothing will be done at all. For the lady of the vicarage, who has her own garden gods, one of whom is by name Robinson, has discovered in the early chapters of his sacred work an attack upon formalists.

Eugenia was shown, when she last called, a passage where her own idols, Messrs. Blomfield and Thomas, were spoken of as no better than they should be. This is the inevitable consequence of making a religion of what is purely a matter of taste. Mr. Robinson appeals to nature. But weeds are as natural as flowers. A lawn left to nature would soon become a meadow. A hedge left to nature would become monstrous and useless because pervious. A well-grown yew-tree is undoubtedly a beautiful object, but a yew clipped intelligently is quite as beautiful, and if a tree will clip it is not unnatural to clip it. A garden given up to "topiary" work, such as Levens, is dull enough; but nothing could be finer or more majestic (say) than the green court at Canons Ashby (Sir H. Dryden's), with its double line of cone-clipped yews, each ten feet in diameter. I suppose they are two hundred years old; in which case glorious John may have seen them planted, when he visited at his uncle's; Richardson, at any rate, must have speculated on their chances of survival to a green old age, for he was a frequent guest. But Mr. Robinson, I presume, would not deign a glance at such deplorable distortion.

22nd.—In all our digging the treasure-trove was *nil*, but to-day in cutting down an ancient hedge we came upon a set of quoits. Quoits would in old days have been as common a game at the farm as bowls were at the vicarage,¹ or cock-fighting in the churchyard. I am not, as a rule, lucky in finding things, not having long sight, and not having contracted the Mammon-like habit of walking with my eyes on the ground. One hears such marvellous tales of things being found after many days by their losers, that one half fancies the fairies may have something to do with the whole process. Is not this, for instance, a Puckish trick? An old friend of mine, who lived in Manchester, lost the stone out of his signet ring, and found it in the street, but not until he had had another engraved. Sometimes the fairy is more kind. I know of a lady who has a bad habit of dropping a ring as she gets into her carriage to go out to dinner, and always finds it when she reaches home. The gift, as one would expect, sometimes runs in families. P.'s father found a gold coin (Roman); he himself found a silver shilling of Edward VI.; and his infant son recently picked up a halfpenny in copper, or, as the police say, "bronze." Now, I suppose, the virtue will have departed from the fairy-gift. It is interesting to observe that this familiar scale of metals is, therefore, not merely human and conventional, but has a validity in the ideal world. As Sophia and I approach nearer to our golden

---

[1] *Cf.* Costard of Sir Nathaniel: "There, an't shall please you; a foolish mild man; an honest man, look you, and soon dashed! He is a marvellous good neighbour, faith; and a *very good bowler.*" ("Love's Labour's Lost," v. 2, 587.)

wedding, I see more and more reason for emphasising its genuinely metallic aspect. It is a pure fiction of the poets, and bears its refutation on its face, that the so-called golden age was the age before the discovery of gold. But this is to digress; I was speaking of finds. My esteemed friend and neighbour, the late rector of ———, told me he once found in a newly ploughed field a coin he could not identify. It was of pewter, and bore a trireme on one side and on the other a head. He kept it for years in his cabinet, and exhibited it from time to time to many antiquaries, who all pronounced it unique. One day he saw some little boys in his own parish playing with new coins precisely similar. They were called "dumps" and came from Birmingham.

It is rather unkind of the reporters to say that the skull of Voltaire, recently exhumed, was recognised by its sneer, for skulls have no choice. And Voltaire was always so emaciated, that his sneer was probably the natural sneer of his skull. Still it suited his temper admirably; as his friend, Dr. Young (the author of "Night Thoughts"), put it, referring to their controversy on the merits of the Sin and Death episode in "Paradise Lost":

> "You are so witty, profligate, and thin,
> At once we think you Milton, Death, and Sin."

It is extraordinary how Englishmen of all classes

have lost the taste and the capacity for keeping festivals. To turn over the pages of "Brand's Popular Antiquities" is to lose oneself in a foreign land; one wonders how our forefathers, who practised all these elaborate customs, found time to do anything else. We still deck our houses and churches with evergreens at Christmas, but among evergreens we do not discriminate. The beautiful carol of the contest between the holly and ivy,[1] first printed by Ritson from a MS. of Henry VI.'s reign, would be unmeaning to us; at least I know I was asked to save all the ivy I had stripped off my trees to help decorate the church. But quotations given in Brand from churchwardens' accounts show that ivy was used for church decoration as early as the sixteenth century; in 1656 we have mention of yew, and in 1734 of cypress. Probably it saved trouble to fetch branches into church from the churchyard. But what becomes of the symbolism?

January 1st, 1898.—"*Semper ego auditor tantum, nunquamne reponam?*" Am I to be besieged with New Year's greetings and not return the compliment? Christmas cards I will never send: no, not even in revenge; and I have a hope the custom may soon die now that hospitals and foreign missions (as I am informed) have declined any

---

[1] "Nay, ivy, nay; it shall not be, I wis;
Let holly have the mastery, as the manner is.
Holly stand in the hall, fair to behold;
Ivy stand without the door, she is full sore a-cold," &c.

longer to relieve the British household of its last year's hoard. Perhaps this accounts for the new form they are taking. Instead of "herald angels" (who really, the Vicar tells us, ought not to be "herald angels" at all, but a "welkin"), and instead of the merry hunter out with the hounds in a hard frost, the postman now brings the good wishes of Mr. and Mrs. Jones embossed in gold with a smudgeograph of the new baby. But this must surely be the beginning of the end. The New Year seems to offer greater scope to the fancy. One friend signalises the season with a Pindarique Ode of his own compounding; another with a calendar of his particular saints and worthies; another—and this is what has haunted me—with a text by way of motto. As the New Year approaches I find myself uneasily forecasting whether it shall be Carlyle, or Sir Thomas Browne, or Ruskin, that must guide my pained steps through the fresh year of grace, and whether the motto will be printed in violet or magenta.[1]

To-night I gave a little feast to the village handbell ringers. The talk was very interesting; but all I remember was a literary judgment on Shakespeare. Somebody praised "The Merchant of Venice," but P. dissented. He thought poor old

[1] The postman has resolved the doubt. It is Bacon, and in scarlet, as befits a Lord Chancellor. This year my mind is to "move in charity, rest in providence, and turn upon the poles of truth." It makes me giddy to think of it.

Shylock very hardly used. His favourite play was "Hamlet." There was no favouritism in that. Shakespeare killed a man on one side and then killed one on the other; gave this fellow a slap in the face, and then that other a punch in the ribs. For insight this is worthy of G. B. S.

4*th*.—I noted some weeks ago [1] the departure of my garden-boy for the crusades, but by an oversight I did not record his return. I went for my usual stroll round the garden after breakfast three days later, and found the young hopeful digging away as if nothing had happened. "Good morning, Sidney" (every boy here is Sidney who is not Albert Edward); "we have missed you these three days." "Yes, sir." "What has happened to you?" "Went to enlist, sir." "Well, why have you come back again?" "Wouldn't have me, sir." William, who is himself in the reserve, told me in confidence, "he expected as how he were too meek-hearted like." All the old soldiers in the neighbourhood who have served in India are much in request now for legends of the Pathans. I bought the New Year's editions of those invaluable works "Whitaker," "Hachette" (for Sophia), and "Who's He." I feel sure that a comparison of "Whitaker" with "Hachette," if one had leisure to make it, would throw light on some fundamental differences in

[1] November 10th.

genius between the two peoples. It might even account for the Dreyfus case.

6th.—I went to look at the lambs. Did anybody in England ever see a shepherd playing upon a pipe? My experience of shepherds is that they are what we call in Berkshire "drew" men, sombre spirits, given perhaps to psalmody on Sundays, but not likely on working-days to "fool away the light" with pipe and tabor, or any other combination of instruments. Somehow the hideous structures, like bathing-machines, with corrugated iron roofs, which roam our wintry meadows like the wheeled house of the Scythian on the wide steppe, seem an unfit tabernacle for any spirit of song. It would be unimaginable in the background (say) of that lovely little Raphael drawing of a shepherd boy with a bagpipe which Mr. Mackail printed for a frontispiece to his version of the "Eclogues," or of the flute-player by Campagnola reproduced in the "Pageant" for last year. Nor do I find that our shepherd's sons incline to take at all a more romantic view of their father's calling. The eldest, who is still at school, hopes in time to be a butcher, and on his holidays dons a blue apron and goes round for orders. Still the old pastoral convention, though unreal, has its charm, and I would not willingly lose a single Hobbinol or Cuddy from any "Shepherd's kalendar" of them all.

9th.—I picked out of the twopenny box at———'s a

volume which I have found more entertaining than I expected. It was "The Secretary's Vade-mecum," a letter-writer of the year 1697. The book was strange to me, but from internal evidence I should judge that it has been reprinted, for not a few letters that appear in the daily papers seem to be studied from its pages. The letters of the knight who corresponds with Mr. Farrow about the money-lending among ironmasters are undoubtedly modelled upon the "Letters Comminatory," which (as the book says) "must be written full of Resentments of Injury, in an angry, passionate Stile, to terrifie the Person to a submission." One of them accordingly begins: "Ungracious offspring of an infernal brood, whom Heaven permitted for a plague, and the Earth nourished as a peculiar mischief," &c. Mr. K., again, who writes to the Bishop of London about ritual questions, has, I should say, perused with no little profit the "letters mandatory or Commanding in which you expect to have your will absolutely obey'd." Besides these, there are letters accusatory, excusatory, reprobatory, petitionary, letters of advice, and "mixed letters," of all of which, and especially of the last, the press affords daily examples.

Nor are there wanting specimens in every style of that very important branch of correspondence which deals with the art and mystery of lovemaking. We are offered "a letter of address from a gentleman to a lady" with "the answer in a doubtful manner;" perhaps the volume would be of more practical use to-day, in view of Sir F. Jeune's court, if it were the gentleman's letters that were in the "doubtful manner." There is one, however, that opens ominously and, as it were prophetically, with the words, "My breach of promise," &c. In a higher key we have one from a passionate lover to his mistress beginning "Gracious object of my pleasing thoughts, and mistress of my affection;" another in the pastoral style to a "fair nymph," and "a plain country-letter" from "Honest John" to "Honest Joan." A curious sidelight is thrown on manners by a letter of introduction from a gentleman recommending a friend to a lady as "her servant for life." But the gem of the collection is "a letter to a lady much grieved for the impairing of her beauty by the small-pox." It should even make an anti-vaccinationist shudder to know that a letter on this topic was considered useful in a "vade-mecum."[1] The consolation for the ravages of the "inexorable distemper" is not very consoling.

"What if some dimples are impressed by the Disease! *Venus's* Beauty consisted, to her Praise, as Poetical Gayness sets it forth, in that particular, though not happening by the same Means. Observe the Face of Heaven, when the numerous Hoast of Stars stud it over with Seeds of Light, how beautiful

---

[1] See page 297.

and gay it represents itself to our admiring Eyes? So your Face, adorn'd or studded o'er with little Rounds indenting it make it lovely and desirable," &c.

The book includes some specimens of Caroline—or perhaps it would be more accurate to say Low Dutch—banter and repartee, and a collection of songs as far out of the present taste as the banter. One, however, is interesting, not for its merits, poetical or linguistic, but as showing how early our literature was captured by the Scots siren.

> "When anent your Love you came,
>   Ah, *Sawney!* were you true,
> What though I seem to frown and gloom,
>   I ne'er could gang from you.
> Yet still my Tongue, do what I can,
>   With muckle Woe denies;
> Wae's me, when once I'se like a man,
>   It boots not to be wise."

17th.—Should not the excited behaviour of the Parisian students give pause to the gentlemen who are for departing from the wisdom of our ancestors by setting up a university in the capital? The head masters of our public schools met not long ago in solemn session, and denounced the new degree that Oxford and Cambridge are granting for cricket and football; those ancient universities having at last adopted the discipline of Plato (whom they have long praised with their mouth), and admitted Gymnastics to be a recognised branch of education. Tom is much excited over the decision, and hopes we may at length get back to the fine old fortifying curriculum of the Magi, which, if we may credit Herodotus, comprehended only three items, riding, speaking the truth, and drawing the (short) bow. Tom is never tired of pointing to the Clarendon building in Oxford as a crying instance of the deference we pay to the wishes of pious founders; Clarendon having left his bequest to endow a riding-school. I am not sure that some defence might not be made for the Oxford authorities in the matter, since Oxford hardly needs a riding-school so long as it has Shotover. Moreover, both Oxford and Cambridge have accessible rivers (of sorts) on which to practise rowing; and they have playing fields. But London is in a different case; and the present demonstrations in Paris should convince sensible people that no new charter ought to be granted to London till a guarantee has been given for a sound training in athletics. Let our present Lord Chancellor found a riding professorship. We do not want undergraduates parading Pall Mall and Piccadilly shouting an English version of "Conspuez Zola." Spitting (apart from its unpleasantness) must be, except perhaps in a vacuum, a miserable form of exercise.

18*th*.—A letter to the *Times* very happily parallels the Dreyfus case for muddle-headedness with the trial in "Alice."[1]

---

[1] The parallel has since been drawn still closer by the flinging of inkpots in the Chamber.

19th.—In looking down the list of deaths (I find, as I advance in years, I look at the deaths before the marriages: the births are of no interest to anybody) I saw the name of Mr. Dodgson ("Lewis Carroll"), who was in everybody's mouth yesterday. The *Standard*, however, vouchsafes no obituary notice; but as Mr. Dodgson resented nothing so much as a hint that he was interested in any but mathematical literature, perhaps this is taking the correct line. I once committed the indiscretion of confounding the humourist with the don, and was properly snubbed. An Oxford bookseller had told me that Mr. D. was extremely nice about the printing of his "Alices," and that every copy not up to his ideal was withheld from sale and given to the poor. I, coveting some of these for our village children, and being in Oxford, sent a note to Christ Church asking if I had been accurately informed, and received in reply the following printed circular, which is now among my most cherished possessions:—

"Mr. C. L. Dodgson is so frequently addressed by strangers on the quite unauthorised assumption that he claims, or at any rate acknowledges, the authorship of books not published under his name, that he has found it necessary to print this, once for all, as an answer to all such applications.

"He neither claims, nor acknowledges, any connection with any 'pseudonym,' or with any book not published under his own name.

"Ch. Ch., Oxford."

23rd.—The influenza is with us. What impresses me about the disease is, that it picks out the strongest people as though it were a spirit of compensation. One of Tom's labourers, originally a navvy, and perhaps the toughest man in the place, is now tottering about with a stick like a grandfather. Another sign of discretion is that it spares—at least in our neighbourhood—the doctors and the parsons. There is a droll story (one of those which hurt some people with much laughing, while others see nothing to laugh at) in a book called "Random Recollections," by the Rev. George Huntington, which I have had lent me, of a parson whom Mr. H. saw hanging as far as he could out of a window in the top storey of a house to avoid infection, while he read the office of "Visitation of the Sick." The clergy one reads about in these pages are delightful old gentlemen, of whom the type is as extinct as the dodo. Amongst them my favourite is an old Canon Wray. "I heard him tell the Dean that he thought four thousand a year a most desirable income, with which any one might be content. 'You have enough,' he said, 'for your necessities and a few luxuries. No man need wish for more.'" This is quite in the temper of Cowley, who says in his essay "Of Greatness":—

"When you have pared away all the Vanity, what solid and natural contentment does there remain which may not be had with five hundred pounds a year? Not so many servants or horses, but a few good ones, which will do all the business as well; not so many choice dishes at every Meale, but at several meals all of them, which makes them both the more healthy and the more pleasant; not so rich garments, nor so frequent changes, but as warm and as comely and so frequent change too as is every jot as good for the Master though not for the Tailor or *Valet de Chamber;* not such a stately Palace, nor guilt rooms, or the costliest sorts of Tapestry, but a convenient brick-house, with decent Wainscot and pretty Forest-work hangings. Lastly (for I omit all other particulars, and will end with that which I love most in both conditions), not whole Woods cut in walks, nor vast Parks, nor Fountain, or Cascade-gardens, but herb, and Flower, and fruit-gardens, which are more useful, and the water every whit as clear and wholesome, as if it darted from the breasts of a marble Nymph, or the Urn of a River-God."

I used to wonder at Cowley's moderation in fixing the ideal income at five hundred pounds a year, until I reflected that the purchasing power of money was in his day five or six times what it is now.

28*th*.—I am sorry to see the *Standard,* for whose criticism of life I have great respect, laying down to-day as a truth of experience that a person who has suffered great sorrows is braced by them to bear little worries. "A man who has known what it is to lose a wife is not so likely to worry over the loss of a portmanteau; and one who has had to go without food for a couple of days will keep his temper though the soup be cold or the joint burnt to a cinder." This is in the high pulpit manner, and conceals a not very subtle fallacy. The play upon the word "loss" reminds me of Johnson's famous epigram—

> "If a man who 'turnips' cries,
> Cry not when his father dies,
> 'Tis a proof that he would rather
> Have a turnip than his father."

The fact is, man is a social animal, and when something goes wrong, his inbred integrity at once impels him to inquire, "Whom can I blame for this?" Now, when he "loses" a wife, misusing that word in the ordinary way, there is usually no question of blaming any one, and his indignation is not wasted. But when he "loses" a portmanteau, there is an almost inexhaustible series of objects for his indignation to lighten and thunder round—his servants at home, his hackney-coachman, the railway officials, his fellow-travellers, and so forth. Similarly, for his two days' hunger probably no one is in fault; but for the wasted victuals there is the offending cook. And the very condition of his patience under the one set of circumstances is the condition of his wrath under the other—I mean his high sense of duty. Surely, my dear *Standard*, it is only your indifferent Radical, bred in the mistaken doctrine of *laissez-faire*, who tolerates the incapacity of his servants, whether public or private. Edward Fitz-Gerald was fond of quoting a passage from Wesley's journal, which garnishes the *Standard's* doctrine with an amusing anecdote. "A gentleman of large fortune, while we were seriously conversing, ordered a servant to throw some coals on the fire. A puff of smoke came out. He threw himself back in his chair and cried out, 'Oh, Mr. Wesley, these are the crosses I meet with every day.'" Now, allowing a little touch of exaggeration in the expression, due perhaps to the "serious conversation" that was interrupted, I cannot see the gentleman to be as absurd as he is represented. My experience is that masters who pass over *gaucheries* because they seem too trifling to complain of are worse and worse served. Who does not know the domestic who never comes into a room without leaving an open door to retreat by, and advances to your chair with a note or a card like the Spirit of the North Pole with all the Arctic winds in "her tempestuous petticoat"? Who does not know the domestic who forgets to attend to the drawing-room fire till the moment before dinner is done, and you come in to find it black and cold? And if I resent such want of consideration, I shall not find myself less able to bear the next fit of the gout, or the next fall in the stock-market, or the next variation of ――'s undisciplined temper.

February 1st.—It has been found convenient to name the peacocks, so I have called them "Thomas" and "Love." To induce them to stay at home, I was advised to give them company, and accordingly I bought some guinea-fowls—birds, as I think, of singularly beautiful plumage. In Berkshire we call them *gallinis*, which, oddly enough, was the name of a dancing-master who, some time last century, ran away with one of Lord Abingdon's daughters and came to live in Berkshire. Gallinis are apt to be wild, and have a trick of wandering far afield and laying their eggs (your eggs) in your neighbour's preserve; but these were warranted home-keeping, and so they have proved. But I could sometimes wish they would visit other places. At night they roost in the old oak, and about twelve o'clock begin their lugubrious recitative—

> "vexing the ethereal powers
> With midnight matins at uncivil hours."

The doctor, who lives at the other end of the village, tells me he finds them of service in keeping him from falling asleep again after he has been called up, and I cannot but be glad that my loss should in any way subserve another's gain. But peacocks or no peacocks, doctor or no doctor, those birds must die.

3rd.—I saw an amusing scene this afternoon at our railway station. My companion X., who is a keen grammarian, fell a-laughing at a sentence on the notice-board, which is certainly Lindley Murray "a little scratched." It runs: "If passengers are desirous of leaving luggage or parcels under the charge of the Company, they must themselves take, or see them taken to and deposited in, the cloak-room." Looking round for some one to share his glee (I being engaged at the ticket office), X. spied the local postman, and began showing him the absurdity of the thing; but the postman could see no absurdity. "They must themselves take," says X.; "take what?" "Why, take the luggage," says the postman. "It doesn't say so," says X. "Yes, it does," says the postman. "Well, where are they to take?" says X. "Why, to the cloak-room," says the postman. "It doesn't say so," says X. "Yes, it does," says the postman. After this dialogue in the manner of Sterne they were both very red; but X.'s indomitable spirit would not give way, and the postman became every moment more convinced he was being made a fool of. Happily the train soon solved the situation by ambling in. Public inscriptions have been of interest to me from very early years. I recollect that my first letter to a newspaper was to point out the misplacement of an apostrophe in a notice board of the South Coast Railway. But things that interest me have never interested editors, and my first letter fared no better than my last. There is a notice hanging in our village post-office to the effect that "Postmasters are neither bound to give change nor authorised to demand it." This seems to the unofficial mind to lead to an *impasse*. If I present a half-sovereign for a five-shilling postal order, and the postmaster has no small silver, what is to happen? He says, "I am not bound to give change;" to which I retort, "Nor are you authorised to demand it." But a notice that gave me more pleasure even than this was one sent round when the telegraph wires were first brought to us; it was so non-committal: "After January 1st telegrams will be *dealt with* at this office." There were no idle tradesmanlike promises about promptitude or accuracy, or even about the transmission of the messages. They would be "dealt with"; I presume, on the merits.

6th.—"Verbum non amplius"—*influenza*.

12th.—It has been a fairly mild attack, and I have not grudged a few days in bed, still less a few days of convalescence; for as there is no infectious peeling in influenza, I have had no scruple in ordering a variety of light literature from the circulating library. "Send something cheerful," I said. At the top of the heap came

"Weeping Ferry." I remembered a passage in Herrick, where Charon says—

> " Thou and I'll sing to make these dark shades merry,
> Who else with tears would doubtless drown my ferry."

So I took heart, hoping Charon—if it was Charon's ferry—might still be in the mood for a song. Well, I am not going to dethrone " Esther Vanhomrigh " ; but I am confirmed in my opinion that Mrs. Woods is one of the very few writers of to-day who write English. After "Weeping Ferry" I read "The King with Two Faces"—a story that has justly become popular. And then I read Mr. Wells's "Certain Personal Matters." Mr. Wells's uncle is a very old friend, and I was gratified to make the acquaintance of his aunt Charlotte, with whose taste for mahogany I sympathise. Then, being deeply interested in the Scotch, I fell back on Chambers's new " Biographical Dictionary," for this dictionary includes all the Scotsmen who ever lived, with just a sprinkling of Medes and Elamites, like slaves in the triumphal chariot, to avert the evil eye. There are some interesting stories of Bright in Mrs. Simpson's "Many Memories"; it is vastly entertaining to see how a tribune, who was never weary of bullying the country gentry, appealed to all the gods when it was proposed to interfere with his own omnipotence by Factory Acts.

14*th*.—The doctor told me this morning an anecdote which may interest psychologists. He had been attending for some considerable period a country parson, and, according to a fashion now becoming antiquated, attending him *gratis*. When in due course the parson died, his widow wrote to inquire how much the doctor would allow her for the medicine bottles. When I recalled Wordsworth's lines—

> "Alas! the gratitude of men
> Hath oftener left me mourning"[1]—

the doctor observed, first, that Wordsworth was not in medical practice, and secondly, that he says nothing about women. In regard to the first point, I believe it is a fact that country doctors find great difficulty in collecting their fees; and in regard to the second, as gratitude depends upon imagination, it may well be that women, having less imagination than men, are less grateful. The doctor told me "intermittent heart" is a not uncommon female ailment. Sophia, to whom I communicated the anecdote, will have it that it makes nothing against women in general, but only against a particular species with sharply defined

---

[1] 17*th*.—In defence of the maligned sex I should like to record a case of gratitude in a woman that left me a little mournful. I had sent Charlotte a book for her birthday last autumn, and at breakfast to-day she said: "Oh, thank you for that delightful book you sent me." "Oh," I said, "what was it?" "Dear me," said C., "I have quite forgotten."

virtues and defects, the country parsoness. But for this lady I would very gladly hold a brief, even against Sophia. It is easy enough to caricature her as a sort of ogress fattening up the peasant on beef-tea and milk puddings to make a meal for her husband; for, no doubt, she is often as keen a partisan as Mr. Arch himself, or the gentlemen who go round the villages in red vans making fun of her and her blankets, or the amiable celibates who point the finger at her in Socialist church magazines. But let her be ill and have to leave home for a month, as sometimes happens to our good "Vicaress," and hear the clamour of the village mothers!

16*th*.—I came up to Charlotte's for a few days. There are two flies, trifling and absurd, which yet somewhat mar the ointment of my infrequent visits to town. The first is that the ancient doorkeeper at my club is too often off duty, leaving his place to a buttons who insults me by asking my name; the other, that my friends become indignant if I do not pay visits. Now, as some of them reside as far north as the Regent's Park, and others as far south as Chelsea, to pay calls I must either run the risk of bronchitis in a hansom, or of asthma in the Underground Railway. Of the two on this occasion I dreaded asthma least, and have in consequence spent much time on the Inner Circle of that inferno. I observed there that ladies never open a carriage-door (for fear, I presume, of soiling their gloves), but wait until a door opens from within and then make a rush for it. If they are a party of six, and the compartment is already full, while others are empty, this makes no difference; nor does it concern them if the carriage they invade is one where men are smoking. In fact, I saw yesterday a posse of ladies carry by assault a smoking-carriage, from which one man had alighted, all the rest beating a sullen retreat into the adjoining compartment. I should judge that if a person had time to spend and could breathe the atmosphere, he would glean a rich harvest of humours there below the streets. In my short journey to-day I saw a man who turned his hat the front side to the back when he got in, and reversed it again when he got out; I saw another who took down the number of the carriage in case of accidents; and a third who was "the very model" of an old Leech picture with Dundreary whiskers. Perhaps one might find down there buried examples of all the forgotten fashions.

17th.—To the Millais Exhibition. Many of the pictures are old friends or old enemies, but one which I had never seen before fascinated me. It was the portrait of an elderly lady, much wrinkled, with a parrot; and suggested nothing so much as that picture of which Mr. Anstey tells in "The

Fallen Idol," into which Chalanka, the wicked image, got himself painted as an accessory, and then transferred his features to the sitter. It would be interesting to know who the sitter was, and whether the picture has a romantic history. As it is against my principles to enrich the Academy, I forbore to purchase a catalogue. One great charm of the exhibitions at Burlington House is that they may appeal to more than one sense; when the eye is satisfied with seeing, the ear may take its turn of pleasure. The waifs and strays of conversation that have from time to time reached me without any deliberate eavesdropping, although never so delightful as those recorded in "Voces Populi"—for a jest lives in the ear even more than on the lips—have often been as interesting as the pictures, and quite as artless. This morning the first words to fix my attention were these: "Do you know, I feel quite sure it is coming on; Mary is down with it and the nurse; and if I had not pledged myself to bring you here to-day I should have stayed in bed. However, I shall turn in as soon as I get home." I felt I was intruding on domestic mysteries, and moved away to the farther end of the room. Then, while I was looking at the beautiful dove-coloured picture of Mr. Ruskin in a prospect of rocks and waterfalls, two young ladies stationed themselves in front of me, and began to discuss a sister art. Said A.: "I see that the Poet-laureate is about to give up writing in the *Standard*, in order to devote more time to the Muses." Said B.: "Oh, who is the Poet-laureate?" A.: "For shame, Sylvia; what ignorance! His name is Alfred Austin. Isn't it strange that both he and Tennyson should have been called Alfred? and so many poets, too, are called Austin. There is Alfred Austin, and Austin Dobson, and" (after a pause) "Jane Austin.[1] It is rather a poetical name, don't you think?" B.: "Yes, dear. But we always take the *Standard* at home, and I have never seen any poetry in it." A.: "Oh no; that's just it. The Poet-laureate has not had time to write any poetry yet, because he has had to write the *Standard*. But now he's going to begin. You see, the Poet-laureate in these days has to be such a political person. My father said, when Mr. Austin was appointed, that it was a happy return to the sound Conservative principles that prevailed in Mr. Shadwell's time; and he hoped the Government, with their large

---

[1] Besides these, there was a William Austin of Lincoln's Inn, who wrote three capital Christmas carols; and a Samuel Austin, of whose "steropegeretick poetry" that sadly misnamed poet, Flatman, wrote—

> "The beetles of our rhimes shall drive full fast in
> The wedges of your worth to everlasting,
> My much Apocalyptiqu' friend, *Sam. Austin*."

The father of this Samuel and the son of this William were also poets, and probably the "Dictionary of Biography" would extend the list. All these, not excepting Jane, seem worthy scions of the great saint and rhetorician whose name they bear.

majority, would have the courage to make the post a genuinely party one, so that Sir Lewis Morris might come in when Mr. Austin went out." B.: "Oh yes, I do so hope he will. I do so dote on his wall-papers. But who was Mr. Shadwell?" A.: "Oh, Sylvia, do look at the marvellous stratification of these rocks," &c.

This conversation has given me, what I very much wanted, a subject for a paper due at the Lit. and Phil.; it shall be "Poetry and Politics: their Mutual Relations and Antipathies." I know at least one anecdote that will be useful in illustration. Young —— was on a steamer with the late William Morris, who very much took to him, and after some days revealed to the youngster that he was a poet. "Oh!" replied ——, not to be outdone, "so is my grandfather." "And who is he?" asked Morris. "The D. of A-g-ll." Morris turned on his heel and had nothing more to say to the poor lad.

Pursuing for a moment the subject of poets' names, would it be fair to say that the recurrence of the patronymic particle "-son" in so many poets' names to-day points to a certain absence of Apollonian inspiration, as who should say *terræ filii*? I but throw out the suggestion for what it is worth; at any rate, a poet whose own name is pontifical has found a good deal of appropriateness in the names of the "Poetæ Majores."

> "For I must think the adopting Muses chose
>   Their sons by name, knowing none would be heard
> Or writ so oft in all the world as those :
>   Dan Chaucer, mighty Shakespeare, then for third
> The classic Milton, and to us arose
>   Shelley with liquid music in the word."[1]

18th.—To Her Majesty's Theatre. All plays deserving the name were written to be acted, and so it is not wonderful that even at this date we gain new lights on Shakespeare from any decent representation. To-night I gathered without difficulty why they killed Cæsar. His nose, his walk, his voice, his false emphasis, deserved each a several murder. The only wonder is that he was ever tolerated till the third act; and, indeed, at Her Majesty's he is got rid of in the second. The gentleman who played Brutus was often excellent in a rhetorical way; and how rare it is to find an actor whose rhetoric is tolerable. I remember him in Hotspur, when he was even better. The only speech he gave really ill was the orchard soliloquy, which he recited as if Brutus had made up his mind before he began to think. And so, indeed, he had. And that may have been the actor's subtle meaning. Still, he should put the stress on the emphatic words in the argument. Cassius, too, was quite presentable. What a pathetic figure he is,

---

[1] Another poet is said to be writing an epic which opens thus—

> "Ye nine, with whom upon Parnassus romp,
>   The sons of Wat, of David, and of Thomp."

with his affection for Brutus and desire to be loved back again!—the one human spot in his conspirator's nature—which yet ruins the whole by making him, time after time, sacrifice his better judgment to his idol. And so that prig of paragons, his brother-in-law, is allowed to spoil the conspiracy by sparing Antony, and, worse, by letting him speak in the forum, and then spoil the campaign by bad generalship both in the council and in the field; while, to crown all, his colleague has to submit to the charge of peculation at the same moment that he is asked for money—

> "I did send to you for gold to pay my legions,
> For I can raise no money by vile means;"

and when he tries to explain, is lectured on his bad temper. Of course, it is all retribution. Cassius wanted a moral cloak for his plot, and Brutus supplied what was necessary—

> "He covered, but his robe
> Uncovered more."

Lucius seemed preoccupied most of the time in rehearsing for private theatricals; I should guess that he was practising the part of Ariel, for he skipt and tript about in an airy, fairy manner, not like any, even the most soaring, human boy that ever wore buttons. Antony necessarily lacked the one characteristic of Antony—genius; but its absence was amply atoned for by the excellent coaching of the crowd, so that his oration came off just as well as if it had been the real thing. By the way, I could not help thinking how useful it would be to Parliamentary candidates if their audiences could in the same way be taught their proper responses. Julius Cæsar had not been seen on the stage for many years, and one incidental result of the revival has been an enlargement of the *répertoire* of journalists. One comes on lines and half-lines now in the most unexpected places. It was only at the beginning of the year that a certain journal celebrated the solemn season by asking distinguished people for mottoes, and Sir Edwin Arnold chose the desolate speech of Brutus—

> "O that a man might know
> The end of this day's business ere it come!
> But it sufficeth that the day will end,
> And then the end is known."

On which a contemporary, whom I will not name, commented thus: "We wonder from which of his fathom-deep Buddhist books Sir Edwin Arnold disinterred this cheery chirp."

In reading to-day the preface to Dryden's "Absalom and Achitophel," I was amused to find the Tories referred to as Anti-Birminghams. "The longest chapter in Deuteronomy has not curses enough for an Anti-Birmingham." Thus does history repeat itself—at least in the country districts—where we look upon Liberal Unionists as neither flesh, fowl, nor good red-herring.

19th.—My friend S., who is the incarnation of hospitality, makes a point of arranging a little dinner when I am in town. Being a person of reserved manners, and ignorant of the town interests of the hour, I sometimes find myself a little embarrassed for topics of table talk. On this occasion my blushes were saved by the generosity of my neighbour, an actor of distinction, who at once put me at ease by asking how I liked him in his new part. S. had warned me that it was against etiquette to confess to an actor that you had not seen him, and so I replied: "Oh, amazingly! it seemed to me to revive the best traditions of the stage." "Ah, then," said he, "you didn't care for my last piece!" "On the contrary," I replied, "those were the classical traditions I referred to;" and I bowed, thinking that compliment could no further go, and that I had done all that could be expected of me. But my interlocutor resumed: "*Classical*, did you say? I should have called the play romantic myself." "But surely," said I, "there is a *ne plus ultra*, even in the romantic drama, that we may speak of as *classical*." He looked dubious, and I mopped my face. I feared I had been laying it on with a trowel, but I saw that more was expected. If I had only been told what his last pieces were! Still, a risk had to be run, and I proceeded: "It is remarkable, when one looks at the pictures in the Garrick Club, how inferior in grace and dignity and how immature in conception they appear when compared with the renderings of the same parts to which we are accustomed." He looked mollified, and assented. "As far as Shakespeare and Sheridan and other Elizabethans are concerned, that no doubt is so; but, you see, they didn't act Jones and Pinero, and so such a comparison can hardly be made." "Well, no," I said, "not in particulars; but we can judge the general style very well, and eke out our observation by the criticisms that have come down to us—on which you have only to consult Mr. Joseph Knight—and, without wishing to flatter, I should say that there are one or two actors to-day who combine a learning and polish due to study in the best schools with a spontaneity and *verve* that are altogether of our own time." "Two, did you say?" inquired he. "No," I said; "I was exaggerating—one." By this time I did not know if it was I who was smoking or the soup.

In the country one has few opportunities of meeting these children of nature. Occasionally one sees an individual or a company at the railway stations, and then it is curious to note how instinctively they treat the platform as a stage, and take up the important positions on it. I wonder if acting now is as lucrative a profession as it was under Elizabeth. Shakespeare, we are told, got nothing to speak of for his plays, but made his fortune as an actor; and Alleyne, another actor, after providing for his family, founded Dulwich School. Another curious point about actors is that they should not be content with their own names, like painters and writers, but take names (the ladies especially) that belong to other people. Is there no property in names?

21*st.*—It was to be positively the last dance before Lent, and positively we must go; and when Sophia is positive, it boots not that there are higher degrees of comparison. I suppose, if a man has a grown-up daughter, he must not repine if the privilege now and then entails a twenty-mile drive on a winter's night. Happily the season is clement, though the sky this morning looks as if it could snow if it would. I feel more resigned to my fate since I read in Saturday's *Literature* a poem by the famous Rabbi ben Ezra, called "Sursum Cauda," in which that learned gentleman maintains, with a fine adaptation of Oriental fatalism to Western social life, that man, being but a grasshopper, must hop—

> "Nunc pede libero
> Pulsanda tellus."

Or, as the Rabbi has it—

> "No matter what the flight,
> Nor where the feet alight,
> To leap and pause and leap is all our human care."

Our old vicar used to have an unreasonable prejudice against dancing, based on the story of King Herod and John Baptist; but, as I once told him, no dancing I had ever seen in Berkshire houses was good enough to make the onlooker swear rash oaths, though I allowed that a bad performance had sometimes that effect upon other performers. Moreover, if any reliance can be placed on the evidence of a very old window in Lincoln Cathedral, Herodias's daughter danced upon her head; which was, to say the least of it, not pretty manners. It shows how skin-deep the boasted Herodian Hellenism really was, that Herod took such a barbarian exhibition for fine art. The true Greek gentleman would have been disgusted; for Herodotus tells the story of a certain Hippocleides who thought to show his cleverness at a banquet by dancing on his head among the plates and dishes, a proceeding which so disgusted his future father-in-law that he at once broke off the match.

23rd.—The Zola case has come to its inevitable conclusion, and Englishmen must be forgiven if they think it more than ever to their credit that they are not as these Frenchmen. English soldiers are often, and perhaps justly, charged with contempt for civilians; but as a rule they confine themselves to generalities, as when the Commander-in-Chief says in his "Pocket-Book" that a soldier's profession is the only one that could not be as well followed by his grandmother. But in this amazing trial the service has been swaggering over the Bar, over men of letters, and, oddly enough too, over dentists. "You bring against us," said General de Pellieux, shaking with fury, "foreigners and dentists." The contempt for foreigners was once supposed to be a peculiar mark of the barbarous free-trading Englishman, and it is interesting to find it in the civilised and cosmopolitan French. The contempt for dentists is a more interesting symptom. It looks like a survival from feudal days, when the only surgeon was the barber, who, like the corn-cutter, exercises what is still held to be a menial function. The conduct of the judge has been censured no less than that of the generals; but on a closer view it deserves some praise. For what has he done? While preserving his own roof by apparent concessions to the mob, he has allowed all manner of things to come out in evidence that ostensibly he was hushing up. We in England do not know the terror of a Parisian mob; our own roughs, though individually ferocious, seem somehow to exude a saving humour when they collect in masses. The fact is, one nation can never understand another. This conclusion was forced upon me last spring, when I was in Paris. I was sitting down near the Arc de Triomphe, and on the same seat was a gentleman whom I took to be French. He was intently watching a long *queue* of people taking omnibus tickets. Suddenly he burst out, in the English tongue, "What fools these people are!" He could understand taking tickets for the railway before getting into the carriage, but it was clear that no one but a fool would take a ticket for an omnibus till he was well inside. Well, that is roughly one's feeling about French justice—that it is probably all right for Frenchmen.

THE END

Printed by BALLANTYNE, HANSON & Co.
Edinburgh & London